PRAISE FOR *THE RISE OF SUPERMAN*

"A thrill ride of a book, empowering in its implications of what any individual can achieve."

—*Kirkus Reviews*

"A fascinating primer on how athletes of extreme sports use flow to accomplish what seem like impossible goals, such as skiing down cliffs or surfing 100-foot waves. But a close reading of the book also provides great insights into how everyday athletes can use flow in their workouts and the rest of their lives."

—*Financial Times*

"Kotler takes on the latest research on flow through the lens of action and adventure athletics . . . [writing] primarily about flow in high-stakes sports like surfing—where focus and concentration can be the difference between a tubular ride and a watery death—but the concept could also have big implications for the business world."

—*Fortune*

"In this high-octane study, Steven Kotler explores 'flow,' a neurochemically rich state in which cognitive and physiological processes mesh. The stupendous physical feats of the late ski-base jumper Shane McConkey and others are riveting. Equally surprising is what we know of flow science, such as how the brain's superior frontal gyrus deactivates to speed decision-making."

—*Nature*

"*The Rise of Superman* is full of scientific explanations about why flow helps athletes perform at their peak, why this is on the upswing in recent decades, and how almost anybody can better tap their ultimate potential."

—*Surfer Magazine*

"Kotler focuses on extreme sports for good reason. These athletes face a constant choice, 'flow or die,' and his book contains some compelling characters . . . Flow is rooted in the brain, and Kotler does a good job of explaining that science."

—*The Washington Post*

"In Kotler's riveting and beautifully written book, he explains the neuroscience behind the mystery of the flow state, and provides the key to unlocking innovation, creativity, and ultimate achievement for leaders, entrepreneurs, and anyone interested in the big and bold."

—Peter Diamandis, *New York Times* bestselling author, founder of the X Prize, cofounder of Singularity University.

"*The Rise of Superman* is an electrifying book about a potent state of mind. If you aren't inspired to brainhack your way up to the next level, start again at page one."

—David Eagleman, neuroscientist, *New York Times* bestselling author of *Incognito*

"*The Rise of Superman* is a page-turning, game-changing account of the secrets of ultimate human performance—a must read for anyone interested in seriously raising the level of their game.

—Ray Kurzweil, director of engineering at Google, author of *How to Create a Mind* and *The Singularity Is Near*

"In *The Rise of Superman*, Steven Kotler breaks down the elusive and ecstatic 'flow state' that so many high performance athletes, musicians, and artists refer to as indispensable to their creativity and virtuosity—and in doing so, offers us a map to achieve massive upgrades in our capacities and potential."

—Jason Silva, futurist, host of National Geographic's *Brain Games*

THE RISE
OF
SUPERMAN

THE RISE OF SUPERMAN

OF

SUPERMAN

STEVEN KOTLER

amazon publishing

Published by Amazon Publishing, Seattle

www.apub.com

Amazon, the Amazon logo and Amazon Publishing are trademarks of Amazon.com, Inc. or its affiliates.

ISBN-13: 9781542032940
ISBN-10: 1542032946

Cover design by Faceout Studio, Spencer Fuller

Printed in the United States of America

Contents

The tools for managing paradox are still undeveloped.

– KEVIN KELLY

Preface: The Why of Flow

This is a book about the impossible, but it starts with the invisible. Over the past three decades, an unlikely collection of men and women have pushed human performance farther and faster than at any other point in the 150,000-year history of our species. In this evolutionary eyeblink, they have completely redefined the limits of the possible. But here's the stranger part: this unprecedented flowering of human potential has taken place in plain sight, occasionally with millions of people watching—yet almost no one has noticed.

The reason for this is simple: virtually all of this massively accelerated performance has occurred within the world of action and adventure sports. Certainly, surfing and skiing make for good recreation, and the X Games look excellent on TV, but when it comes to riding 100-foot waves and hucking 100-foot cliffs, most of us see daredevil magic: unfathomable stunts, insane athletes—enough said.

Yet what appears to be impossible is actually progressive. Behind each of these feats is a litany of small steps: history, technology, training—and not just physical training, mental training as well. Success in these danger-fueled activities requires incredible psychological and intellectual talents: grit, fortitude, courage, creativity, resilience, cooperation, critical thinking, pattern recognition, high-speed "hot" decision making—on and on, and all under some of the most extreme conditions imaginable. Researchers recently coined the phrase "Twenty-First-Century Skills" to describe those myriad abilities our children need to thrive in this century–abilities not currently taught in school, but desperately needed in society. Action and adventure sports demand them all.

Yet even this is just the beginning. Of all the things these athletes have accomplished, nothing is more impressive than their mastery of the state known to researchers as *flow*. Most of us have at least passing familiarity with flow. If you've ever lost an afternoon to a great conversation or gotten so involved in a work project that all else is forgotten, then you've tasted the experience. In flow, we are so focused on the task at hand that everything else falls away. Action and awareness merge. Time flies. Self vanishes. Performance goes through the roof.

We call this experience *flow* because that is the sensation conferred. In flow, every action, each decision, leads effortlessly, fluidly, seamlessly to the next. It's high-speed problem solving; it's being swept away by the river of ultimate performance. "Flow naturally catapults you to a level you're not naturally in," explains Harvard Medical School psychiatrist Ned Hallowell. "Flow naturally transforms a weakling into a muscleman, a sketcher into an artist, a dancer into a ballerina, a plodder into a sprinter, an ordinary person into someone extraordinary. Everything you do, you do better in flow, from baking a chocolate cake to planning a vacation to solving a differential equation to writing a business plan to playing tennis to making love. Flow is the doorway to the 'more' most of us seek. Rather than telling ourselves to get used to it, that's all there is, instead learn how to enter into flow. There you will find, in manageable doses, all the 'more' you need."

Flow is an optimal state of consciousness, a peak state where we both feel our best and perform our best. It is a transformation available to anyone, anywhere, provided that certain initial conditions are met. Everyone from assembly-line workers in Detroit to jazz musicians in Algeria to software designers in Mumbai rely on flow to drive performance and accelerate innovation. And it's quite a driver. Researchers now believe flow sits at the heart of almost every athletic championship, underpins major scientific breakthroughs, and accounts for significant progress in the arts. World leaders have sung the praises of flow. Fortune 500 CEOs have built corporate philosophies around the state. From a quality-of-life perspective, psychologists have found that the people who have the most flow in their lives are the happiest people on earth.

Put differently, a recent Gallup survey found that 71 percent of American workers were "not engaged" or "actively disengaged" from their jobs. Think about this for a moment: two out of three of us hate what we do with the majority of our time. This is a crisis of commerce, to say the least. Yet we already know where the solution lies. The other 29 percent of workers have jobs that generate flow. Flow directly correlates to happiness at work and happiness at work directly correlates to success. As CNN recently reported: "A decade of research in the business world proves happiness raises nearly every business and educational outcome: raising sales by 37 percent, productivity by 31 percent, and accuracy on tasks by 19 percent, as well as a myriad of health and quality-of-life improvements."

Yet there's a rub. Flow might be the most desirable state on earth; it's also the most elusive. While seekers have spent centuries trying, no one has found a reliable way to reproduce the experience, let alone with enough consistently to radically accelerate performance. But this is not the case with action and adventure sports athletes. Quite simply, the zone is the only reason these athletes are surviving the big-mountains, big waves, and big rivers. When you're pushing the limits of ultimate human performance, the choice is stark: it's flow or die.

Ironically, this is very good news. Scientists have lately made enormous progress on flow. Advancements in brain-imaging technologies like fMRI and consumer "quantified self" devices like the Nike Fuel band allow us to apply serious metrics where once was merely subjective experience. Until now, there's been no way to tie all this disparate information together, but recent events in action and adventure sports solve this problem. Knowing that survival demands flow gives us a hard data set with which to work. We don't have to wonder if our research subjects are really in flow: if they live through the impossible, we can be certain. Moreover, by mapping this new science onto these extreme activities, we can start to understand exactly how flow works its magic. Finally, if we can figure out exactly what these athletes are doing to reliably reproduce this state, then we can apply this knowledge across the additional domains of self and society.

In other words, despite the unusual "them" at the center of this story, this book is really about us: you and me. Who doesn't want to know how to be their best when it matters most? To be more creative, more contented, more consumed? To soar and not to sink? As the deeds of these athletes prove, if we can master flow, there are no limits to what we can accomplish. We are our own revolution.

Toward these ends, this book is divided into three parts. Part One examines just how far action and adventure sports athletes have pushed the bounds of the possible and explores the science of *why* (this work is based on over a decade of research; unless otherwise noted, all quotes come from direct interviews between the subject and the author or historical documents). It's here that we'll see how flow works in the brain and the body, how it massively accelerates mental and physical performance, how its allows these athletes to accomplish the impossible. As capturing lightning in a bottle is not easy, Part Two of this book probes the nature of the chase: how these athletes have mastered flow, how they have redesigned their lives to cultivate the state, and how we can too. Finally, Part Three looks at the darker side of flow, wider cultural impacts, and the future.

The great civil rights leader Howard Thurman once said, "Don't ask what the world needs. Ask what makes you come alive. Because what the world needs most is more people who have come alive."

The data is clear. Flow is the very thing that makes us come alive. It is the mystery. It is the point. Put another way: There are difficult and dangerous activities described in the pages of this book. The people involved are highly trained professionals. So please, please, please, try them at home. Because what the world needs most is Superman.

It is time to rise.

Episode One:

FLOW 101

Introduction: Before the Flow

SHANE MCCONKEY

We like our geniuses a certain way here in America. If they are scientifically minded, we prefer them wild-coiffed, calculation-spouting, so far beyond the confines of standard intelligence that only exotic metaphors may apply. If they are artistic, we like them like we've always liked them—exiled on Main Street, melancholy and misanthropic, occasionally drug-addled, often drunk. If they are rich geniuses, we prefer them having begun poor. If they are poor geniuses, we want them once rich and now, having lost it at all, tenaciously staging a comeback. What we don't want, at least not often, is genius naked and spreadeagle and forty feet off the ground—but that, my friends, is where this story begins.

Actually, it begins a few days earlier. The year is 1993. A twenty-four-year-old skier named Shane McConkey was putting on quite a show at the Crested Butte Extremes. Within a decade, McConkey would become one of the most beloved and revered athletes in the world: a dual sport master of the impossible, one of the greatest skiers to have ever lived, one of the most innovative skydivers in history. Back then, though, almost no one knew his name.

Steve Winter, who co-runs the ski filmmaking company Matchstick Productions, certainly didn't know his name. But he was impressed enough with McConkey's performance that he invited him to film with MSP after the conclusion of the event. During that session, the first thing they did together was hike out to a cliff band in the Colorado backcountry. Winter and his crew set up the camera below a large cornice. McConkey hiked up top. There was a countdown–*three, two, one, dropping*–and McConkey dropped all right. He blasted off the cliff. His goal appeared to be a double back flip, but a few things should be mentioned: The first is that back in 1993, no one was throwing double backflips and certainly not off forty-foot cornices. The second: Neither was McConkey.

"Shane did one and a half rotations and landed on his head," says Winter. "We were all thinking the same thing: Holy shit, this guy's gonna kill himself."

Many things can help a skier's career–being stupid in the backcountry is not among them. "There are a lot of unexpected risks out there," says Winter. "The last thing we want is some kook going crazy for the camera. But Shane kept demanding a second shot at the double backflip. We kept trying to talk him out of it–saying the cliff's not big enough, he didn't have the trick, there was no way to get enough speed."

McConkey wasn't hearing any of it. He stomped off and hiked up. Winter stayed below. He had a bad feeling in his stomach. Above him, out of sight, McConkey got ready. The feeling got worse. Through his headset, Winter heard the countdown. That's when it happened. McConkey blazed off the cliff–wearing nothing but his ski boots. He did not throw a backflip. He threw what would soon become his signature: a giant, naked spread-eagle.

"What can I say?" asks Winter. "It was fucking genius."

THE NEW HIGH BAR

Genius? Really? According to Dictionary.com, *genius* is defined as "an exceptional natural capacity of intellect, especially as shown in creative and original work in science, art, music, etc." But that doesn't help us much in athletics, especially when the sports in question are of the action-adventure variety. What does genius look like when snowboarding? What does creativity mean for a skydiver? How can we tell if a particular surfer is doing original work when the proof of that work vanishes with the crashing of a wave?

Well, for starters, the obvious: we all seem to agree genius begins with feats of mental greatness. The thinking needs to be novel, so the results need to be beyond what most can envision. As it takes courage to push past the confines of culture, the thinking must also be brave. Because an athlete's canvas is nothing more than his body moving through space and time, then an act of genius must also be defined as an act of redefinition–redefining what is possible for the human body. Which is to say, in the world of action and adventure sports, the easiest way to hunt genius is to look for those athletes consistently betting their asses on the impossible.

And this is where things start to get strange–because quite a few asses have been on the line these last two decades. Not too long ago the idea of anyone jumping a motorcycle over a bunch of school buses was so incredible that the whole world tuned in every time Evel Knievel decided to give it a go. These days, on any given weekend, in arenas all over the world, you can watch dozens of riders jumping similar distances–only backflipping as they go. Go back twenty-five years in skiing and the 360 was just about the hardest trick anyone could throw. These days, it's the entry point to jib skiing–meaning kids age six are pulling them off routinely. On the other side of that coin, in 1998, when ski-industry giant Salomon introduced the 1080–their first twin tip ski–they were given that name because three spins (1080 degrees) was jib skiing's Holy Grail, an impossible. Well, been there, done that. In 2011, Bobby Brown threw the world's first Triple Cork 1440–which is four spins and three flips, and all off-axis.

Along the way, world records have been broken and broken again. Many of these are records no one thought should even exist: records that were beyond the pale, beyond the possible. Kayakers paddling straight-drop waterfalls are a good example. In 1997, Tao Berman blew minds when he sent an eighty-three-footer on the El Tomata River near Vera Cruz, Mexico. It should have been a world record, but as close to an official measurement as anyone got was noting that a seventy-foot rope tossed over that cliff "appeared" to end ten feet above the ground. While that argument was going on, Shannon Carroll popped off Oregon's Sahalie Falls–a mere seventy-eight feet–but still staggering and highly visible, and the record was hers. Two years later, Berman stormed back, dropping all ninety-eight feet and four inches of Upper Johnson Falls in Banff National Forest. That record stood for nearly ten years–an eternity in today's game–but then eight or nine athletes (the ninth belonging to, according to *Canoe & Kayak* magazine, "the creepy German guy on YouTube whose footage cannot be confirmed") battled the number up to 108 feet, only to be fought off in 2009 by Pedro Olivia's 127-foot launch on the Rio Sacre in Brazil. Olivia entered the water at seventy miles per hour, which was so far beyond what most thought a kayaker could survive that this record too was believed unbreakable. That thinking lasted three months, until Tyler Bradt plunged 189 feet off Washington State's Palouse Falls, marking the occasion with a short video of his own, telling audiences: "[T]his is a major step up from what anyone's done before. It's kind of an unknown realm for kayaking and what the human body can take off of a waterfall."

Yeah, you think?

Oddly, though, here in the early twenty-first century, there's plenty of talk about our sports becoming softer, milder, less deadly. Interest in boxing, for example, continues to wane. The new illegal-hits rules in the NFL protect "defenseless players," which more and more seems to include anyone wearing pads. The 2011 technical-foul changes in basketball make even aggressive gestures–punching the air, jumping up and down, waving arms in disbelief–off-limits. As a result, point guards, almost by definition the smallest guys on the court, are having their greatest seasons ever and the NBA enforcer Ron Artest–infamous for cold-cocking a fan–officially changed his name to Metta World Peace.

But that's only half the picture. At the same time that competitive ball sports have become less dangerous, action and adventure sports have become increasingly harebrained. In rock climbing, skydiving, snowboarding, skiing, motocross, mountain biking, mountaineering, skateboarding, surfing, windsurfing, kite surfing, cave diving, free diving, parkour, etc., the list of once-impossible feats continues to shrink. "In this day and age," says Micah Abrams, former ESPN.com senior editor for action sports, "the upper echelon of adventure sport athletes are grappling with the fundamental properties of the universe: gravity, velocity and sanity. They're toying with them, cheating death, refusing to accept there might be limits to what they can accomplish."

These athletes...well, that's the great irony, right? Many people don't even consider them that. They're the poster children of the slacker generation, the ones marked with an X, who still, some two decades after the fact, continue to smell like teen spirit. But along the way, they have somehow become so much more: a force pushing evolution further, the tip of the spear, the ones charged with redefining what it means to be human. As Mike Gervais, one of the world's top peak-performance psychologists, says: "There's a natural urge to compare athletes to athletes, but trying to compare a guy like Shane McConkey to a guy like Kobe Bryant misses the mark entirely. It's almost apples and oranges. McConkey's got more in common with fourteenth-century Spanish explorers than anyone playing on the hardwood. You want to compare these athletes to someone, well, you've got to start with Magellan."

ULTIMATE HUMAN PERFORMANCE

Even if you start with Magellan, comparisons are still problematic. The issue is evolution, specifically the snail's pace at which it typically proceeds. As athletic ability is directly shaped by natural selection, for most of the 150,000 years our species has been on this planet, progress has been incremental at best. Historically, our ancestors performed pretty much the way their ancestors performed. Certainly, there has been some improvement, but when plotted on a graph the results show slow change stretched across centuries. At no period in human history did we add an extra foot to our vertical leap between generations. Daughters could not outpace mothers and mothers could not outpace grandmothers, and this was just the way things were.

But in the world of high adrenaline, this is no longer the way things are.

Examples are helpful. The sport of platform diving debuted at the 1904 Olympics. That year, an American eye doctor named George Sheldon took gold with what was then considered a difficult and dangerous dive: the double front somersault. Today, slightly more than a hundred years later, the reverse four and a half occupies a similar spot.

If you measure progress using degrees of rotation, then a single flip (or spin) produces 360 degrees of rotation and Sheldon's 1904 double totaled out at 720 degrees. Meanwhile, the 2004 reverse four-and-a-half produces 1,620 degrees (180 for the direction change, an additional 1,440 for the flips). This means the sport of diving took more than a century to advance by 900 degrees of rotation.

Now compare this to the past decade in "Big Air" skiing. Exactly as it sounds, a Big Air competition is nothing more than a giant jump, with skiers–much like divers–judged on the maneuvers they can execute between takeoff and landing. In 1999, Canada's JF Cusson won the first ever X Games Big Air competition with a Switch 720. "Switch" means he took off backward (and landed backward), while the 720 is a measure of degrees of rotation. And forget difficult and dangerous; in 1999, the Switch 720 was considered downright insane.

That designation didn't last long. Just twelve years later, during the 2011 X Games, TJ Schiller took Big Air silver with a Double Cork 1620. Cork is an off-axis flip (meaning the athletes tumble through the air sideways instead of vertically), so a double cork is two off-axis flips, or 720 degrees of rotation. The 1,620 measure refers to flat spins–in this case, four and a half. If you discount the added difficulty of flipping while spinning and simply measure progress in rotations, from takeoff to touchdown, Schiller's trick measured out to 2,340 degrees of rotation. Think about this for a moment. Diving took a century to add 900 degrees to its tally, but skiers somehow pushed their total up 1,640 degrees in slightly more than a decade?

Such eye-popping progress isn't just found in skiing. The Baker Road gap is one of snowboarding's most iconic jumps. Situated on Mount Baker, deep in the Cascade Range, the gap measures forty feet end to end and is conveniently positioned on the road that runs between the resort's main lodge and upper lodge. In 1990, when Shawn Farmer first cleared this chasm, his was one of the biggest jumps anyone had ever undertaken. In 2005, the appropriately nicknamed Norwegian rider Mads "Big Nads" Jonsson launched 187 feet, setting a new world record along the way and raising an obvious question: When, in the history of sport, has athletic performance quintupled in fifteen years?

Then there's freestyle motocross. Since the invention of the motorcycle, the backflip has been the sport's Holy Grail. Because of the weight of a bike and the aerodynamics involved, everyone from professional scientists to professional athletes considered the feat impossible. Then both Travis Pastrana and Mike Metzger landed backflips during the 2002 X Games. The following year, athletes added a midair heel click to the trick. They were soon doing them one-handed and no-handed and no-footed and off-axis. Just four years later, Pastrana doubled down on impossible and pulled off the world's first double backflip. "There's just no easy way to describe what we're seeing in motocross," says Dr. Andy Walshe, head of athletic performance at Red Bull. "The sport is so challenging and the risk of serious injury so high, it'd be ridiculous to expect anything but incremental progress. It took riders decades to close in on the back flip. To get to double backflips four years later? It's hard to wrap your head around that."

And there you have it, the central mystery of this book: How is any of this possible? Why, at the tail end of the twentieth century and the early portion of the twenty-first, are we seeing such a multisport assault on reality? Did we somehow slip through a wormhole to another universe where the laws of physics don't apply? Where gravity is optional and common sense obsolete?

These are more than idle curiosities. If the term *impossible* means anything here, it means the barriers being shattered exist beyond the confines of both biology and imagination. These feats are paradigm-shifters. Historically, in science and culture, breakthroughs of this ilk emerge once or twice a century. Not five times a decade. So decoding these phenomena tells us something deep and important about accelerating human potential, creativity, and innovation—but it tells us more than that.

The past three decades have witnessed unprecedented growth in what researchers now term *ultimate human performance*. This is not the same as *optimal human performance*, and the difference is in the consequences. *Optimal* performance is about being your best; *ultimate* performance is about being your best when any mistake could kill. Both common sense and evolutionary biology tell us that progress under these "ultimate" conditions should be a laggard's game, but that's not exactly what the data suggests.

Instead, over the past thirty years, in the world of action and adventure sports, in situations where asses really were on the line, the bounds of the possible have been pushed further and faster than ever before in history. We've seen near-exponential growth in ultimate human performance, which is both hyperbolic paradox and considerable mystery. Somehow, a generation's worth of iconoclastic misfits have rewritten the rules of the feasible, not just raising the bar but often obliterating it altogether. And this brings up one final question: Where—if anywhere—do our actual limits lie?

THE QUESTION OF COST

If you want to really understand this question of limits, you have to understand December 23, 1994—the day the game changed. The epicenter of this shift was Maverick's, a dark, gray beast of a wave, located two miles off Pillar Point Harbor, twenty-two miles south of San Francisco, deep in the shark-infested waters of California's Red Triangle. *Surfer* magazine once described the spot as "gloomy, isolated, inherently evil," and the website Mavericksurf.com explains why: "With waves cresting as high as fifty feet, ridiculously strong currents, dangerous rocks, perilously shallow reefs, and bone-chilling water temperatures, Maverick's is like no other place on earth."

It's also a place that wasn't supposed to exist. "Since the beginning of modern surfing," says professional surfer and surf filmmaker Chris Malloy, "if you wanted to ride big waves, you were going to Hawaii, because everyone knew that was the only place in the world with real big waves. When stories about Maverick's started hitting the islands, no one believed them. The idea that there was a true beast breaking off the coast of Northern California was heresy."

And then it wasn't.

Maverick's was first discovered back in 1962, but only a local named Jeff Clark was crazy enough to paddle out. And he kept paddling out. Clark, in as close to a definition of madness as can be found in the sport, surfed Maverick's *alone* for over fifteen years. In the early 1990s, he finally decided some company was in order, so he invited a few friends along for the ride. It was quite a ride. Pretty soon, as Jon Krakauer penned in *Outside,* "rumors started to drift up and down the coast about a mysto surf break near Half Moon Bay that generated thick, grinding barrels tall enough to drive a bus through. They were reputed to be at least as big as the famous waves that rumbled ashore at Hawaii's Waimea Bay, the Mount Everest of surfing."

For the surfers who made their names riding giants in Oahu, Maverick's was the wave they refused to believe in, the wave that threatened their territorial hold on unparalleled excellence. But the rumors didn't stop, and something had to be done. So in December of 1994, when a monstrous Aleutian storm sent furious pulses down the California coast, three of the world's most famous Hawaiian big-wave riders–Ken Bradshaw, Brock Little, and Mark Foo–boarded red-eye flights to San Francisco to see for themselves.

Of the trio, Foo was arguably the most well known. This wasn't just about talent. All three were ferocious watermen, but Foo was equally ferocious about fame. In the late 1980s, when he quit the pro tour and decided to make his bones in big surf, his strategy was twofold. Until his arrival, big-wave riders had taken a no-frills, shortest-path-out-of-danger approach to their craft. Wipeouts were avoided at all costs, because wipeouts could kill. But Foo carried his small-wave slasher's style into the larger surf. He took bigger risks and–the other portion of his strategy–he bragged about them too. "If you want to ride the ultimate wave," said Foo–as often as possible, always when there were journalists around– "you have to be willing to pay the ultimate price."

Foo cultivated fame. His Rolodex contained the names and numbers of the world's best surf photographers. Rarely did he venture into the waves without making a few phone calls first. On December 23, 1994, he didn't have to bother. Throughout the 1990s, Maverick's fearsome reputation had been growing, but the winter of '94 brought some of the biggest waves in history to California's coast. December's four weeks would soon be dubbed "the month full of monsters" and the media couldn't resist. By the time Foo, Bradshaw, and Little made it out to the lineup, there was a helicopter buzzing overhead and three boats filled with photographers parked just outside the impact zone.

Despite the hype, that morning turned out to be disappointing. A few big beasts rolled through, not the bedlam that had been expected. This changed a few minutes before noon. Black lines appeared on the horizon, and someone onshore screamed, "Set!" The events that would make this date famous in history were only, horribly, moments away.

The gentlemen from Hawaii wasted no time. Both Foo and Bradshaw started paddling for the second wave of the set. According to surfer's code, because Bradshaw was positioned deeper–that is, closer to the wave's curl–the ride was his. To be sure, there were plenty of days when Bradshaw would have staked that claim–hell, there was a river of bad blood between Bradshaw and Foo–but during the past year the two had become close. To honor that friendship, in a decision he'll spend the rest of his life second-guessing, Bradshaw pulled out of the wave.

Foo dropped in.

Ironically, the wave wasn't much by local standards. Faces there have been measured to eighty feet–the size of an apartment complex. This one was merely a house. But surf legend Buzzy Trent said it best: "Waves are not measured in feet and inches, they are measured in increments of fear." And Maverick's, no matter the size, is the stuff of nightmares. Just the hydraulics alone are ridiculous. In seconds, the wave can radically change shape: wall, drop, lift, kink, shimmy, shake. And for first-time riders, there's really no telling what's coming next.

In this particular case, the wave jacked up and the bottom fell out. In the resulting chop, Foo dug a rail and pitched himself headfirst into hell. For a moment, it looked like he had enough speed to punch straight through the wave, but he didn't dive deep enough. The curl caught him, snatching him up, hurling him over the falls. In photographs of the event, Foo can be seen just then, in ghostly silhouette, trapped inside the very belly of the beast.

These photographs are the last time anyone saw Mark Foo alive. Exactly what killed him, no one knows. Maybe he hit his head on the reef and blacked out; maybe he snagged his leash on a rock and couldn't pull free. Whatever the case, his body was found an hour later, floating facedown in the water outside the harbor entrance.

Word of his death traveled fast and far. Newspaper stories, magazine articles, television features–the coverage kept coming. "The publicity surrounding the event was unprecedented," wrote Jason Borte at *Surfline*. "The story quickly spread around the world. Although [Foo] wasn't around to enjoy it, it was the sort of fame he always wanted." It was, without question, the most public moment in surf history. It was also something of an "I told you so" moment.

Since the early 1980s, action and adventure athletes had been pushing into increasingly dangerous territory. If for no other reason than the law of large numbers and the frailties of the human body, it was only a matter of time. Everybody knew, sooner or later, somebody was going to die. "The fact that someone had died surfing Maverick's was a shock," wrote big-wave rider Grant Washburn in *Inside Maverick's: Portrait of a Monster Wave*, "but not surprising. That it was Foo, one of the most experienced and prepared athletes in the sport, was hard to grasp. He was one of the best, and that left us all more vulnerable than we had hoped."

Thus the plot thickens. The theory of evolution says we exist to pass along our genes. Fundamental biology tells us that survival is the name of the game. So potent is this dictate that in 1973 the psychologist Ernest Becker won a Pulitzer Prize for *The Denial of Death*, arguing that everything we think of as civilization–from the cities we build to the religions we believe in–is nothing beyond an elaborate, symbolic defense mechanism against the awful knowledge of our own mortality. A chorus of researchers has since seconded this opinion. These days, scientists consider the fear of death *the* fundamental human motivator, the most primary of our primary drives.

Then Mark Foo died.

Before his passing, it could be said that the consequences of tickling the edge were still somewhat unknown. Certainly, others had died for these dreams. Mountain climbers went by the dozen. Skydivers too. And skiers? In Chamonix alone, nearly sixty perished every year. Somehow, though, there had always been a way to rationalize these events. Inexperience, bad equipment, bad weather, freak accident, whatever. Mark Foo, though, was a household name. When he went, he took plausible deniability with him.

Evolutionary science tells us his extremely well-publicized death should have produced a serious downtick in the pursuit of the dumb and the dangerous. Athletes, realizing their lives really were on the line, should have started backing away from the line. But–um–that's not what happened.

Not even close.

In 1994, the number of big-wave riders in the world totaled less than a hundred. These days, it's well into the thousands. The same holds for the extreme wing of every other action and adventure category. The phenomenon is ubiquitous. Right now, more people are risking their lives for their sports than ever before in history, and, as Thomas Pynchon wrote in *Gravity's Rainbow,* "It is not often that Death is told so clearly to fuck off."

Trying to explain why this is happening is not easy. In the years since Darwin published *The Origin of Species,* survival and procreation have become the only scientifically acceptable answers to "What is the meaning of life?" This recent upswing in gleeful, wanton abandon pushes hard on these answers, challenging foundational notions in biology, psychology, and philosophy. This, then, is the gauntlet thrown by the likes of Mark Foo and Shane McConkey, the very far frontier, the razor's edge of our knowledge, the uneasy and somewhat spiritual truth that for an ever-burgeoning segment of the human population, these sports really are worth dying for.

PART ONE

HE IS THIS FRENZY

Where is the lightning to lick you with its tongue? Where is the frenzy
with which you should be inoculated? Behold, I teach you the overman:
He is this lightning; he is this frenzy.

— FRIEDRICH NIETZSCHE

The Way of Flow

DANNY WAY AND THE SHORTEST PATH TOWARD SUPERMAN

It's the last day of the women's team gymnastic competition in the 1996 Olympics. In the history of the games, the United States has never beaten the Russians in this particular contest, but that record looks about to fall. Going into the final rotation, the US has a significant 0.897-point advantage. Only a complete collapse on the vault stands between these women and their dreams. Then the unthinkable begins to happen. The first four American gymnasts all take extra steps on their landings. Next, Dominique Moceanu falls on her first vault, then again on her second. That commanding lead has been erased. It's down to Kerri Strug, but hers is a difficult trick, and she underrotates, lands awkwardly, and hears a loud snap. Her ankle is now badly sprained. She is limping, in considerable pain, but if she doesn't stick her next attempt, the Russians will take home gold.

The United States is in a tough spot. Strug, a four-foot-nine gymnast from Tucson, Arizona, has always been their weakest link. As *ESPN The Magazine* once wrote: "Strug . . . does not possess the fearlessness, the toughness, the aggressiveness, the heart and the threshold of pain as her teammates." All of this changes on her second attempt. She tears down the runway, nails her back handspring, flawlessly flips over the vault, and perfectly lands a difficult twisting dismount. On impact, she hears another snap. Gingerly, like a dancer, Strug tucks that leg behind her, never losing her balance. She hops in one direction, then another, both times raising her arms in the traditional judges' salute. An instant later she collapses, but not before scoring a 9.712 and taking home the hardware.

I mention all of this in a book about action and adventure sports because, again, comparisons are helpful. Strug's vault is considered one of the greatest moments in gymnastics history and the defining moment of the 1996 games. The entire women's team is now remembered as the Magnificent Seven, and Strug herself earned the athletic trifecta: her face on a Wheaties box, a *Sports Illustrated* cover, and a trip to the White House. Danny Way has none of these things. In fact, unless you are a serious skateboarding devotee, there's a pretty good chance you don't know his name, let alone what he accomplished on July 12, 2005.

So let's return to Strug's final vault. Imagine a similar set of circumstances with a few key differences. Instead of a bad sprain, the ankle is shattered. Fractured into pieces. The foot is the size of a cabbage and the knee isn't working quite right. Instead of having to weigh an injured joint and stumble fifty feet to the start of the runway, imagine having to climb ten long flights of stairs on a broken bone. The pain is agonizing, but the view from the top even worse. The launch pad is a wobbly platform a couple hundred feet off the ground. No safety nets either, so any fall could be fatal.

Just to keep things interesting, let's make a few more changes. Strug later told reporters she'd performed that exact trick over a thousand times, a fact not difficult to understand because the vault doesn't change between attempts. But what if it did? Instead of the same old apparatus, imagine a brand-new one — the largest ever constructed: longer than a football field, with a springboard capable of pitching a human body some seventy feet into the air. Suddenly, this is not a vault that anyone has done a thousand times — it's a "megavault" no one has ever done before. A completely de novo experience, an unknown, an impossible — and one with exceptionally dangerous consequences. Now, hopefully, you're starting to understand what Danny Way was up against when he attempted to jump the Great Wall of China on a skateboard.

If not — well, you're not alone.

Danny Way, considered by many to be the greatest skateboarder of all time, first introduced the world to the MegaRamp in the 2003 skate flick *The DC Video*. Very few knew what to make of it. At first glance, the contraption is utterly befuddling, more like an outtake from a surrealistic painting than anything anyone would ever skate down. "It was like three times the size of anything I had ever seen in skateboarding," pro Australian rider Jake Brown told the *New York Times*. "It was crazy. It still is crazy." Brown, it should be mentioned, once crashed fifty feet straight down on a MegaRamp miscalculation. He hit so hard that his sneakers shot off and he was knocked out cold. Many who witnessed that fall thought he was dead.

In 2004, Way convinced the X Games to make the MegaRamp the center of their skateboarding competition, claiming it was the only way he'd ever consider competing in the event. Not surprisingly, he took home gold. That same year, he also saw the Great Wall from an airplane window and decided that jumping over it was the next thing he wanted to accomplish. He went to China on an inspection trip, trying to find a suitable launch point, finally settling on the majestic Ju Yong Guan gate. "It's the widest spot in the wall," said Way, "which I think does the most justice to skateboarding and the possibility of breaking a world record."

It turned out the spot was actually a little wider. A few weeks into the ramp's construction, the architects realized they'd made a measurement mistake and the distance required to jump the wall was considerably greater than first imagined. Way, now back in the States, was reached via satellite phone. "I think you're going to have to clear more than seventy feet to make it," he was told, "isn't that, I mean, just too gnarly?" Danny didn't even pause. "No," he said, in a statement that has since ended up printed on T-shirts: "Nothing's too gnarly."

Still, when completed, the Great Wall MegaRamp *was* pretty gnarly. The roll-in stretched more than 100 feet, roughly the same size as an Olympic ski jump. This led to a seventy-foot gap jump over the wall, which dropped into a thirty-two-foot quarterpipe, the largest ever constructed. According to Way's calculations, the pipe would launch him some thirty-five feet straight up — almost seventy feet off the deck — so, of course, there's no margin for error. But here's the tricky part: skaters make errors.

"Skateboarding is a game of failure," says Way. "That's what makes this sport so different. Skaters are willing to take a great deal of physical punishment. We'll try something endlessly, weeks on end, painful failure after painful failure after painful failure. But for me, when it finally snaps together, when I'm really pushing the edge and skating beyond my abilities, there's a zone I get into. Everything goes silent. Time slows down. My peripheral vision fades away. It's the most peaceful state of mind I've ever known. I'll take all the failures. As long as I know that feeling is coming, that's enough to keep going."

And Way keeps going. That is his trademark. He arrives in China one day before the event and climbs to the top of the MegaRamp. The platform is unsteady. He bounces up and down; the whole structure starts to shake. This is not a good sign. Two years prior, a BMX rider tried to jump the wall, but shoddy ramp construction sent him over the landing pad and into the side of a mountain. He died from massive internal organ failure a few hours later. Despite all of this, Way decides to take a practice run.

It will be his only one.

Way trained in the desert, where the air was thin. In China, with the humidity, it is far too thick. The denser atmosphere slows him down and Way under-jumps the gap, pancakes hard, and rag-dolls for more than fifty feet. His ankle is fractured, his ACL torn, his steering foot swollen beyond belief. He is rushed to the hospital, but, not wanting to know the extent of the injury, hobbles out before treatment. While this is going on, construction workers get busy. The roll-in is lengthened, the gap is shortened, and, if Way decides to try again, it'll be another first descent.

Of course, he tries again. Twenty-four hours later and barely able to walk, Way climbs those ten flights of stairs a second time. He moves slowly, his breathing labored, his head hanging down. More than 125 million Chinese are watching; most hold their breath. Atop the launch platform, Way paces like a caged animal. Finally, he decides it's time. A one-arm salute to quiet the crowd, a shift of his weight forward, and the lonely thump of his board contacting the ramp.

One Mississippi, two Mississippi . . .

It takes five painfully long seconds for him to hit the edge of the jump. Five seconds after that it is over. Danny Way, under ridiculously adverse conditions and with considerable aplomb, just became the first person to leap the Great Wall of China on a skateboard. He broke two world records along the way.

And if this were typical athletic fare, this is where our story would end. But the triumph of the podium is rarely what drives action sport athletes. Way doesn't skate to break records or win championships. He skates. Period. Plus, MegaRamps cost over half a million dollars to build—so the opportunity to play on one doesn't come along every day. Thus, with nothing left to prove and his life on the line, Danny Way drags his sorry ass up ten stories once again, this time throwing a perfect 360 over the gap. And just to make sure that one wasn't a fluke, he did it three more times.

"Look," says freestyle motocross legend Travis Pastrana, "on that ramp, with totally healthy limbs, Danny's risking his life. But he destroyed his steering foot and knee. Once he sets himself on the board, if either the ankle or the knee gives by even a fraction of an inch, he's going to fly off the side and die. If you want to talk about pushing limits, most people can't even stand on a broken ankle. Danny not only stood, he withstood four Gs of pressure going into that quarter-pipe—five times in a row."

One G is the force of Earth's gravity—the force that determines how much we weigh. Formula One drivers, when cornering, pull two. Astronauts, on takeoff, suffer three. Most people black out at five. The four Gs that Way experienced equate to more than 800 pounds of added pressure—all supported by a shattered limb.

And forget the external pressures; what about the internal ones? Way, believe it or not, is afraid of heights. "I've been with Danny on location scouting trips," says Darryl Franklin, one of Way's managers, "we'll be up high and he'll turn white as sheet. He's terrified, can't wait to get down." But to keep that fear in abeyance while standing atop the Great Wall MegaRamp—200 feet up and wobbly? To have the confidence to make that run, when no one has ever done anything like this before? On a broken limb? When the last guy who tried died for his effort? Again, the question at the heart of this book: How is any of this possible?

Well, to start where most start, the psychological: the undisputable fact that the ghosts that hunt for Danny Way are unremitting. They are legion. The ghosts of his injured brother, his alcoholic mother, his dead father, his dead stepfather, his first coach, the man who saved him from himself, T-boned at a stoplight and dead also, his best friend in jail for murder, his broken neck, his broken back, his umpteen surgeries, his anger, his pride — a relentless roar only truly silenced by the salvation of the edge.

The edge is the one place these ghosts can't follow.

And, to be certain, this alone provides plenty of motivation, but it still doesn't answer our question. The weight of Way's past and his desire for escape merely explain part of the why — why he started skating, why he kept skating — but little of the *how*. Way feels the same. "You want to know how I did something like jump the Great Wall on a fractured ankle," he says. "I can't really answer that. All I can tell you is what I already told you: When I'm pushing the edge, skating beyond my abilities, it's always a meditation in the zone."

This, then, is our answer. This is our mystery: a rare and radical state of consciousness where the impossible becomes possible. This is the secret that action and adventure athletes like Way have plumbed, the real reason ultimate human performance has advanced nearly exponentially these past few decades. The zone, quite literally, is the shortest path toward superman.

And this is a book about that zone.

ALBERT HEIM, WILLIAM JAMES, WALTER CANNON, AND THE HISTORY OF PEAK PERFORMANCE

Albert Heim found the zone as well — found it when he fell off the side of a mountain. This was in the early spring of 1871. Heim, his brother, and three friends had set out to climb the Santis, the twelfth-highest peak in Switzerland. All five men had been playing in the Alps since childhood, but none were considered experienced mountaineers. That issue was historical — almost no one was considered an experienced mountaineer in 1871.

While the first recorded climb in history was Roman emperor Hadrian's 121 CE scamper up Mount Etna (to watch the sun rise), historians date the sport to Sir Alfred Wills's 1854 summiting of the Wetterhorn. For certain, local guides had already topped that peak, but Sir

Alfred was an Englishman, and it was the English who were then keeping score. Either way, Wills's conquest marked the birth of "systematic mountaineering" and the start of the "Golden Age of Alpinism," a decade-long stretch wherein most of the first ascents in the Alps were completed.

Albert Heim, meanwhile, arrived a few years too late for the Golden Age. No peak-bagging exploits are credited to his name. In fact, he's not remembered for his contribution to mountaineering history. Rather, he's remembered as the point when that history took a turn for the weird.

The events that earned Heim this distinction took place just above treeline, at the point where the Santis' verdant lower flanks give way to an enormous blade of rock. By the time his party had reached the bottom edge of this massif, sunny skies had turned to heavy snow. Whiteout conditions trapped them in the middle of a rocky ledge. The way forward was down a dicey slope, steep and narrow, with cliffs on all sides. An argument broke out about what to do next, but they were underdressed and overexposed, and Heim decided to push on. Just as he lifted his leg to take a step, a gust of wind snatched his hat from his head. And Heim, without thinking about it, tried to snatch it back.

The sudden motion unbalanced him and the angle of the perch did the rest. Heim fell sideways, flipped upside down, and spun around backward. Before anyone could react, he was rocketing toward the lip of a massive cliff, no way to slow down. His ice axe was out of reach. He tried driving his head and hands into the ground, but his skull slammed into rocks, his fingers ground to pulps. Even before that pain could register, he was airborne.

Heim's actual flight covered sixty-six feet and lasted no more than a few seconds, but that wasn't his experience. The first thing Heim noticed was that he'd dropped into another dimension. His senses were exquisitely heightened, his vision panoramic. Time had slowed to a crawl. He could see his brother and his friends and the horrified look on their faces, but — as he explained later — felt "no anxiety, no trace of despair or pain ... rather calm seriousness, profound acceptance and a dominant mental quickness."

With his life unfolding in slow motion, Heim had time to survey the territory and begin making rescue plans. He imagined scenarios for slight injuries, others for serious injuries: where would he land, how would he bounce, and how his companions would make it down to his body. Then he realized he was never going to survive this fall and thus would be dead and unable to deliver the lecture he was supposed to give in five days. At Oxford University, no less, his first major Oxford lecture. He'd have to find a substitute. Then again, he'd be dead, so someone else was going to have to find a substitute. Next he tried to take off his glasses — to protect his eyes, of course — but was unable to reach them. Instead, he said goodbye to his family and his friends, and was that heavenly music he heard? But wait, if he did survive the fall, then he probably would be stunned by the impact. Since he didn't want to go stumbling off another cliff, the first thing he needed to do was revive his senses. A few drops of vinegar on his tongue should do the trick, and on and on until, as he later recounted: "I heard a dull thud and my fall was over."

Heim survived the impact, but the mystery never left him. Panoramic vision? Time dilation? Heavenly music? None of this made any sense. He was a scientist by training, a geologist who would go on to do fundamental work on the structure of the Alps and become a member of the Oxford Royal Society, yet his experience seemed beyond the bounds of the rational. Not knowing what else to do, Heim conducted a survey of thirty-two others who had all survived near-fatal falls. A staggering 95 percent reported similar anomalous events. What was causing them would remain a matter of long debate, but Heim's work marks the first scientific investigation into the fact that high-risk activity can profoundly alter consciousness and significantly enhance mental abilities.

Heim wrote this all up in a long essay entitled "Remarks on Fatal Falls," which was published in 1892. Historians consider it the first written account of a "near-death experience," but that term is misleading. Many of Heim's subjects reported these profoundly altered states without being in actual jeopardy — they only *thought* they were in life-threatening situations. This was a key detail. These experiences seemed mystical. If they only arose solely in dire straights, then perhaps they really were communiqués from beyond the beyond. Yet if perception and psychology were the triggers, then the puzzle was more physiological than paranormal — and that opened the door to considerably more interesting possibilities.

One of the first to notice these possibilities was philosopher, physician, and psychologist William James. This was perhaps appropriate. While James taught at Harvard, he was also one of science's wilder men, an extreme sensation seeker who often ran experiments on himself. In the early 1880s, those experiments involved psychedelics, primarily nitrous oxide, but he toyed with mescaline as well. Concurrently, James had been conducting a broad survey of the world's spiritual literature, trying to come up with an accurate catalog of all possible types of mystical experiences and their psychological ramifications. He noticed that it didn't seem to matter what drug he tried or spiritual tradition he studied, all of these so-called mystical experiences seemed to share deep commonalities: all variations on the same themes that Heim reported.

James also noted two more key details. The first was that these experiences were profound — people were radically different on the other side. Happier, more content, significantly more fulfilled. The results were undeniable. No matter the seemingly fantastic nature of the events, James was certain they produced changes that were undeniably psychologically real.

Secondly, high-risk adventure tended to amplify not only mental performance, but physical performance as well. This discovery made James curious about the limits of human potential and led him to his famous conclusion: "Most people live in a very restricted circle of their potential being. They make use of a very small portion of their possible consciousness, and of their soul's resources in general, much like a man who, out of his whole organism, should get into a habit of using and moving only his little finger."

But, James critically realized, people were not doomed to stay that way. "Our normal waking consciousness, rational consciousness as we call it, is but one special type of consciousness, whilst all about it, parted from it by the flimsiest of screens, there lie potential forms of consciousness entirely different. We may go through life without suspecting their existence; but apply the requisite stimulus, and at a touch they are there in all their completeness."

What is the requisite stimulus? Psychedelic drugs certainly provoke these experiences, as do a host of spiritual practices. But if it's truly a question of unlocking hidden abilities, James shared Heim's opinion: high-risk activity seemed the most likely path, once writing, "Great emergencies and crisis show us how much greater our vital resources are than we had supposed."

The work of Heim and James laid the foundation for a deeper inquiry into human potential, but it was the discovery of one of James's students, Walter Bradford Cannon, that truly changed the nature of the game. Cannon was interested in the strange physiological changes produced by powerful emotions. In all mammals, rage, anger, and fear produce an assortment of peculiarity: heart rates speed up, pupils dilate, nostrils flare, muscles tighten, digestion ceases, senses perk and sharpen — the list goes on. Around 1916, Cannon decided these disparate reactions were actually a global response by the nervous system to extreme stress, a response with a purpose: increase strength and stamina.

Cannon had discovered the "fight-or-flight response" and this rewrote the rule book. Until then, performance enhancement had always been divine in origin. Want to write a sonnet? Talk to the Muses. Want a better time in the 100-yard dash? Hermes can help. But the fight-or-flight response changed the equation, turning a gift from the gods into a byproduct of standard biology.

And biology was hackable.

The trail of Heim to James to Cannon went from psychology into physiology. It was a trail of mechanism: mindset impacts emotion, which alters biology, which increases performance. Thus, it seemed, by tinkering with mindset — using everything from physical to psychological to pharmacological interventions — one could significantly enhance performance.

Out of this work emerged one of history's stranger movements: the epic quest to hack ultimate human performance — a giant, global, mostly underground, often DIY, 100-plus-year effort to decode the mysteries of the zone. Adventurers, artists, academics, bohemian outcasts, maverick scientists, credentialed scientists, the psychedelic underground, paranormal researchers, the military's special forces, the

Pentagon's top brass, the CEOs of major Fortune 500 companies, all got involved. Yet out of this hodgepodge — for reasons that comprise the bulk of this book — action and adventure sport athletes have become the most advanced practitioners of this art, an elite cadre of zone hackers, masters of the state now known to scientists as *flow*.

THE WAY OF WAY

Three weeks after returning from Asia, his ankle broken, his knee torqued, his foot still plenty sore, Danny Way has a decision to make. The fifteenth installment of the Summer X Games are being held in downtown Los Angeles, the MegaRamp the centerpiece of the skateboarding competition. Way had taken home the gold the previous year, but with the injuries sustained in China, no one expects him to defend his title. No one, that is, except Way himself.

Way won his first contest at age eleven, was twice selected as *Thrasher Magazine's* Skater of the Year, five times an X Games gold medalist, six times an X Games podium finisher, and seven times a world record breaker. He remains the only skateboarder to have his name inscribed in gold in the Great Wall of China, "bomb drop" sixty-five feet off the guitar in front of Vegas's Hard Rock Casino, or have sideline careers in professional motocross and snowboarding. But of all the things Way's done, nothing is more impressive than his ability to triumph over injury.

"Danny Way single-handedly invented sports medicine for skateboarders," says Jacob Rosenberg, who directed the excellent Danny Way documentary *Waiting for Lightning*. "When he broke his neck — that was a career-ending injury. Athletes retired for far less. But Danny wouldn't accept that. He found his own doctors. He pioneered his own methods."

Way's methods are legendary. On a number of occasions, in order to gain a better understanding of his injury, he chose to have surgery without anesthetic. Big-wave rider Chris Malloy tells a story about the time he and Way had the exact same procedure on their knee. "I have a pretty high threshold for pain," recounts Malloy, "I kind of enjoy seeing what I can endure. But when I got home from the hospital, I was semiconscious, in extreme agony, about the worst I've ever felt. A few days later I called up Danny and mentioned how grueling that was. He said, 'Yeah, the drive home was gnarly.' We had the same procedure. I was in so much pain I kept blacking out. Danny drove himself home from the hospital."

Thus, perhaps not surprisingly, just three weeks after returning from China, Way steps onto the X Games MegaRamp launch platform and surveys the scene. His appearance sends the crowd into a tizzy; he barely notices. "I've gotten really good at pulling the veil down," says Way, "at camouflaging reality, locking out my conscious mind and riding my focus into the zone."

The same must be true for Jake Brown. Moments later, he kicks off the contest with a seventy-foot, 360 mute grab over the gap and a McTwist—an inverted backside 540 with another mute grab—out of the quarterpipe. There's an electronic height meter positioned behind the ramp. At the apex of Brown's McTwist, the meter blinks twenty-two feet—and that's above a twenty-seven-foot quarterpipe. So yeah, game on.

But not quite. Bob Burnquist drops in next, comes off his board midway over the gap, and goes headfirst into the landing. Typical Burnquist. Known for extremely technical tricks in extremely dangerous situations, he survives due to catlike reflexes and seriously good karma. This time is no different. Burnquist gets his knees down at the last moment and rides the fall out on his pads.

Next up is Way. He sails cleanly over the gap, stomps the landing, and blazes into the quarterpipe. Then everything goes sideways. He soars twenty-two feet into the air, but drops down at a bad angle and smashes his foot on the edge of the pipe—the same foot he mangled in China. The impact rebreaks the ankle, then flips Way upside down. He flies another ten feet, slams hard, bounces twice, and doesn't move. The medical staff rushes over, the air sucks out of the stadium. Atop the ramp, Burnquist buries his head in his hands.

Eventually, three people help Way to his feet, but he shakes off the assistance, nearly stumbles, then drags himself to the side of the ramp. It's a brave performance, yet the announcer says what everyone is thinking: "I don't know how in the universe Danny could come back from that."

A good question.

In 1907, William James challenged psychologists to explain why certain people can draw on deep reservoirs to accomplish significantly more than others. As an example, he reflected on the idea of the "second wind."

> [F]atigue gets worse up to a certain critical point, when gradually or suddenly it passes away, and we are fresher than before. We have evidently tapped a level of new energy, masked until then by the fatigue-obstacle usually obeyed. There may be layer after layer of this experience. A third and a fourth "wind" may supervene. Mental activity shows the phenomenon as well as physical, and in exceptional cases we may find, beyond the very extremity of fatigue-distress, amounts of ease and power that we never dreamed ourselves to own, sources of strength habitually not taxed at all, because habitually we never push through the obstruction, never pass those early critical points.

Danny Way has spent his life pushing past obstruction. Skating gave him a family and a sense of belonging, and he feels strongly that the only way to honor that debt is to continue progressing his sport. To that point, the medical staff checks out his ankle. It's clearly destroyed. They tell him he needs to go to the hospital, that he should seriously consider calling it a day. Way shakes his head against the idea.

"That's not my style," he says.

Thus, not much more than ten minutes later, Way returns to the top of the MegaRamp, shakes off the pain, and throws a rocket air backflip over the gap. On its own, in his condition, just a rocket air would have been a victory. Invented by Christian Hosoi in 1986, the trick requires a skater to stand with both feet on the tail of the board, while both hands grip the nose, and then, by shoving the board forward, the skater and his board form the rough outline of a rocket. But adding a broken ankle and a backflip to this mix? It's the rough equivalent of Leonardo da Vinci painting the *Mona Lisa* with a steak knife shoved into his eye.

"That's part of the problem with trying to discuss the level of performance in action sports today," says Travis Pastrana. "Danny Way did a seventy-foot backflip on a broken ankle. But how many people in the world can even throw a backflip? On flat ground? Over a seventy-foot gap? How about a rocket air? None of these are everyday skills. To put them together in front of a live audience, in gold medal competition? Most people would say that's a home run to win the World Series, but Danny wasn't even done; he still had the quarterpipe ahead of him."

The quarterpipe throws Way about twenty feet into the air, and Way throws a varial 540 — meaning, at the same time that he's doing one and a half spins, he's also reaching down between his legs and spinning his board 180 degrees — then laces (comes in smooth) the landing. Pandemonium erupts. "If ever you say you can't do something," shouts the announcer, "remember Danny Way."

But there's no need to remember — because Way isn't done. Over the next hour, he and Burnquist and Brown enter into one of the greatest duels in X Games history. In the middle of it, Way takes another fall, stunningly hard, but comes back a second time. He has one run left. To pull back into first place he needs to pull off something spectacular. He does not disappoint.

Way backflips over the gap and soars out of the quarterpipe and throws . . . well, no one is still sure. He spins around twice and sails too far from the vert wall, then tries to alter his flight path by torquing sideways. This added momentum over-rotates his torso, his feet sail up toward his head, his body spins nearly upside down. He's fifty feet above the deck and falling fast. The announcer says, "Oh no." The entire stadium braces for impact. Then Way — as calmly as a geisha pouring tea — sets his feet back on the board and stomps the landing.

"I've been shooting action sports for twenty years," says photographer Mike Blabac, "I've never seen anyone do something like it." Not many have. It's been said that the four-week stretch from Way's first attempt at the Great Wall to the X Games landing of his 540 miracle is one of the most astounding examples of athletic performance in action sport history. Maybe, some say, the most astounding. Ultimately, it's probably too difficult to make such comparisons, but, if nothing else, Way's performance demonstrates the depth of our ignorance. We really have no idea how deep our reservoir runs, no clear estimate of where our limits lie. You want more proof? In the Big Air competition, Danny Way placed second.

Bob Burnquist, on the last run of the contest, busts out a move he has yet to attempt, either in warm-ups or at any point during the contest. He goes switch over the gap and switch into the quarterpipe, then tosses an indie backside 360 off the vert wall — one of the harder tricks in skateboarding (ironically, it's a trick invented by Way in the early 1990s). Landing one requires coming in backward and blind. Burnquist threw the biggest indie backside 360 ever, falling more than twenty feet before the ramp snapped into view. Watching from the side, Way just shakes his head and starts clapping.

"Every good athlete can find the flow," continues Pastrana, "but it's what you do with it that makes you great. If you consistently use that state to do the impossible, you get confident in your ability to do the impossible. You begin to expect it. That's why we're seeing so much progression in action sports today. It's the natural result of a whole lot of people starting to expect the impossible."

THE GODFATHER OF FLOW

It was Mihaly Csikszentmihalyi (pronounced *Me high, Chick-sent-me-high*), the former chairman of the University of Chicago Department of Psychology and now at Claremont Graduate University, who first coined the term *flow*. This was in the late 1960s. Csikszentmihalyi was in the midst of what would soon become the largest global happiness study ever conducted, though this was a somewhat accidental outcome. To borrow Daniel Gilbert's phrase, Csikszentmihalyi had merely stumbled upon happiness. What he'd really been searching for was the meaning of life.

It had been quite a search.

Csikszentmihalyi was born in Flume, Italy, which is now Rijeka, Croatia, on September 29, 1934. The son of a Hungarian diplomat, his childhood was war-torn, spent in flight from both the Nazis and the Russians. One of his brothers was killed, another exiled to Siberia. When he was seven years old, Csikszentmihalyi was sent to an Italian prison camp.

In the camp, Csikszentmihalyi learned to play chess. He became obsessed with the game. When at the board, nothing else seemed to penetrate his consciousness: no missing siblings, no armed guards, no prison he couldn't leave. Chess allowed him forget the tumult, to make the best of a bad situation. This, he noticed, was something of a rare talent.

"In prison," Csikszentmihalyi told audiences at TED, "I realized how few of the grown-ups around me were able to withstand the tragedies the war visited upon them, how few of them had anything resembling a normal, contented, satisfied life once their job, their home, and their security was destroyed. So I became interested in understanding what contributed to a life worth living."

After the war, Csikszentmihalyi read philosophy, studied religion, got involved in the arts — all the things that supposedly gave life meaning. Nothing quite satisfied. Then, one Sunday afternoon in Zurich, he attended a free lecture by Carl Jung, the founder of analytical psychology. Csikszentmihalyi enjoyed the talk, started reading Jung's books, and pretty soon decided psychology was the best way to answer his question.

In the coming years, his studies took him to the University of Chicago, where Csikszentmihalyi zeroed in on one of the hot topics of the time: motivation. After Freud's unconscious had been dethroned by Skinner's behaviorism, psychologists began having a hard time explaining why people did the things they did. The behaviorists said it all came down to need and reward. We do X to get Y. This is known as "extrinsic motivation," but the conclusion never sat right with Abraham Maslow.

One of the greatest psychological thinkers of the past century, Maslow began his career in the 1940s on staff at Brooklyn College, where he was mentored by anthropologist Ruth Benedict and Gestalt psychologist Max Wertheimer. Back then, most of psychology was focused on fixing pathological problems rather than celebrating psychological possibilities, but Maslow thought Benedict and Wertheimer such "wonderful human beings" that he began studying their behavior, trying to figure out what it was they were doing right.

Over time, he began studying the behavior of other exemplars of outstanding human performance. Albert Einstein, Eleanor Roosevelt, and Frederick Douglass each came under his scrutiny. Maslow was looking for common traits and common circumstances, wanting to explain why these folks could attain such unbelievable heights, while so many others continued to flounder.

High achievers, he came to see, were *intrinsically* motivated. They were deeply committed to testing limits and stretching potential, frequently using intensely focused activity for exactly this purpose. But this focused activity, Maslow also noticed, produced a significant reward of its own: altering consciousness, creating experiences very similar to those James had dubbed "mystical." Except, the key difference: few of Maslow's subjects were even religious.

So Maslow secularized James's terminology. "Mystical experiences" were out; "peak experiences" were in — the sensation, though, was the same. "During a peak experience," Maslow explained, "the individual experiences an expansion of self, a sense of unity, and meaningfulness in life. The experience lingers in one's consciousness and gives a sense of purpose, integration, self-determination and empathy." These states, he concluded, were the hidden commonality among all high achievers, the source code of intrinsic motivation:

> The peak experience is felt as a self-validating, self-justifying moment. . . . It is felt to be a highly valuable — even uniquely valuable — experience, so great an experience sometimes that even to attempt to justify it takes away from its dignity and worth. As a matter of fact, so many people find this so great and high an experience that it justifies not only itself, but even living itself. Peak experiences can make life worthwhile by their occasional occurrence. They give meaning to life itself. They prove it to be worthwhile. To say this in a negative way, I would guess that peak experiences help to prevent suicide.

Csikszentmihalyi arrived on the scene a few years later. The birth of his happiness study was a more pedestrian version of Maslow's inquiry. Csikszentmihalyi wasn't just interested in high achievers, he was curious about what motivated the average citizen: What activities produced their deepest enjoyment and greatest satisfaction? This was the birth of his happiness study — the desire to ask people about the times in their lives when they felt their best and performed at their best.

He started out interviewing experts: rock climbers, dancers, artists, surgeons, chess players, and the like. Next, he expanded his search to include Italian farmers, Navajo sheepherders, Chicago assembly-line workers, rebellious Japanese teenagers, elderly Korean women — a gargantuan assortment in total. Surprisingly, and regardless of culture, level of modernization, age, social class, or gender, all of these people told him the same thing: when they were at their best and felt their best was when they were experiencing sensations very similar to Maslow's peak experiences.

This was a fairly startling finding. It meant that while the things people found enjoyable varied completely — the Japanese teenagers liked to swarm around on motorcycles and the elderly Korean women preferred meditation — the feeling the activity produced, the *why* behind the enjoyment, was globally ubiquitous. In fact, when Csikszentmihalyi dove deeper into the data, he discovered that the happiest people on earth, the ones who felt their lives had the most meaning, were those who had the most peak experiences.

Moreover, this did not come down to chance or luck. The happiest people on earth worked hard for their fulfillment. They didn't just *have* the most peak experiences, they had devoted their lives to *having* these experiences, often, as Csikszentmihalyi explained in his 1996 book *Creativity*, going to extreme lengths to seek them out:

> It was clear from talking to them, that what kept them motivated was the quality of the experience they felt when they were involved with the activity. The feeling didn't come when they were relaxing, when they were taking drugs or alcohol, or when they were consuming the expensive privileges of wealth. Rather, it often involved painful, risky, difficult activities that stretched the person's capacity and involved an element of novelty and discovery.

In his interviews, to describe these optimal states of performance, *flow* was a term his subjects kept using. When everything was going right, the work was effortless, fluid, and automatic — flowy. So Csikszentmihalyi, in keeping with tradition, renamed "peak experiences," instead calling them "flow states." He defined the state as "being so involved in an activity that nothing else seems to matter. The ego falls away. Time flies. Every action, movement and thought follows inevitably from the previous one, like playing jazz. Your whole being is involved, and you're using your skills to the utmost."

And those skills are significantly magnified. Physical skills, mental skills, psychological skills, social skills, creative skills, decision making skills — the list goes on. A ten-year study done by McKinsey found top executives reported being up to *five* times more productive when in flow. Creativity and cooperation are so amplified that Greylock partner venture capitalist James Slavet, in a recent article for Forbes .com, called "flow state percentage" — defined as the amount of time employees spend in flow — the "most important management metric for building great innovation teams."

Flow also has an incredible yet unsung impact on our economy. "When we watch a live concert or a traditional sports event," says former head of innovation at Yahoo and Singularity University global ambassador Salim Ismail, "we're essentially paying to watch people in a flow state. Whether it's Kobe Bryant, Roger Federer, Jay-Z, or a jazz crooner, they've all put in endless hours of work so that when performance time comes, they are fully present and in flow. An actor with screen presence is there, too. A great poet can deliver flow to the reader just through the power of words. We pay to watch, read, or be in the presence of a flow experience. If quantified, you'd find it's a major chunk of the GDP."

Of course, flow's effects extend beyond profits turned and abilities enhanced. The data Csikszentmihalyi collected was clear. Flow is more than an optimal state of consciousness — one where we feel our best and perform our best — it also appears to be the only practical answer to the question: What is the meaning of life? Flow is what makes life worth living. "There are moments that stand out from the chaos of the everyday as shining beacons," wrote Csikszentmihalyi, alongside psychologist Susan Jackson, in *Flow in Sports*. "In many ways, one might say that the *whole effort of humankind through millennia of history* has been to capture these fleeting moments of fulfillment and make them part of everyday existence."

Flow was a groundbreaking discovery, and one with considerable impact. In the coming years, it would quietly reshape our world, radically altering our thinking about everything from the limits of human performance to the neurobiology of religious experience. It would launch outstanding scientific debate and either wholly create or significantly impact a half-dozen fields of academic research. Corporations like Patagonia, Toyota, Ericsson, and Microsoft would make flow a critical piece of their strategy and culture. Entire industries would benefit: coders in flow built the Internet, gamers in flow built the video game industry, and, of course, the sports world has never been the same.

For athletes hunting the zone, books and training programs appeared by the score. Flow in golf. Flow in tennis. Flow in archery. In 1993, coach Jimmy Johnson credited Csikszentmihalyi with helping the Dallas Cowboys win the Super Bowl, and suddenly, flow in football. Temple University sports psychologist Michael Sachs, who made an extensive study of these states, summed this up nicely: "Every gold medal or world championship that's ever been won, most likely, we now know, there's a flow state behind the victory."

Yet, out of all of these groups, it's action and adventure sport athletes who have taken things the farthest. Some of this was accidental, some intentional, but if you're looking for one reason why there has been near-exponential growth in ultimate human performance over this past generation, the first thing to know is the most straightforward: while finding flow may be the goal of every athlete on the planet, for action and adventure sports athletes it's a necessity.

In all other activities, flow is the hallmark of high performance, but in situations where the slightest error could be fatal, then perfection is the only choice — and flow is the only guarantee of perfection. Thus, flow is the only way to survive in the fluid, life-threatening conditions of big waves, big rivers, and big-mountains. Without it, equipment like the MegaRamp remain a pipe dream or a death sentence. Necessity, as they say, is the mother of invention.

Or, as Danny Way explains: "It's either find the zone or suffer the consequences — there's no other choice available."

2

The Wave of Flow

THE MILLENNIUM WAVE

In the annals of find the zone or suffer the consequences, there is little that can compare to Teahupoo (pronounced *cho-poo*). The word translates from the French Polynesian as "wall of skulls" or "place of severed heads," but neither description quite captures. Surfers describe Teahupoo as "hideous," "deadly," "a war zone," "liquid napalm," "the grinding eye of doom," and, of course, "up there with anything for tons of brutality per square inch of skin." The website Surfline might have said it best: "This isn't your father's perfect wave, and unless seeing your next birthday doesn't rank on your list of priorities, it isn't yours either."

Teahupoo sits a quarter mile off the southwestern coast of Tahiti. It is not a cold-water wave like California's Maverick's, nor a tall wave like Hawaii's Jaws. Instead of exploding vertically, Teahupoo detonates laterally, producing a barrel that has accurately been compared to the Lincoln Tunnel. It is also the heaviest wave in the world — the most mass, the most power, the most ferocity — but unlike other famous big-wave destinations (Jaws, Waimea Bay, Maverick's), Teahupoo breaks in incredibly shallow water. Less than three feet below the surface of the water sits a razor-sharp coral reef. Surf legend Laird Hamilton summed up the issue nicely: "Jaws is all about the hold down, Teahupoo is all about the bounce."

And it was Hamilton, who, on August 17, 2000, just seven days after surfer Briece Taerea died from Teahupoo's bounce, tucked his feet into his foot straps, grabbed hold of a tow rope, and headed out to this famed lineup. Hawaiian big-wave charger Darrick Doerner was piloting that Jet Ski and, considering what would soon unfold, this was perhaps appropriate.

Some eight years prior, Hamilton and Doerner had together made the discovery that made surfing Teahupoo even possible. The issue was one of physics. Catching a wave requires paddling a surfboard to a speed roughly equal to the wave's speed, but big waves travel far faster than a human being can actually paddle. As a result, since the early days of surfing, waves in excess of twenty-five feet have been deemed uncatchable, thus unridable. As author Susan Casey explained in *The Wave:* "Anything bigger is simply moving too fast; trying to catch a sixty-foot wave by windmilling away on your stomach is like trying to catch the subway by crawling."

To get around this problem, in the mid-'90s, Laird Hamilton, Darrick Doerner, and Buzzy Kerbox invented the sport of tow-in surfing. Instead of having to paddle into monster waves, these surfers could hitch a ride on a tow line hung behind a Jet Ski. The ski could then whip the surfer into the wave with exacting precision and more than enough speed to catch the behemoth. The result was a paradigm shift akin to Danny Way's invention of the MegaRamp — it meant that once off-limits monsters were suddenly open for business.

And business was good.

If you're looking for another example of the recent and accelerated progress in ultimate human performance, consider that Pat Curren's 1960 ride of a twenty-five-footer at Waimea Bay had long been deemed the biggest wave ever caught. "In 1996," wrote surf historian Matt Warshaw in *Surfriders,* "Laird Hamilton caught the biggest wave of the year — a thirty-five-footer. A ten-foot jump after thirty-six years doesn't seem like much. The fact that a full three quarters of that height jump was made from 1993 to 1996, however, is nothing less than amazing."

It was also just the beginning. Hamilton, Doerner, and Kerbox were soon joined by Dave Kalama, Brett Little, Rush Randle, Mark Angulo, Mike Waltze, Pete Cabrinha, and Brian Keaulana — an exceptional bevy of big-wave talent who together formed the "strapped crew," a reference to the foot straps used to hold these surfers on their boards. These men pioneered both tow-in surfing and the next phase of big-wave rescue, an attempt to make the colossally dangerous merely exceptionally dangerous. Others soon borrowed their techniques and by decade's end, waves in excess of fifty feet were being toyed with on a semi-regular basis.

But nothing accomplished in the 1990s compared to the madness Doerner and Hamilton awoke to that sunny day in 2000. When both men got to the beach, the surf was big. Too big. "The day started out with us being told Teahupoo was completely unridable," recounts Hamilton. "They said: 'We don't go out there when it's like this.' But all the people who do what we do, who do things that no one has done before, we're not the type to accept that answer. All no means is they don't know for sure or there's a secret being kept, like someone's trying to hide something really good. Either way, we have to try."

And by "we" he means, of course, himself.

Hamilton grew up in Hawaii. His adopted father, Bill Hamilton, considered the most stylish surfer of his era, had no problem taking his son to the beach. At the time, the beach was the legendary Bonzai Pipeline, one of the more vicious breaks in surfing. But Pipeline was Bill's playground; thus it became Laird's as well.

"People always ask me if I feel fear in the big waves. Of course, I'm afraid. If I was out in fifty-foot surf and I'm not feeling fear, then I'm not properly assessing the situation. But it's different when you're raised in these conditions. When I was a kid, I was rescued every four or five days at Pipeline. The currents would catch me and drag me out and the lifeguards would have to come get me. Eventually, they got so pissed off, they told my father to lock me up while he surfed."

Little has changed. When it comes to the questionable edge of big waves, even among his exceptionally talented group of friends, Hamilton has remained, as he puts it, "the crash-test dummy." In this particular case, he had an early morning session riding beastly Teahupoo and no problem. He loved every minute. So the rest of the crew went out to see for themselves.

That session went well. After his friends had their fill, Hamilton decided he wanted another go. His timing couldn't have been better. Or worse. Right when he grabbed the tow rope to begin his second session, the real heart of the swell arrived. "Imagination," says futurist and philosopher Jason Silva, "allows us to conceive of delightful future possibilities, pick the most amazing one, and pull the present forward to meet it." But the wave that Hamilton chose — it wasn't a future anyone wanted to meet.

Doerner, from his position on the ski, saw what was about to happen and tried to shout Hamilton out of the way. Others did as well. Even before what is now known as the "Millennium Wave" rose anywhere close to its final height, a chorus of "Don't go!" erupted from surfers and spectators sitting in the channel. But it was too late. Hamilton was already gone.

The Millennium Wave was a rogue wave, a freakish titan, the product of two different swells intersecting and stacking atop each other. The results looked less like a product of hydrodynamics than a very special effect cooked up by wizards in Hollywood. "On any normal wave," says Matt Warshaw, "the lip — the part that is pitching ahead and forming the tube — is only a tiny fraction of the wave. On the Millennium Wave it was almost half. It was like a dam bursting, like someone had dropped the seafloor by thirty feet and the ocean was desperately trying to find level ground."

So much force was being generated that Hamilton, as he was trying to get into position for the tube ride, found himself getting sucked up the wave's face. To hold steady, he had to reach down, to the outside of his surfboard, and drag his right hand in the water. It was the perfect move and the only reason he's alive today — but here's the thing: no one had ever made that move before.

"Laird had to drag his backhand," says former *Surfer* editor Sam George in Stacy Peralta's film *Riding Giants*, "on the opposite side of the board, to keep himself from getting sucked up in that hydraulic. In the middle of that maelstrom how did his mind say this is what I have to do? No one had ever ridden as Laird rode on that wave before. He couldn't practice. So it was his imagination dealing with that unimaginable energy and coming up with the plan spontaneously."

And then things got really crazy. That monster lip cantilevered into the reef, and the resulting thunderclap splash went off like a megaton bomb. Shock waves pulsed into the channel. The spray shot up almost sixty feet. As far as anyone could tell, Hamilton had been swallowed whole.

Seconds later, though, the mists parted, and out he rode, tall and triumphant. It is no exaggeration to say nothing has been the same since. "Laird's wave at Teahupoo was the . . . single most significant ride in surfing history," continues George. "More than any other ride. . . . [W]hat it did was completely restructure our entire, collective perception of what was possible."

Or, at least, that's how the history books tell the story. The real truth is even more peculiar. "We don't talk about it much because of the film and all the press attention that followed," explains Hamilton, "but I rode two other waves that day that were bigger than the Millennium Wave. One of them had boat wakes running through it. So not only was it bigger, but, just to mess with my mind a little more, I had to jump these little rollers as I was riding down the face."

I AM TRYING TO FREE YOUR MIND, NEO

By now, it should come as no surprise that Hamilton found himself in a flow state while riding those Teahupoo waves. Flow tends to be the psychic signature of world-class performance and paradigm-shifting breakthroughs, and clearly Hamilton's effort falls into both categories. Moreover, as Danny Way pointed out, there's just no other way to survive such a situation. But the goal of Part One of this book is to understand how flow makes these things possible, so these facts don't take us very far. Instead, to get at the answers we want, we're going to need to draw a much more detailed map of the experience.

Flow cartography begins in the brain. Of course it does. To paraphrase author Diane Ackerman: That little huddle of neurons calls all the plays. But how it calls a play like flow is a complicated affair. The brain sends messages (i.e., calls plays) electrically and chemically and both are important here. Moreover, where in the brain these messages are being sent further affects the experience. So to complete our map of flow, we need to understand how the state impacts neuroelectricity (later in this chapter), neuroanatomy (Chapter Three), and neurochemistry (Chapter Four). Yet, before we can answer these specific questions, we must first address a few general concerns.

For starters, why are we examining events like the Millennium Wave? After all, many of us will never surf a day in our lives, let alone paddle into anything nearly as fearsome as Teahupoo. But that doesn't mean we have nothing to learn. Action and adventure athletes have used flow to push performance faster and farther than any group in history, so their triumphs can become our teachers. These events are our yardsticks (so we can see what's actually achievable) and case studies (so we can figure out how to achieve similar heights). The point is not that the impossible is possible for these athletes alone — if we diligently apply the lessons detailed herein — it's actually possible for all of us.

Our next general concern is the definition of terms. What is flow exactly? Scientists describe it either as a "state of consciousness" or an "altered state of consciousness," though neither phrase completely satisfies. Consciousness itself is a slippery subject. There is no agreed upon definition of the term, nor accurate taxonomy of its various states. Traditionally, researchers divide consciousness into sleeping, waking, and dreaming, then further subdivide by degrees of focus and alertness. The results are a progression of attentional categories from the "total unresponsiveness" of a vegetative coma to the "hypervigilance" of the fight-or-flight response. Flow states fall on this scale, but not exactly.

The zone requires attention, but of a very specific kind. When it comes to the task at hand, concentration is nearly total. Laird Hamilton saw every nuance of detail of the Millennium Wave's face. Yet, beyond this field, his awareness dropped off precipitously — i.e., he never heard the cries of warning coming from the spectators in the channel. Hamilton was hypervigilant and totally unresponsive and both at the same time. So unlike most other states of consciousness, which are defined by a singular type of attention, flow breaks boundaries, straddling multiple categories at once.

Nor does flow fit comfortably into the standard definition of an "altered state of consciousness," which, using psychologist Charles

Tart's classic description, is a "*qualitative* shift in the pattern of mental functioning" [Tart's italics]. The issue is that most of these shifts are emotionally unstable. While sleeping, we have good dreams and bad dreams; while taking psychedelics, we have good trips and bad trips. Flow, on the other hand, is always a positive experience. No one ever has a bad time in a flow state. So while the zone provides a qualitative shift in mental functioning, it's a far more consistent shift than can be found in other altered states of consciousness.

Consider, for example, how Hamilton describes the experience of riding giants, be they at Teahupoo or otherwise: "When you're in that moment, there's no beginning and no end. It starts off where it left off. When you go to that place, there's no time, and there's definitely no thought. It's just pure. You are and it is and that's why we continually seek it out, and always search for it, and need it. We need it to feel alive and to feel complete and to bring it all into perspective — it just makes everything else fall in line, fall in place. It makes everything else tolerable."

In his words, we hear plenty of familiar echoes. Just like Heim, Hamilton experienced time dilation. Just like Danny Way, he vanished into the moment. The same intrinsic motivation that fascinated Maslow shows up, as does Csikszentmihalyi's meaning-of-life ramifications. So while flow might be different from both traditional and altered states of consciousness, the stability of these component parts allows us to zero in on the phenomena.

To do just that, let's pry deeper into Hamilton's tale. Here's his memory of the takeoff: "I remember letting go of the rope just as Double D (aka Darrick Doerner) yelled out, 'Don't let go!' And other people were shouting, 'Don't go! Don't go!' I remember seeing the magnitude of the wall as it stood up, a double wall, and then putting myself in position . . . and then time just stood still. Then it was like I had an angel on one shoulder and a devil on the other as I thought about what I should do next, and they were saying, 'Jump off! Stay on! Jump off! Stay on!' Eventually the angel won and I stayed on, and that's the only way I made it."

Within this experience, we discover three of the more curious and basic properties of flow: the profound mental clarity provided by the state (note the calm, rational nature of the mental argument); the emotional detachment that tends to accompany this clarity (Hamilton watched his own mind debate itself from a removed position); and a hint of its automatic nature—how one right decision always leads to the next right decision. Within the zone, all of these elements are standard fare, turning up in thousands upon thousands of anecdotal reports. In fact, despite the ephemeral nature of the experience, so consistent are its various features that Csikszentmihalyi was able to sift through the data and isolate ten core components which demarcate the state. Here's his list:

Clear goals: Expectations and rules are discernible and goals are attainable and align appropriately with one's skill set and abilities. Moreover, the challenge level and skill level should both be high.

Concentration: A high degree of concentration on a limited field of attention.

A loss of the feeling of self-consciousness: The merging of action and awareness.

Distorted sense of time: One's subjective experience of time is altered.

Direct and immediate feedback: Successes and failures are apparent, so behavior can be adjusted as needed.

Balance between ability level and challenge: The activity is neither too easy nor too difficult.

A sense of personal **control** over the situation.

The activity is **intrinsically rewarding,** so action is effortlessness.

A **lack of awareness** of bodily needs.

Absorption: narrowing of awareness down to the activity itself.

Other researchers have since validated these ten categories and they stand as close to a working definition of flow as anyone has yet produced. Still, out of this total, three of the components — clear goals, immediate feedback, and the challenge/skill ratio (all of which we'll explore in greater detail later) — are considered "conditions for flow." They do not actually describe the state itself. Moreover, flow exists on a continuum, so not all of the remaining seven elements need to be present at the same time. Csikszentmihalyi uses the terms *microflow* and *macroflow* to explain these variations. In microflow, only a few of his categories are fulfilled — say clear goals, concentration, and absorption, or what would happen if Laird Hamilton paddled out for an afternoon of mellow Malibu surf. Macroflow, on the other hand, is what occurs when all of Csikszentmihalyi's conditions arrive at once — it's the full Teahupoo.

Yet still missing in this description is the one element that truly sets flow apart: the creative, problem-solving nature of the state. Because flow requires action — otherwise action and awareness cannot merge — there's decision making involved at every step. This is not a consistent feature of any other state of consciousness, altered or otherwise. Psychedelics, meditation, and dreams may bring fresh insight, but none requires that knowledge be immediately acted upon. Even in those waking states where decision making occurs, the process is not consistent enough to be considered part of the state's definition. But remember Csikszentmihalyi's explanation of the zone: "Every action, movement, and thought follows inevitably from the previous one, like playing jazz." What is jazz? It's the acoustic result of high-speed problem solving, of near-perfect decision making.

So, if we're really hunting for qualities that distinguish flow from other states of consciousness, the place to start may not even be with its individual components, rather with its practical value. Flow is an extremely efficient and effective decision-making strategy. But this does raise an additional question: How does flow enable us to make such good decisions? After all, as Hamilton himself pointed out, if the angel and the devil arguing on his shoulders had reached the wrong conclusion, we'd still be picking pieces of him out of Teahupoo's reef.

BRAIN WAVES AND BIG WAVES

Leslie Sherlin studies the brains of people making decisions — very, very good decisions. He's one of the world's leading experts in the neuroscience of high performance, having spent his career trying to figure out what separates guys like Laird Hamilton from the rest of us. "It's not just talent and training," says Sherlin, "it's something else. And, whatever that something else is, I sure don't have it."

Yet he almost had it — which was exactly the problem.

Sherlin grew up in Powell, Tennessee. While neither of his parents played an instrument, both felt music to be an important part of a child's education and introduced their son to the piano at age five. It was love at first sound. Sherlin was a natural. He displayed a significant aptitude for the instrument, though soon switched his attention to the trumpet (also the upright bass and guitar).

During those early years, Sherlin's music teacher was deeply involved in the local scene. "Even before I was out of middle school," he says, "I was being groomed for a spot on the University of Tennessee's marching band." Once in high school, Sherlin continued to outshine his classmates. Certainly, he practiced, but progress came effortlessly. So did advancement. By the time Sherlin was out of high school, he'd earned himself a free ride to the University of Tennessee and a spot on their 400-piece marching band. But it was the end of the line.

"In college, I experienced what my classmates had felt in high school. I maxed out. Other kids in the music department were learning much faster than was possible for me. I had to work and work and work and still couldn't keep up. They barely had to practice, yet continued to excel. And I got to know these kids, a lot of us had similar backgrounds — high-quality instruction, innate talent, similar hours of practice, similar socioeconomic status — but there was still something fundamentally different in our abilities."

Sherlin became obsessed with figuring out the exact nature of this "something." He changed directions, replacing baroque and classical with psychology and neuroscience, specifically focusing on qualitative electroencephalography (EEG) — which had the benefits of being cheap, easy, reliable, and the exact right tool for the job.

"Whenever you encounter stimuli or have a thought," explains Sherlin, "the brain has an electrical response. EEG measures those responses down to the 1/1000 of a second range, which allows us to track how the brain changes across time. When someone is decision making—and this can be an athlete solving a physical problem or an artist solving an aesthetic one—we can see everything that leads up to a decision, the decision itself, and everything that happens as a result. No other technology can do that."

As those electric responses occur in bursts, they create waves—technically "brain waves"—which is what an EEG actually measures. There are five major brain-wave types, each correlating to a different state of consciousness. "Delta," the slowest brain wave (meaning the one with the longest pauses between bursts of electricity), is found between 1 Hz and 3.9 Hz. When someone is in a deep, dreamless sleep, they're in delta. Next up, between 4 Hz and 7.9 Hz, is "theta," which correlates to REM sleep, meditation, insight, and (as is often necessary for insight) the processing of novel incoming stimuli. Between 8 Hz and 13.9 Hz hovers "alpha," the brain's basic resting state. People in alpha are relaxed, calm, and lucid, but not really thinking. Beta sits between 14 Hz and 30 Hz, and signifies learning and concentration at the low end, fear and stress at the high. Above 30 Hz there's a fast-moving wave known as "gamma," which only shows up during "binding," when different parts of the brain are combining disparate thoughts into a single idea.

EEG has another feature that makes it useful for decoding decision making: it is very good at detecting networks. While it doesn't have the detailed spatial resolution of functional magnetic resonance imaging (fMRI), the technology can see which parts of the brain are talking to one another at any given time. Thus, when decisions are being made, EEG can help determine the structure of the network involved in the process. In fact, it was this network detection ability that gave us our first neurological insights into flow.

Back in the 1970s, Csikszentmihalyi used EEG to examine the brains of chess masters midgame. He found a significant decrease in activity in the prefrontal cortex, the part of the brain housing most of our higher cognitive functions. This may seem surprising. Chess is a game of reasoning, planning, and strategy, three things that appear to require higher cognitive functions. But this isn't the only way the brain can make decisions.

Human beings have evolved two distinct systems for processing information. The first, the *explicit system,* is rule-based, can be expressed verbally, and is tied to conscious awareness. When the prefrontal cortex is fired up, the explicit system is usually turned on. But when the cold calculus of logic is swapped out for the gut sense of intuition, this is the *implicit system* at work. This system relies on skill and experience, is not consciously accessible, and cannot be described verbally (i.e., try to explain a hunch). These two systems are often described as "conscious" versus "unconscious," or "left brain" versus "right brain," but neither comparison is entirely accurate.

"Think of a factory," says Sherlin. "If all the workers are broken into little pods and they're all doing unique things at unique times, that's the explicit system. On an EEG, it shows up as beta. Replace those pods with a giant assembly line, one where the work is extremely rhythmic, fluid, and collaborative — aimed at a collective goal — that's the implicit system. It's usually denoted by a low alpha/high theta wave."

There are two advantages to the brain using the implicit system. The first is *speed.* "When the brain finds a task it needs to solve," writes Baylor neuroscientist David Eagleman in *Incognito,* "it rewires its own circuitry until it can accomplish this task with maximum efficiency. The task becomes burned into the machinery. . . . Automatization permits fast decision making. Only when the slow system of consciousness is pushed to the back of the queue can rapid programs do their work. Should I swing forehand or backhand at the approaching tennis ball? With a ninety-mile-per-hour projectile on its way, one does not want to cognitively slog through the different options."

Efficiency is the second advantage. Our brain is 2 percent of our body by weight, yet consumes 20 percent of our energy. As a result, it's always looking for ways to conserve. Using the explicit system to think through decisions burns a lot of calories, but switching to the implicit minimizes the energy required to solve problems.

This is also why Csikszentmihalyi found little activity in the prefrontal cortex of chess masters. After years of playing, they'd internalized board patterns and move sequences and didn't have to rely on their conscious mind to work through every option. Instead, their explicit system went offline, and the implicit system turned on. Since low alpha/high theta is the dominant brain wave produced by the implicit system, this frequency has long been considered the signature of both high performance and flow states. But this idea is now starting to change — and Sherlin is part of the reason why.

While he runs a number of different companies and holds four different academic appointments, Sherlin also serves as chief science officer for Neurotopia, a leader in the research and use of EEG for improving athlete performance. In 2009, he got a call from Red Bull's director of athletic high performance, Dr. Andy Walshe. The energy-sports-drink company has been a longtime supporter of all things action and adventure, sponsoring many of the world's most accomplished athletes. Walshe wanted to help these athletes get better — and that's where Sherlin fit in.

Together, Red Bull and Neurotopia established a neuroscience skunk works. Their goal was straightforward: use EEG to figure out what the brains of top action and adventure athletes were doing and help them do more of it. To this end, thousands and thousands of subjects were analyzed. Bat and ball athletes were compared to action and adventure athletes. Amateurs against elites (top 5 percent) against superelites (top 1 percent). In the beginning, they examined resting states, but beyond more low alpha/high theta in the baseline of experts — which, for the aforementioned reasons, was to be expected — there wasn't much to see. Once they got those athletes moving, though, that story started to change.

For this portion of the study, Sherlin used a simple target-acquisition task. Subjects had to stare at a screen as images flashed by. If the image was a target (twelve pink squares arranged as a cube), they had to react. If the image wasn't a target (eleven pink squares arranged as a cube, with the center square missing), they had to suppress the reaction. "It sounds really simple," says Sherlin, "but there's actually a lot going on. It requires speed, stamina, focus, and really good decision-making abilities."

When any of us make decisions, our brains go through a six-stage cycle. Before the novel stimuli shows up (which is what starts the whole process), we're in a baseline state. Then we move to problem-solving analysis, pre-action readiness, action, post-action evaluation, and back to baseline. Each of these stages requires different parts of the brain and produces different brain waves: theta for processing novel stimuli, beta for analysis, alpha for action, etc. When Sherlin and his team examined the data, what became clear was that the best athletes moved through this entire cycle fluidly, seamlessly transitioning from step to step.

"That's the secret," says Sherlin, "extremely fluid brain control. Most people can't make it through the whole cycle. They get hung up somewhere. They either can't generate all the necessary brain states or they can't control them. Elite performers can produce the right brain wave at the right time, vary its intensity as needed, then smoothly transition to the next step. Mentally, they just take total charge of the situation."

Flow states, which can be considered elite performance on overdrive, take this process one step farther. "In the zone," says Sherlin, "you still see this same fluidity in the transitions between states, but you also see even more control. Instead of producing all these other brain waves, really great athletes can transition smoothly into the zone, creating that low alpha/high theta wave, and then hold themselves there, sort of in suspended animation, shutting out the conscious mind and letting the implicit system do its stuff."

To illustrate this further, consider Hamilton's experience on the Millennium Wave. "Before he grabbed the tow rope," says Sherlin, "he was assessing the situation, trying to predict the future, feeling fear — that classic beta. But once he was being pulled toward the wave, when he started to shut out outside stimuli and focus on the task at hand — that's a burst of alpha. The angel/devil argument was really about alpha versus beta. The angel was alpha. It was the implicit system saying 'let's go for it, we know what to do.' The devil was beta — it was the explicit system saying 'hold up a second, let's just gather more data.' But the angel won. Hamilton made the right decision, suppressed that beta wave and got himself to alpha/theta — the zone — and held himself there."

Of course, the Millennium Wave didn't end when Hamilton found the zone. Moments later, he was getting sucked up that wave's face. So while the implicit system is capable of high-speed pattern recognition — which helped him realize what was happening a little sooner — it took more than just that to survive. He still had to have a creative insight no one had ever had before and pull off a difficult move that no one had ever attempted before — which, as it turns out, is par for the course for Laird Hamilton.

SUDDEN DEATH OR SUDDEN INSIGHT

Off the shores of northern Maui, beyond the sugarcane fields and the muddy roads and the tall cliffs, lies a reef break known as Jaws. It too is a terrifying colossus, long considered an impossible. For more than fifty years, surfers have been staring at this spot — it's hard not to. When powerful northern Pacific storms blast down from the Aleutian Islands, the results travel thousands of miles unhindered, only to run smack into a fan-shaped reef. Two deepwater channels on either side of the break increase the upward pressure. The combination creates perfect monsters: waves that can reach eighty feet in height; waves that crash with so much force that the sound has been compared to the explosion of an atomic bomb. Surf legend Gerry Lopez is known for his fearlessness in heavy surf, but back in the 1960s he said he got nauseous just looking at the place.

One of the first to brave these waves was Dave Kalama, a former world-champion windsurfer and one of the most accomplished watermen on the planet. Back in 1998, Kalama and a couple of friends decided to windsurf Jaws. It was a small day, maybe fourteen feet, but that was enough. He didn't go back for years. And when he did return, he brought reinforcements.

Kalama was a founding member of the "strapped crew," actually part of the reason the crew got its name. In 1991, while Hamilton, Kerbox, and Doerner were experimenting with towing a surfer behind an inflatable Zodiac (later a Jet Ski), Kalama, Brett Little, and Mark Angulo had begun toying with foot straps on normal surfboards. When the two groups decided to combine their innovations, it was with one purpose in mind: to surf Jaws.

No one had ever surfed Jaws before — not when it was big. On those days, the wave punched across that reef at over thirty miles per hour, far beyond the paddling speed achievable by surfers. But Jet Skis tipped those odds, and the strapped crew used this advantage to attack—literally. "When you let go of the rope and drop in," Kalama once said, "you go into warrior mode—you flex your muscles, you grit your teeth, you're ready for anything. I'm so focused I can't hear the wave when I'm riding it. It feels like riding in an elevator when the cables break—all of a sudden you're falling and screaming, and then the cable reengages and you slow down and step off and try to recover from a heavy dose of adrenaline."

Adding to that dose is barrel height. If Teahupoo produces the heaviest tube in the world, Jaws produces one of the tallest, also the meanest. Imagine being in the middle of a ten-story building when it collapses. And collapse it will. "[L]ike all sets of Jaws," explains author Susan Casey, "this one had a tendency to snap shut, swallowing anything unfortunate enough to be inside it. And its teeth . . . well, they were more like fangs."

Which is why, if you mentioned the Millennium Wave to Dave Kalama, if you ask him about Hamilton's creative insight, his out-of-the-blue outer-hand drag, he just chuckles and says: "Sure, the Millennium Wave was significant. It changed surf history, but all Laird really needed to do was not screw up. It takes an incredible amount of skill to stand there and take it and not screw up, but if we're talking about moments of absolute creative brilliance, of truly astounding, I've seen Laird come up with stuff that is far more significant."

And then he'll tell you a story about Jaws.

It was a big day, waves in the forty- to fifty-foot range. Kalama and Hamilton had been there all morning, experimenting with the barrel, getting deeper and deeper, getting more comfortable as the hours went by. "We were definitely in the zone," recounts Kalama, "but maybe too in the zone. I towed Laird into a forty-five-footer, and he got so deep in the tube, was so relaxed, it was almost like he forgot where he was. He let himself get pulled up the face—just way, way too high."

The problem with getting pulled up the face is there's a point when the wave becomes vertical—it *walls*, in the lingo—and this leaves surfers only two options: get pitched straight into the impact zone or ride that rollercoaster over the falls. Either way, on a wave like Jaws, the results can be horrific.

But when Jaws walled, Hamilton didn't get pitched into the impact zone or sucked over the falls. Instead, with his feet still in his foot-straps, he did something no one has ever done before: jumped forward, hopping the board clear out of the wave and then dropping fifteen feet straight down. He did this while still inside that roaring barrel. Stuck the landing too. Absorbed the impact and rode off clean.

"To me," says Kalama, "the Millennium Wave might have started a revolution, but in the history of Laird making shit up on the fly, what he did that day at Jaws? I've been around surfing almost my entire life, I've never even heard anybody talk about anything like that. And I was watching the whole time. Laird never panicked, never even said 'Oh, shit!' He just jumped out of the wave, dropped to the bottom, and rode off. Nothing to it."

Of course, there was something to it and it was the exact same kind of something that saved Hamilton's ass on the Millennium Wave — a moment of sudden, creative insight. Often these moments are important enough to make history. Isaac Newton sees an apple fall and BAMMO: the theory of gravity arrives fully formed in his brain; Archimedes climbs into the bathtub and SHAZAM: the solution to the mathematical puzzle of volume pops into his head. But, seriously, Newton was lazing around an orchard and Archimedes was having a hot soak. Hamilton, meanwhile, had his creative insight while riding down the gullet of Godzilla. It was an impossible tucked inside of an impossible — which makes one wonder how it could have happened at all.

Turns out, over the past decade, we've learned a great deal about how such things happen — including how flow may make them happen more frequently. Not surprisingly, our creativity lies deeply rooted in the right side of the brain: the side dominated by the implicit system. The reason has to do with the structure of neural networks. When the explicit system (mostly on the left side of the brain) handles a problem, the neurons involved are very close to one another. This much proximity leads to linear connections, logical deductions, and all the other keystones of standard reasoning. When the implicit system is at work, its reach is much broader — far-flung corners of the brain are talking to one another. This is known to experts as "lateral thinking" or, to the business executives who so crave this talent: "thinking outside the box." It means that novel stimuli can combine with random thoughts and obscure memories and the result is something utterly new.

Creativity has a brain wave signature as well: alpha waves pulsing out of the brain's right hemisphere. This is considered the readiness state for sudden insight — meaning not the revelation itself, rather its precursor condition. Interestingly, Kalama's observation — that Hamilton never panicked — may also play a role, as it now seems that without a calm, relaxed frame of mind, the brain is incapable of switching from beta-dominant localized networks to alpha-driven widespread webs.

But this isn't where the process ends. Whether we're speaking about Hamilton's hand drag on the Millennium Wave or his decision to jump out of the barrel at Jaws, that moment of sudden insight comes with a different brain wave signature. Exactly thirty milliseconds before the breakthrough intuition arrives, EEG shows a burst of gamma waves. These ultrafast brain waves appear when a bunch of widely distributed cells — i.e., novel stimuli, random thoughts, and obscure memories — bind themselves together into a brand-new network. It is the brain-wave signature of the "Aha!" moment.

"But the interesting thing about a gamma spike," explains Leslie Sherlin, "is that it always happens inside of theta oscillations. The two waves are coupled. It makes sense. Theta processes novel incoming stimuli; gamma is what happens when those stimuli snap together into new ideas. But it's hard to do any of this on command. It takes meditators a long time to get that kind of control. This is where athletes in flow have a huge edge — their brain is already in alpha/theta. They're holding themselves in the only state that can produce that gamma spike."

When you add these elements together it's easy to see why flow is such an effective decision-making strategy. Not only does it elevate our problem-solving abilities, but — by holding themselves in low alpha/ high theta needed to produce that gamma spike — people in the zone are already "neurologically" poised on the brink of breakthrough. This means flow packs a double punch: it doesn't just increase our decision-making abilities — it increases our *creative* decision-making abilities.

Dramatically.

In flow, we are our resourceful, imaginative, ingenious best. Better still, the changes stick. According to research done by Harvard Business School professor Teresa Amabile, not only are creative insights consistently associated with flow states, but that amplified creativity outlasts the zone. People report feeling extraordinarily creative *the day after* a flow state, suggesting that time spent in the zone trains the brain to consistently think outside the box.

This is why creative insights are par for the course for Laird Hamilton, but it's also why we're seeing accelerated growth in ultimate performance in action and adventure sports. Pushing the limits of human potential requires considerable innovation and imagination. By spending so much time in the zone, these athletes have found a way to amp up these abilities. Moreover, by consistently using that creativity to push limits, these athletes have taken things even farther.

"Everybody who has ever spent any time in flow," explains NBC action sports commentator and professional skateboarder Chris Miller, "knows it's a deeply creative place. You're just tapped into that creative force on such a larger scale. But there's a difference between when this happens in an artist's studio or on the tennis court versus inside the barrel of a fifty-foot wave. When you tap into that much force while pushing the absolute limits of human performance, that's more than just an imaginative breakthrough — that's bending reality to your will. And when you do that frequently, which is what guys like Danny Way and Laird Hamilton can do, imagine what that does for your confidence."

Or, as Laird Hamilton once explained in an interview with *Bon Hawaii:* "[T]he true challenge is how you continue doing it, after you've ridden the biggest wave, crossed the longest distance. You set up challenges that are more than what you ever did before. And by getting through it, you get the sensation you've completed something. And if it's dangerous, then other things that scare you, the experience will strengthen you for those situations."

3

The Where of Flow

DEAN POTTER

Mount Fitz Roy, the tallest mountain in Patagonia, is a daunting blade of rock — jagged and ragged and mean. On the list of the world's most dangerous climbs, Fitz Roy always ranks in the top twenty, often in the top ten. It is cold. It is isolated. And getting to its zenith demands crossing a vertical ocean of granite protected by some of the most ferocious weather on earth.

In the early 2000s, a climber by the name of Dean Potter thought he'd solved that puzzle: "Patagonia's weather is terrible. If you get a break it's only going to last a day or two. That's not a lot of time for a traditional mountaineer's approach (i.e., multiple people on the team, ropes, protection). But I had been developing a style of rapid big wall free soloing (i.e., alone, no ropes, no protection) that I thought might work well on these more traditional routes."

Free soloing is the mother of all death sports. The equation is simple: you fall, you die. It is also, at least for a certain breed of athlete, deeply pure and undeniably enticing. Without ropes or gear in the way, there is only the climber and the rock, as intimate and personal a relationship as can be had with big nature. "Up on the High Lonesome," explains author John Long (in his appropriately titled book: *The High Lonesome*), "the soloist answers to his own standards, the climbing at hand, and God, in that order."

Many have answered to God. Over the past few decades, the desire for this relationship has claimed a bevy of our best climbers, the majority of them dying on shorter, smaller routes. Very few people have played this game in the bigger mountains. That Potter wanted to test out his style of rapid big wall free soloing in Patagonia? On a beast like Fitz Roy? Well, let's just say he had his reasons.

To understand those reasons, we need to understand more about the man. Potter was born in Kansas in 1972, the son of an army colonel and a yoga teacher. Before he was four years old, Potter was copying his mom's moves, adding breadth to stretch and twisting himself up like a pretzel. "I think yoga gave me my first taste of the zone," he recounts, "but I definitely got a runner's high [now considered a low-grade flow state] out training with my dad and the troops."

The high stayed with Potter, shaped him, began to define him. "I noticed there was a pattern to it," he says. "I'd be running and it would be hard and then I'd check out for a little while. I saw early on that being exhausted made it easier to quiet the mind and get to the zone."

His most poignant lesson occurred the first time his father took him fishing. Getting to their desired spot meant stepping across a series of slime-covered rocks. Dean was nervous, lost his footing, and plunged into the river. The cold knocked the wind from him; he scrambled up the bank and started crying. "I don't like fishing," he bawled, "I want to go home."

Potter's father shook his head no; instead he gave his son some advice. "Put everything aside. There's nothing to be afraid of except a little cold water. Just focus on the next steps you are taking." Focus was the key to getting past the fear—and everything else as well. Pretty soon Dean was skipping from stone to stone, his body automatically going where it needed to go. By day's end, he was racing around the river, playing in rapids, all of his senses remarkably heightened. "That gave me a lot of confidence," he says now, "but it also gave me a glimpse of the superpowers, and my first memory of *the Voice*."

The Voice—the voice of intuition—the center of the zone's mystery. Everybody who has ever been in a flow state has heard it—a voice very different from the mind's normal chatter. Neuroscientist David Eagleman likes to quote Pink Floyd when describing this facet: "There's someone in my head, but it's not me," while the Indian philosopher

Jiddu Krishnamurti refers to this someone as "the Tyrant." Certainly, both statements track with Potter's experience: "Right before I have to make a move, the Voice tells me what to do. And it's never wrong. When the Voice tells you to do something, you do it: right then, don't think, no questions asked. Not listening to the Voice is what'll get you killed. I learned that really early in my climbing career."

So what is the Voice? Carl Jung defined intuition as "perception via the unconscious" and the Voice is the end result of that perception — the unconscious mind broadcasting its perceptions to the conscious mind. Of course, it's not always a voice. Some people see images; others get strong feelings. Occasionally, the information arrives by multiple channels. And that information arrives constantly. Intuition is a permanent feature of standard brain function — meaning the Voice is always communicating with us — yet we can rarely hear it. The data is diluted and distorted by everything else the mind is considering. But in flow, for reasons we'll explore in this chapter, the signal is stronger, the message clearer, and for those on the receiving end, the feeling accompanying that broadcast is often one of profound relief — a sense that finally, at long last, someone else is driving this bus.

Potter has been listening to the Voice over a career that's had few parallels. As a climber, his reputation hinges on speed and daring. In 1998, he ran up Yosemite's legendary Half Dome in four hours and sixteen minutes — the previous record was twenty hours and fifty-six minutes. In 1999, it was Half Dome and The Nose on El Capitan in twenty-three hours, marking the first solo one-day assault of both routes. In 2000, Potter went alone and ropeless up Blind Faith, the Rostrum, and Astroman — three notable terrors that would surely kill most mortals. The following year he broke the four-hour mark on The Nose (three hours, fifty-nine minutes, thirty-five seconds), which would be a lifetime achievement for most and, for him, was just the beginning.

In 2002, with these warm-ups behind him, Potter took his one-man band down to Patagonia. Within a few days of arrival, he became the first person to free solo Mount Fitz Roy, sending Supercanaleta — a classic, mile-long ice-and-rock route — in an astounding six and a half hours. Next, after little rest and a twenty-four-hour hike including a pitch-black glacier crossing, he tackled the Solos Compressor route up

Cerro Torre — a nearby mountain that ranks just below Fitz Roy on the climber's list of terrible tyrants. Potter didn't seem to mind. He topped out in a record-breaking eleven hours, then happened to glance across the valley and back at Fitz Roy.

The most famous route up Fitz Roy is known as Californian. Directly below it sits the deadly Poincenot couloir. Linking the two together has been a longtime dream of climbers, but a giant serac overhanging the couloir makes the danger extreme. Over the years, an uncomfortable number of athletes have lost their lives trying to join these routes. Making matters more complicated, the couloir and the Californian are connected by a featureless stretch of stone over 250 feet high. Only when a rare ice flow (a frozen waterfall) forms can the section be crossed. While Potter is admittedly not much of an ice climber, when he glanced across that valley and saw the ice flow in place, well, what other choice did he have?

"I was following the Voice," he recounts, "and more focused than I'd ever been. I was doing everything I could to cultivate that heightened awareness. I was down there alone, sleeping under rocks, not talking to anyone, meditating — all to help strengthen my intuition. The Voice said climb, so that's what I did."

When Potter started up the route, he didn't need his intuition to alert him to the danger. Above him, the serac was moaning. "It was 100,000-year-old blue ice and it was wailing. Like listening to a ticking time bomb. My body had an instinctive reaction to the sound. I started climbing like a maniac. I couldn't have slowed down if I tried."

Potter zipped up the couloir, and then sailed over the ice flow. It was the hardest ice climbing he'd ever done, but nothing could slow him down. He reached the halfway point on the route in less than five hours — shaving a day and a half off the traditional pace — but the frenzy had come at a cost.

Potter's heart, already racing, started skipping beats. Certain he was about to have a heart attack, he ate all his food, trying to give his body the fuel to calm down. It was a big bet. Still to come was the last big push of the route: a 2,000-foot vertical rock wall. "It was huge," recounts Potter, "and I had no idea which was the right way to go. But I started following the footholds, listening to the Voice and not questioning."

This was no easy task. The wall Potter faced was over one-third of a mile high — or roughly double the height of New York's Chrysler building. He had very little information about the correct way up and it was biophysically impossible for him to judge the quality of the footholds from that far below. If we assume a three-foot height gain per move, getting to Fitz Roy's apex meant the Voice would have to make 670 correct decisions in a row — and Potter could question none of them.

Some of those decisions were fairly unusual. Near the top of that final push, at a point where the traditional route hugged a corner, Potter saw a crack on the face that seemed to be calling to him. Really beckoning. But crack climbing without a rope is often an all-or-nothing proposition. Once Potter committed to the line, downclimbing was not a possibility. The only way to survive was to finish the ascent. But there's no way to judge the depth of the crack, the quality of the rock, or any number of other unfathomables from below. If Potter's gut was the slightest bit wrong, there'd be no retreat. He'd never make it off the mountain alive.

Yet again his intuition was correct.

"The crack was perfect. Whatever I needed to jam in there — my hand, my feet, my knee — like a key slipping into a lock, like the crack had been custom designed for my body."

The crack ended in the rarest of gifts. Potter topped out into a giant crystal garden. He'd never seen anything like it: shimmering fractals of light, all along the wall's face. Arguably, he was the first person in history to lay eyes on this place. Definitely, he was the first person in history to free solo three of Patagonia's biggest routes in a single season. But his ordeal wasn't quite over.

Coming down off Fitz Roy was supposed to be easier. Potter had decided to descend the "friendlier" east face. The route wasn't the issue. The issue was above the route — where a tremendous snowfield sat, jam-packed with loose rock. With nothing beyond a 5mm rope and thirty rappels ahead of him, Potter was concerned. A little sunshine, a little snow melt, a little rock fall — it wouldn't take much to cut that rope in half.

Four pitches into the descent, all that listening to his intuition paid off. Potter's ears started ringing. He looked up; he just knew. A few seconds later there was a deep booming crack and rocks started to fall. Slabs the size of dining room tables were pulling free and tumbling down. A good-size chunk was heading straight for his head.

In this situation, standard protocol is to get small. Climbers try to flatten themselves against the wall. But the Voice had yet to be wrong. Potter was told to kick outward, and again he did as he was told— saving his own life in the process.

By kicking outward, Potter got his head out of the projectile's flight path. Unfortunately, he exposed his torso. The rock clipped his thigh; the pain knocked him unconscious. He came to dangling 4,000 feet in the air, the appendage completely numb. It took twenty rappels to get back to solid ground; Potter could use his leg for none of them.

Unable to walk, Potter still faced a long hike and a dangerous glacier crossing. He slithered across the ice, traversing tiny snow bridges over giant crevasses on his belly. It took him twenty-four hours to reach his base camp. He literally crawled off that mountain. He was deeply satisfied.

"I went to Patagonia to cultivate my intuition—to listen to the Voice. When I'm really in tune with it, really deep in the zone, I get to a place where I disappear completely, where I merge with the rock, when time slows down, my senses are unbelievably heightened, and I feel that oneness, that full-body psychic connection to the universe. It took risking my life to get there, but mission accomplished. And that's why I climb. I crave these experiences. I certainly don't climb to get on top of rocks."

TRANSIENT HYPOFRONTALITY AND THE QUIETING OF DOUBT

The experiences that Potter craves — the disappearance of self, the distortion of time, and that "psychic connection" to the universe — are among flow's more famous qualities, also its most peculiar. While these phenomena are included in most standard descriptions of the zone, they are also the reason William James described the state as "mystical" and Maslow borrowed quasi-Buddhist terms like *self-actualiza-*

tion for its long-term effects. Not surprisingly, trying to understand how the brain produces this peculiarity has been a longtime goal of flow researchers. Unfortunately, until recently, there have been issues.

Neuroanatomy for starters. The brain is specialized. Different areas do different jobs. So understanding how the brain produces an experience requires understanding what parts of the brain are involved in that production and, for most of the past century, our imaging technologies weren't up to the task. Neither, to be honest, were our researchers. The second issue was familiarity: the scientists most interested in studying flow states weren't always that good at having flow states. With neither a technological nor personal window into the experience, the result was a black box and a big puzzle.

Arne Dietrich, though, faced neither of these problems. A tall man with a bald head, Dietrich was born in Germany, studied neuroscience at the University of Georgia, and now teaches at the American University in Beirut. His early work was on learning and memory, his later work on creativity and consciousness. Yet, despite the seriousness of these topics, Dietrich has a casual manner, an easy laugh, and a professional biography that includes the line: "After a wholly uneventful time in college, he spent several years globetrotting, climbing little known mountains, and bushwhacking through the jungle; a lifestyle interrupted only by the occasional date and a few phone calls to his mother."

Dietrich stopped globetrotting and returned to graduate school in the late 1990s, around the same time that high-powered imaging devices like fMRI were revolutionizing the field. For the first time in history, scientists had a concrete picture of neurological structure and function — a picture all earlier flow researchers had lacked. But Dietrich had more than that. As a lifelong athlete, he had actual knowledge of the zone.

A weight lifter and soccer player growing up, Dietrich became a recreational mountaineer after college, and, "because there were no real mountains in Georgia," a serious triathlete while finishing his PhD. In the early 2000s, Dietrich started competing in Ironmans, training over thirty hours a week. Like many endurance athletes, he found long runs were an easy entrance to the zone — and this led to questions.

For most of the past half century, in the "which part of the brain produces flow" sweepstakes, the prevailing wisdom has centered on the prefrontal cortex (PFC). This makes sense. The PFC is the heart of our higher cognitive abilities. It's the place we collect data, problem solve, plan ahead, assess risk, evaluate rewards, analyze thoughts, suppress urges, learn from experience, make moral decisions, and give rise to our normal sense of self. Since the zone is a state of heightened performance and enhanced decision making, it seemed obvious to scientists that the entire PFC was involved, arguably functioning at a maximum level. But this didn't track with Dietrich's experience.

"The prefrontal cortex is where thinking happens," he explains. "It's where we take simple ideas and add all kind of layers of complexity to them. But I was slipping into flow of a regular basis and always amazed by the clarity of the state. All that complexity was gone. Decisions were easy and automatic. It was like the opposite of thinking."

So Dietrich started to wonder how the brain was eliminating this complexity — which is when it dawned on him: the brain wasn't eliminating complexity, it was eliminating the very structures that created this complexity. "We had it backward," he says. "In flow, parts of the PFC aren't becoming hyperactive; parts of it are temporarily deactivating. It's an efficiency exchange. We're trading energy usually used for higher cognitive functions for heightened attention and awareness."

The technical term for this exchange is *transient hypofrontality*, with *hypo* (meaning slow) being the opposite of *hyper* (i.e., fast). In flow, which parts of the brain become hypofrontal determines the nature of the experience — with a quick rule of thumb being: the greater the deactivation of neuronal structures, the more profound (and bizarre) the experience.

In 2006, for example, a team of Israeli scientists discovered that when people lose themselves in a task — be it playing cards or having sex or climbing a mountain — a part of the brain called the superior frontal gyrus starts to deactivate. The superior frontal gyrus helps produce our sense of self, that introspective feeling of self-awareness, which, as the study's lead researcher, Ilan Goldberg, told *New Scientist*, is not always useful: "If there is a sudden danger, such as the appearance of a snake, it's helpful not to stand around wondering how one feels about the situation."

Another breakthrough occurred in 2008, when Johns Hopkins

neuroscientist Charles Limb began using fMRI to examine the brains of improv jazz musicians and freestyle rappers immersed in flow. He found the dorsolateral prefrontal cortex is also deactivated in the state. The dorsolateral prefrontal cortex is an area of the brain best known for self-monitoring and impulse control — both of which are important here. Self-monitoring is the voice of doubt and disparagement, that defeatist nag, our inner critic. Since flow is a fluid state — where problem solving is nearly automatic — second-guessing can only slow that process. When the dorsolateral prefrontal cortex goes quiet, those guesses are cut off at the source. The result is liberation. We act without hesitation. Creativity becomes more free-flowing, risk taking becomes less frightening. In fact, without this structure deactivated, there would have been no way for Potter to "follow the Voice, no questions asked." The job of the dorsolateral prefrontal cortex is to ask those questions, to start the process of second-guessing. It is the enemy of flow junkies everywhere.

Impulse control, meanwhile, is another enemy. In normal life, our ability to resist temptation is critical to survival, but flow is an action state: the Voice tells us what to do and we do it. If we are trying to control our impulses, hesitation would creep into the process. The end result would be much less doing and — for athletes like Potter — far more dying.

There's also a flip side to these events: while parts of the prefrontal cortex are shutting down, others are ramping up — and this too shapes the experience. Limb, for example, found that flow also activates the medial prefrontal cortex, a part of the brain that governs creative self-expression. This is the reason that people in the zone still have individual styles. Even though Sonny Rollins and John Coltrane both experience flow as an automatic process, their sax solos don't sound the same. Instead, a hyperactive medial prefrontal cortex ensures that even with self-awareness out of the way, our personal preferences still leak through.

Beyond these psychological impacts, hypofrontality also confers an equally important physical advantage. Penn State kinesiologist Vladimir Zatsiorsky uses the terms *maximal strength* and *absolute strength* to distinguish between the amount of force one can generate through acts of will and the amount of force our muscles can theoretically produce. Normally, people can access about 65 percent of their absolute strength; trained weight lifters can get this up to about 80 percent. But that's usually the end of the line. If we could access all our strength on command, we could very easily overextend ourselves, pushing beyond our limits and doing serious damage along the way.

Flow changes this entire dynamic. For starters, in the zone, the brain releases a number of powerful painkillers that deaden us to the damage being done and allow us to push our maximal strength closer to its absolute boundary (more on this in the next chapter). Simultaneously, transient hypofrontality removes our sense of self. With parts of the prefrontal cortex deactivated, there's no risk assessor, future predictor, or inner critic around to monitor the situation. The normal safety measures kept in place by the conscious mind are no longer. This is another reason why flow states significantly enhance performance: when the "self" disappears, it takes many of our limits along for the ride.

UNSTUCK IN TIME

In 2002, while dragging his numb leg off Fitz Roy, Potter kept thinking there had to be a better way. It seemed ridiculous that he should be able to free solo up a route this difficult only to nearly die while coming back down. Then it dawned on him. Why bother downclimbing? Forget descending. With help from a parachute, he could finish the climb, find the appropriate launch point, and jump.

Potter called this combination freeBASE, for free soloing meets BASE jumping. There was a small problem. BASE jumping is sky diving's far more dangerous cousin; it means parachuting off a fixed object (the acronym stands for the most popular assortment of fixed objects: *buildings, antennae, spans,* and *earth*). At the time he dreamed up this idea, forget BASE jumping — Potter didn't even know how to skydive.

Learning was not easy. As a free soloist, falling always meant dying. This was a hard notion to shake. On his first free-fall skydive, Potter freaked. He had a coach with him. They jumped at 13,000 feet, with 5,000 feet being the time to throw the pilot chute. But at 5,000 feet, when Potter reached back, he grabbed the leg loop of his harness by mistake. "I started yanking and yanking and nothing happened. My mind froze. Total panic. Coach had to put my hand on the pilot chute so I could pull."

But Potter was committed. He kept at it. He got better. Pretty soon, he decided to try BASE jumping. His inaugural leap was off a 500-foot bridge above Idaho's Snake River. It was love at first flight. "It can take a lot of climbing for me to get into the zone," he says. "On the speed climb of El Capitan, it didn't happen until two-thirds of the way up. But on a BASE jump, it's immediate. Leap off a cliff and WHAM — welcome to a new reality."

In 2003, about a year into his BASE training, Potter and a few friends were given the opportunity to BASE jump into Mexico's "Cellar of Swallows," a gargantuan open-air pit: 1,200 feet deep, and actually misnamed. While some 50,000 birds do make their home in this cave, they are swifts, not swallows. Either way, the cellar is deep enough to house a skyscraper. Wide too. With a diameter running between 170 and 300 feet in length, the cavern provides plenty of room to steer a parachute.

The group spent two days BASE jumping into the cave. At the end of that time, when everyone else was totally exhausted, Potter decided he wanted one last jump. "I never should have done it," he says now. "I was exhausted from all that jumping and rigging and I'd felt sick for almost a day. I'd also had a bad feeling in my gut. It was stupid. I just ignored all these signs."

He also ignored another. When he went to strap on his chute, he noticed the canopy was wet. It should have been the end of his plans. A wet chute is unevenly weighted. When deployed, parts will inflate, others will not. Potter, not thinking clearly, decided the water was evenly dispersed and wouldn't be a problem.

And it wasn't a problem — at least not for the first five seconds of the jump. "When I leaped," he says, "it was right into the zone. Immediately my senses started peaking. I was moving at ninety miles per hour but could see in incredible detail — minute fissures in the rock, tiny patches of lichen, bat guano."

At the six-second mark, roughly 500 feet from the ground, Potter deployed his chute. It opened asymmetrically. The wet sections collapsed, the dry ones inflated. Instantly, with the air currents unevenly distributed, Potter started spinning. From above, his friends started shouting: "Avoid the walls!" Important safety tip. Except, with his guidelines twisted, there was no way to steer.

Then the miraculous intervened: the guidelines began to untwist. Potter seized the moment, yanking the toggles. He knew the better move was to reverse his direction — which would have sent him backward and out into open space — but for reasons he still cannot fathom he turned left instead. He was now heading directly toward the cave wall. Worse, the moment he turned, his chute collapsed, draping itself completely over his head.

But Potter's senses were peaking. In the fleeting instant before his vision vanished, he caught a glimpse of orange. "We were filming the jumps," he recounts, "so we'd hung a rope about 400 feet off the deck for the camera man. It was glowing orange. And that was what I saw: a flash of glowing orange."

He reacted immediately, grabbing for the rope, catching it too. But there was no way to tighten his grip. Potter was less than 300 feet from the ground and closing in on terminal velocity. His hands were already burning from the friction. When he tried to clamp down on the rope, his flesh flayed, then instantly cauterized. The pain was unbelievable.

Above him, his friends were screaming: "Hang on." It was his only option. He used all his strength, every last bit. And Potter did manage to stop himself for a moment — but couldn't hold it.

Again, he started plummeting. Again, he clamped down. Again, he managed to stop. Not a moment too soon. With the chute still covering his eyes, he had no way of knowing, but Potter had halted himself merely six feet above the ground.

His friends shouted down: "Just let go!"

Potter landed in a heap on the cave floor. His hands were destroyed, other parts as well. He'd torn all the muscles in his stomach and his rectum. "I blew out my ass," he says. "I didn't even know that was possible."

But that question again: How is any of this possible?

Potter's survival hinged on the second of flow's famous oddities: a radical shift in time perception. "Everything was moving in super slow motion," he recounts. "I had time to hear the advice my friends were shouting down at me, to think about it, to turn my parachute, to hear more advice, to see the orange rope, to realize what it was, to grab for it, try to hang on, not be able to hold it, hear my friends shouting more instructions, try again. It was a lot to do and a long, complicated conversation. But it was all happening so slowly, I could process all that information and make the right decisions."

The technical name for Potter's experience is "time dilation." Normally, in the zone, after self-awareness starts to fade, temporal awareness tends to follow. In *Flow*, Csikszentmihalyi explains further: "One of the most common descriptions of optimal experience is that time no longer seems to pass the way it ordinarily does. The objective, external duration we measure with reference to outside events like night and day, or the orderly progression of clocks, is rendered irrelevant by the rhythms dictated by the activity. . . . [I]n general, most people report that time seems to pass much faster. But occasionally the reverse occurs."

Why this happens, as Baylor neuroscientist David Eagleman discovered, also comes down to hypofrontality. The same events that erase our sense of self also distort our sense of time. In a series of elegant fMRI experiments, Eagleman found that temporal awareness is not centralized in any one location in the brain; rather, it is calculated by multiple areas working together. This means that time, much like self, is a summary judgment, a democratic conclusion reached by a vast prefrontal caucus. But this also makes temporal awareness vulnerable to interruption. "Because flow deactivates large parts of the neocortex," says Eagleman, "a number of these areas are offline — thus distorting our ability to compute time."

Underlying this loss of time is another efficiency exchange. As focus tightens, the brain stops multitasking. Energy normally used for temporal processing is reallocated for attention and awareness. Instead of keeping time, we are taking in more data per second, processing it more completely, and, perhaps — though great debate rages around this point — processing more of it per second.

It is all this data that actually elongates the current moment. Our sense of how long "the now" lasts is directly related to information processing: The more stuff we're processing, the longer the moment appears to last. And the longer the moment lasts, the better quantity and quality of information we have at our disposal. More data gives us a shot at sudden insights. Better data leads to more creative solutions. Both allow us to fine-tune our reactions. This is the reason Potter could make the leap from "glowing orange" to "climbing rope, grab now" in the millisecond he had to reach that conclusion — it's the reason he's still alive.

THE CLOSING OF THE DOORS OF PERCEPTION

When Potter finally got that parachute off his head, he found himself sitting on the floor of the Cellar of Swallows. Above him, his friends were running around, trying to facilitate his rescue. He paid them little mind. His body was pretty destroyed — again he didn't notice. Instead, his focus was entirely on the ground beside him, where a small swift with a broken wing lay dying.

Instinctively, Potter picked up the bird, cradling it in his shredded palms. The connection was immediate. As soon as their flesh touched, he felt a powerful psychic union, as if his consciousness had merged with the bird's consciousness. In that instant, they were no longer two wounded creatures: they had become one stronger animal.

"I know it's hard to believe," says Potter, "but the experience was so powerful, the connection so true. I just sat there with that bird, holding it while it died. When it died, I died with it. And I don't mean that metaphorically, I mean I became that dying bird."

While Potter's experience may be hard to believe, variations of it are not that uncommon in action and adventure sports. Surfers frequently report becoming one with the waves; snowboarders become one with the mountain. "It was like I reached a place where clarity and intuition and effort and focus all came together to bring me to a higher level of consciousness," says professional kayaker Sam Drevo, "a level where I was no longer me; I was part of the river." In fact, long before the Cave of Swallows, Potter too had familiarity. When he went to Patagonia hunting that "psychic connection to the universe," this was the very experience he desired.

It was Jefferson University neuroscientist Andrew Newberg and University of Pennsylvania neuropsychologist Eugene D'Aquili who gave us our first real insight into this experience. Back in 1991, they were investigating a different version of oneness — the kind produced by meditation. In deep contemplative states, Tibetan Buddhists report "absolute unitary being," or the feeling of becoming one with everything, while Franciscan nuns experience *unia mysica,* or oneness with God's love. So Newberg and D'Aquili put both Buddhists and nuns inside a single photon emission computed tomography (SPECT) scanner to try to figure out if there was biology beneath this spirituality.

The SPECT scan revealed biology all right, and hypofrontality to be exact. In moments of intense concentration, the same efficiency exchange that erases our sense of self and distorts our sense of time begins to impact our relationship to space. Instead of taking place in the prefrontal lobes, this hypofrontality occurs farther back in the cortex, in the superior parietal lobe, a portion of the brain that Newberg and D'Aquili dubbed the orientation association area (OAA) because it helps us orient in space.

When functioning normally, the OAA is a navigation system. It judge angles and distances, maps course trajectories, and keeps track of our body's exact location. But to do this last part, the superior parietal lobe must also produce a boundary line: the border of self, the division between finite "us" and the infinite "not us" that is the rest of the universe.

Obviously, drawing this border is no simple task. So the OAA depends on a constant stream of incoming messages. All of our senses send data here. Incredible calculations occur. But all of this takes a lot of energy. When that energy is needed elsewhere — like during moments of intense focus — the OAA stops performing those calculations because it stops receiving those signals. Without this data stream, this part of the brain is temporarily blinded — it too becomes hypofrontal — and to incredible result. "Once this happens," says Newberg, "we can no longer draw a line and say this is where the self ends and this is where the rest of the world begins, so the brain concludes, it has to conclude, that at this moment you are one with everything."

This is a somewhat startling reversal. Ever since Aldous Huxley told the world about his experiments with mescaline, the idea has been that the *doors of perception* needed to be opened for cosmic unity to be revealed. Newberg and D'Aquili discovered the inverse. With hypofrontality, attention is narrowing. Parts of the brain are shutting down.

Oneness is the result of the narrowing of the doors of perception, not throwing them wide open. Huxley had it exactly backward.

Newberg and D'Aquili also discovered that what you focus on matters. Surfers with their attention entirely on a wave become one with the wave. Meditating Franciscan nuns had God's love in mind so their experience was oneness with God's love. And Dean Potter, at the bottom of the Cellar of Swallows, had his attention entirely upon a dying bird so he did, in fact, become that dying bird.

This also explains why oneness keeps showing up in action and adventure sports. Focus is focus. There's little difference between the amount of concentration needed by a meditator to achieve "ecstasy" and the amount required by a BASE jumper leaping into a cave. Danger heightens attention. Thus the big mountains and big waves allow us to cheat this process, a fact Potter openly acknowledges: "I take the easy way," he says. "I can sit on my ass and meditate for two hours to get a fifteen-second glimpse of this state. Or I can risk my life and get there instantly—and it lasts for hours."

This is not to say these athletes are a new class of enlightened spiritual warriors. Not close. Like most of us, they're wildly fallible and often flawed. But spirituality isn't their intention. Action and adventure athletes want to experience oneness because it enhances their performance—it makes them better athletes.

This performance benefit emerges from a number of different places, but for starters, let's return to where we began: enhanced decision making. Since flow is a fluid action state, making better decisions isn't enough: we also have to act on those decisions. The problem is fear, which stands between us and all actions. Yet our fears are grounded in self, time, and space. With our sense of self out of the way we are liberated from doubt and insecurity. With time gone, there is no yesterday to regret or tomorrow to worry about. And when our sense of space disappears, so do physical consequences. But when all three vanish at once, something far more incredible occurs: our fear of death—that most fundamental of all fears—can no longer exist. Simply put: if you're infinite and atemporal, you cannot die.

This is also why the Voice comes through so clearly in a flow state. With self, time, and space erased from the picture, all that complexity that Dietrich mentioned is edited out. It's not that the Voice is turned up louder in the zone, it's that everything that stands between us and the message is removed from the picture.

Yet this begs an even deeper question — where does the Voice get its information? When Dean Potter was climbing Fitz Roy, he felt "one with the rock" — but was this more than a feeling? His intuition led him straight up a 2,000-foot wall. Foothold to foothold, some 670 decisions in a row, the Voice was never wrong. But the Voice should still be subject to the laws of biophysics. Since the human eye can't detect tiny variations from one-third of a mile's distance — where did the information come from?

To put it another way, scientists assume that unity is an illusion produced by hypofrontality. We feel one with everything, but the merger is sensational rather than actual. Yet blind people claim to *feel* the sidewalk through the tips of their canes and racecar drivers say they *feel* the track through their tires — two bits of anecdotal evidence that suggest the expansion of the boundary of self also expands the reach of our senses. But how far can the process go? Potter felt at one with the mountain and his astounding route-finding suggests that this was more than just an illusion.

There is a final advantage to consider, this one far less esoteric. Everything we're describing here — the loss of self, time, and space — are not the most ordinary of experiences. When most people bump into these phenomena, it's a rare encounter, an astronaut on a moonwalk. Without any frame of reference, the bizarreness of the experience tends to dominate. By consistently putting themselves in flow, action and adventure athletes have gained familiarity with terra incognita. They're mapping the landscape, learning the ins and outs of lunar gravity, turning a one-time trip to the moon into a permanent base — a launch point for further deep-space exploration.

As Potter explains it: "I learned that the zone gave me superpowers when I was a kid. In my early career, I spent a really long time figuring out how to cultivate those powers. Now, the thing that interests me is practicing with them, testing their limits. You've got to wonder. I saved my own life while falling into a cave with a parachute over my head and then, not too long afterward, became one with a bird. If that stuff is possible, well what else is possible?"

4

The What of Flow

THE RED BULL AIR FORCE

The first thing Mike Swanson did when he exited the building was check his reflection in the mirror. This wasn't vanity; it was protocol. The building was the Willis Tower, formerly the Sears Tower, 108 stories of cold steel, black glass, and modern ingenuity. From the ground, Swanson had difficulty looking up. He is severely afraid of heights and just the sight of the Tower's upper edge, some 1,451 feet above, made him nervous. But looking up wasn't the issue just then. That's because Swanson hadn't exited the Willis from the street level. He did not use the main doors. Nor the side doors. Not even the emergency exit. Swanson had just jumped off the roof.

This was in July 2011. A few months earlier, Hollywood director Michael Bay had seen a segment of *60 Minutes* featuring JT Holmes and Julian Boulle flying wingsuits off cliffs in Norway. Bay had never seen anything like it before; then again, not many people had.

The earliest attempts at "human-powered flight" date to the sixth century CE, when Chinese emperor Kao Yang got curious about the potential for large kites to lift human bodies. Yang strapped a number of variations onto prisoners and pushed them off tall towers. One design actually worked. A convict named Yuan Huang-t'ou floated safely to the ground.

His was a rare success.

For the next 1,500 years, birdman aspirants have been strapping on homebuilt wings, stepping off high perches, and dying. Literally everyone who went down this road has been killed along the way. By the tail end of the twentieth century, the body count was so high that merely mentioning the word "wingsuit" at any major skydiving operation was enough to get thrown off the premises.

Change came in the 1990s. Frenchman Patrick de Gayardon copied the wing design of flying squirrels, stretching pliable, nonporous fabric into three triangular wings: two running wrist to armpit, a third forming a giant inverted *V* between the legs. His revolutionary insight was to stitch a series of ribs across these wings. When aloft, ram air inflated the ribs much like modern square parachutes, providing pilots a three-to-one glide ratio (three feet forward for every one-foot drop) and an astounding level of in-flight control.

In 1999, Finnish company Birdman International brought a safer version of this design to market, then established the world's first wingsuit flying school to train potential customers. Interest was immediately high. In the first year alone, 2,000 skydivers took the training. The real tipping point came in 2005, when a group of Norwegian BASE jumpers released *Super Terminal,* a DVD containing footage of proximity flying, piloting a wingsuit a few feet above a cliff face. Proximity flying was the real deal: flying, just like the birds do. And seriously, who doesn't want to fly like a bird?

At the time Michael Bay caught JT and Julian's act, he was working on the third installment of his mega-franchise, *Transformers: Dark of the Moon.* The plot? Well, never mind the plot. Bay's plan was big-budget spectacular. As the Transformers are an alien race of giant robots, much of that budget was spent on computer-generated imagery. But Bay is also an archaic throwback who preferred flesh-and-blood humans to do his stunts. Immediately, he decided to become the first director to put wingsuit flying into an action scene.

Since no one in Hollywood knew too much about wingsuit flying, JT Holmes was brought in to help stretch imaginations. Holmes is both a professional big-mountain skier and a member of the Red Bull Air Force, arguably the greatest assembly of skydivers, BASE jumpers, wingsuit flyers, and paraglider pilots in the world. For teammates, he hired from within. Julian Boulle would remain the cameraman. Jon

Devore, Andy Farrington, and Mike Swanson, three other members of the Air Force, were also brought on board. With over 80,000 jumps and a multitude of national and international titles among them, these five pilots were already the best of the best. But if they were going to survive the Willis Tower, they were going to have to get a whole lot better in a hurry.

For starters, no one had ever jumped the Willis before. In fact, very few wingsuit pilots had even flown through a city. Beyond the legalities, height was an issue: 1,500 feet of vertical clearance is the minimum margin for safety, but not too many buildings stand that tall. With rare exceptions, urban wingsuit flying was terra incognita. Unfortunately, as Jon Devore points out, "once inflated, those wings are extremely rigid. Flying a wingsuit is like piloting an F-16 in a straight jacket. It's not the ideal situation for encountering the unexpected."

More alarming was the wind. In the mountains, wind moves like a river; in the city, like a pinball. Wingsuit pilots, not surprisingly, prefer calm conditions, with gusts higher than fifteen miles per hour being enough to cancel most jumps. "When we put our heads over the side of the Willis for the first time," continues Devore, "it felt like getting punched. The wind was blasting up the building. That was a bad moment. Everyone got really quiet, had a long think."

All of them reached the same conclusion: The hurricane only blew right next to the building. Five feet out, the air was calm. Yet this would make an already tricky exit even trickier. Bay wanted them to fly as a group, so logistics dictated a simultaneous departure. If anyone got blown of course? With speeds well over 100 miles per hour and with little more than inches between them? Yeah, the wind was an issue.

But the real concern was line of flight. Holmes had decided that the most interesting choice lay on the south side of the Willis. "This was a once in a lifetime opportunity," he says. "So I wanted to do something memorable, something that would really push the boundaries of urban wingsuit flying. The jump from the south side was intense. It was gnarly. But I thought it was doable."

Barely.

There were a pair of ledges — one ninety feet down, another 700 feet down — directly beneath the south-side launch point. The plan called for them to fly in a tight diamond formation: JT at the front, Jon and

Mike in the middle, Andy at the rear. With fabric stretched between their legs, running starts were impossible. Yet clearing both ledges required their wings to immediately inflate, which meant prejumping: waddling three feet from the edge and diving over blind. This was why Swanson checked his reflection on the side of the building. He was trying to make sure he was in the right place — his life depended on it.

Within three seconds they would reach terminal velocity, then use that speed to thread the needle between a row of buildings, before making a sharp S-turn: a hard left around a skyscraper, then an immediate right around another. The former was their real concern. It was a *very* hard left: 110 degrees at 150 miles per hour. At the apex of the turn, each would pull four Gs — like being pinned beneath a medium-size motorcycle — and less than ten feet from the side of the building.

JT Holmes, from his position flying point, would initiate all movements. Yet here's the thing: in this tight of a formation, if the team actually waited for Holmes to start his hard left it would be too late. "I need to know what JT is going to do before he does it," explains Swanson. "If I wait for him to actually get through the motion, then I won't be able to turn in time."

His teammate Andy Farmington puts things slightly differently: "We started calling it 'Suicide Corner.' We just had no real idea if it was actually possible to make that turn."

For all of these reasons, before any jumps were attempted, Holmes made a demand unheard of in movie stunt coordination: he wanted the entire team flown to Switzerland for a month of training. He wanted to find near-vertical cliffs to practice formation swooping. Tight turns done in close proximity were also on the rehearsal menu. But mainly, because this was the hardest urban wingsuit flight ever attempted and their survival so clearly depended upon it, they practiced ESP — which, as it turns out, is actually a thing you can practice.

PATTERN RECOGNITION AND ESP

In 2011, a team of researchers at the Beckman Institute for Advanced Science and Technology at the University of Illinois decided to play a little *Frogger*. Actually, they decided to play a big *Frogger*. Life-size big. Their goal was to see how normal college students fared against Division I athletes in a few rounds of "cross a busy city street; don't get splatted."

For the experiment, a treadmill was placed between three ten-foot-high screens, each showing a lively cityscape. Just like in the video game, a bustling boulevard sat center stage. Traffic came from both directions, whizzing by at speeds between forty and fifty-five miles per hour. Athletes from all sorts of sports were recruited. Everyone hopped on the treadmill, donned virtual-reality goggles to increase depth and verisimilitude, and tried to avoid becoming roadkill — ninety-six times in a row.

In the end, there was a huge performance gap between normals and athletes. Normals made it to the other side 55 percent of the time, athletes 72 percent of the time. The more interesting part was why.

The assumption was that physical fitness accounted for the athletes' success. But this wasn't what the researchers discovered. It wasn't that the athletes were quicker or more agile. They didn't dodge and weave through traffic better than the normal students. Instead, they could assimilate and apply incoming information with more speed and accuracy than nonathletes. Neuroscientist Art Kramer, who oversaw this work, told the *New York Times:* "They didn't move faster, but it looks like they thought faster."

How they thought faster has been the subject of an incredible amount of recent research. Over the past few decades, neuroscientists have discovered that the main job of the neocortex is to predict the future. This was a radical revelation. The old idea was interpretation: the senses gather data and then decide what's actually happening in the world. The new idea means the senses gather data and the brain uses that information to make predictions about what's happening in the world *before* it's happened. Imagine, for example, approaching a door. "'Prediction' means that the neurons involved in sensing your door become active in advance of them actually receiving sensory input," writes Jeff Hawkins and Sandra Blakeslee in *On Intelligence:*

> When the sensory input does arrive, it is compared with what was expected. As you approach the door, your cortex is forming a slew of predictions based on past experience. As you reach out, it pre-

dicts what you will feel on your fingers, when you will feel the door, and at what angle your joints will be when they actually touch the door. As you start to push the door open, your cortex predicts how much resistance the door will offer and how it will sound. When your predictions are all met, you walk through the door without consciously knowing these predictions were verified. But if your expectations about the door are violated, the error will cause you to take notice. Correct predictions result in understanding. Incorrect predictions result in confusion and prompt you to pay attention. The door latch is not where it is supposed to be. The door is too light. The door is off center. The texture of the knob is wrong. We are making continuous low-level predictions in parallel across all our senses.

So important is prediction to survival, that when the brain guesses correctly — i.e., when the brain's pattern-recognition system identifies a correct pattern — we get a reward, a tiny squirt of the feel-good neurochemical dopamine. Dopamine feels *really* good. Cocaine, widely considered one of the most addictive substances on earth, does little besides cause the brain to release dopamine and then block its reuptake. This same rush reinforces pattern recognition — it's why learning happens.

But dopamine actually does double duty. Not only does this neurotransmitter help us learn new patterns, it also amps up attention and reduces noise in neural networks, making it easier for us to notice more patterns. And noticing patterns actually prepares the brain to notice more patterns. It's why creative insights tend to snowball. Once we do the hard work of identifying that first pattern, the dopamine dumped in our system primes us to pick out the next.

And the next.

Neurons that fire together wire together. The more times a particular pattern fires, the stronger the connection between neurons becomes, and the faster information flows along this route. This is learning and it leads to "chunking." When the pattern recognition system correctly identifies a pattern, it's stored not as a series of steps, rather as a whole — a chunk. Chunks get added to chunks get added to chunks, until seeing the front edge of a tiny pattern allows us to make very complicated predictions about the future.

It was these predictions that explain why the athletes playing *Frogger* outperformed the normals. Sports usually involve making calculations about approaching objects and reaction times. The athletes already had these patterns down. Thus their brains could take in a tiny bit of information — a very quick glance at that cityscape — and use it to make a very complicated prediction: a safe path across the street.

Something similar happened with the *Transformers* BASE jumpers. The Red Bull Air Force went to Switzerland to learn one another's tics, tendencies, and techniques — their patterns. They did dozens and dozens of practice jumps so these patterns formed into chunks that formed into larger chunks that predicted a very sophisticated future. Take Mike Swanson's experience. In their diamond formation, he was positioned behind and to the left of JT Holmes. This meant his in-flight focus was entirely on the back of Holmes's left shoe. As he says, "it was almost all I saw on the way down." But to avoid dying along the way, Swanson had to learn very subtle patterns — like, say, when JT's heal twitches slightly left and down, he's a second away from initiating a steep dive. The goal is to cut out consciousness. Swanson doesn't have time to see Holmes's twitch, decide what it means, and initiate his own dive. He needs to have learned the patterns so well and trust his predictions so much that even before JT's foot *begins* to twitch, his implicit system has already identified the chunk and triggered the reaction. By the time this information trickles up to Swanson's consciousness, he's already midswoop.

Swanson, though, had another advantage in this effort: he was in flow state during that jump. They all were. It's the reason they survived the trip around Suicide Corner. Flow turns predictive pattern recognition into full-blown ESP.

THE NEUROCHEMISTRY OF FLOW

To understand how flow makes this possible requires understanding a little more neurochemistry, but before we get there it's worth considering the macroscopic perspective. Flow originates in the brain, thus our attempt to unpack the science behind the state has been focused there. As most researchers describe basic brain function with a triumvirate approach — neuroelectricity, neuroanatomy, and neurochemistry (i.e., the two ways the brain communicates internally and the places where those communications take place) — we too have followed that path, with this chapter being the trilogy's last installment. When finished, we'll have our map, but the larger point is that cartography is not reality.

What's being presented here is more than the "minimum viable flow" (i.e., enough information to get everyone on the same page), yet less than a complete picture (i.e., there is over 100 years of scientific research to cover). For niggling particulars, potential caveats, and larger possibilities, check out the endnotes. And if you want more, go to the website for the Flow Genome Project (www.flowgenomeproject.co).

Along these same lines, there are dozens of neurochemical systems involved in flow. Some are still unknown, some irrelevant to this discussion. Our focus here is on a quintet of star performers, the substances that — to reprise our original description — help set flow apart from all other states of consciousness, altered or otherwise. Flow's two defining characteristics are its feel-good nature (flow is always a positive experience) and its function as a performance enhancer. The chemicals described herein are among the strongest mood-boosters and performance-enhancers the body can produce.

Now some details.

At a very simple level, neurochemicals are "information molecules" used by the brain to transmit messages. Mostly, these messages are either excitatory or inhibitory: *Do more of what you're doing* or *Do less of what you're doing.* But these small signals add up quickly, changing emotions, altering thoughts, fine-tuning reactions — essentially shaping our response to external events.

Flow is an extremely potent response to external events and requires an extraordinary set of signals. The process includes *dopamine,* which does more than tune signal-to-noise ratios. Emotionally, we feel dopamine as engagement, excitement, creativity, and a desire to investigate and make meaning out of the world. Evolutionarily, it serves a similar function. Human beings are hardwired for exploration, hardwired to push the envelope: dopamine is largely responsible for that wiring. This neurochemical is released whenever we take a risk or encounter something novel. It rewards exploratory behavior. It also helps us survive that behavior. By increasing attention, information flow, and pattern recognition in the brain, and heart rate, blood pressure, and muscle firing timing in the body, dopamine serves as a formidable skill-booster as well.

Norepinephrine provides another boost. In the body, it speeds up heart rate, muscle tension, and respiration, and triggers glucose release so we have more energy. In the brain, norepinephrine increases arousal, attention, neural efficiency, and emotional control. In flow, it keeps us locked on target, holding distractions at bay. And as a pleasure-inducer, if dopamine's drug analog is cocaine, norepinephrine's is speed, which means this enhancement comes with a hell of a high.

Endorphins, our third flow conspirator, also come with a hell of a high. These natural "endogenous" (meaning naturally internal to the body) opiates relieve pain and produce pleasure much like "exogenous" (externally added to the body) opiates like heroin. Potent too. The most commonly produced endorphin is 100 times more powerful than medical morphine.

The next neurotransmitter is *anandamide,* which takes its name from the Sanskrit word for "bliss" — and for good reason. Anandamide is an endogenous cannabinoid, and similarly feels like the psychoactive effect found in marijuana. Known to show up in exercise-induced flow states (and suspected in other kinds), this chemical elevates mood, relieves pain, dilates blood vessels and bronchial tubes (aiding respiration), and amplifies lateral thinking (our ability to link disparate ideas together). More critically, anandamide also inhibits our ability to feel fear, even, possibly, according to research done at Duke, facilitates the extinction of long-term fear memories.

Lastly, at the tail end of a flow state, it also appears (more research needs to be done) that the brain releases *serotonin,* the neurochemical now associated with SSRIs like Prozac. "It's a molecule involved in helping people cope with adversity," Oxford University's Philip Cowen told the *New York Times,* "to not lose it, to keep going and try to sort everything out." In flow, serotonin is partly responsible for the afterglow effect, and thus the cause of some confusion. "A lot of people associate serotonin directly with flow," says high performance psychologist Michael Gervais, "but that's backward. By the time the serotonin has arrived the state has already happened. It's a signal things are coming to an end, not just beginning."

These five chemicals are flow's mighty cocktail. Alone, each packs a punch, together a wallop. Consider the chain of events that takes us from pattern recognition through future prediction. Norepinephrine tightens focus (data acquisition); dopamine jacks pattern recognition (data processing); anandamide accelerates lateral thinking (widens the database searched by the pattern recognition system). The results, as basketball legend Bill Russell explains in his biography *Second Wind*, really do feel psychic:

> Every so often a Celtic game would heat up so that it would become more than a physical or even mental game, and would be magical. That feeling is difficult to describe, and I certainly never talked about it when I was playing. When it happened I could feel my play rise to a new level. . . . At that special level all sorts of odd things happened. . . . It was almost as if we were playing in slow motion. During those spells I could almost sense how the next play would develop and where the next shot would be taken. Even before the other team brought the ball in bounds, I could feel it so keenly that I'd want to shout to my teammates, 'It's coming there!' — except that I knew everything would change if I did. My premonitions would be consistently correct, and I always felt then that I not only knew all the Celtics by heart but all the opposing players, and that they all knew me. There have been many times in my career when I felt moved or joyful, but these were the moments when I had chills pulsing up and down my spine.

Yet, the *Transformers* BASE jumpers weren't just trying to predict the future, they were betting their lives on their predictions. And this level of psychic confidence takes an additional ingredient: trust. A lot of trust. "Three-fourths of what I saw on the way down was JT's shoe," says Devore. "If I didn't trust him completely, if I decided to look away and double-check one of his actions? Most likely, I just put myself in a very bad situation."

To this end, flow's neurochemistry performs an added function: it accelerates social bonding. Ever fall in love? That high — the sleeplessness, giddiness, hyperactivity, loss of appetite, etc. — that's dopamine and norepinephrine at work. These are the neurochemicals that reinforce romantic love. Endorphins serve a similar function, only showing up in maternal love (in infants) and general attachment (in adults). Serotonin, as well, further reinforces love and attachment (alongside oxytocin). And anandamide, as any pot smoker will attest, makes one feel open, expansive, and empathetic — all of which further improves connection.

This is why the Red Bull Air Force trained in Switzerland. Whenever the team entered a flow state together, these five neurochemicals were tightening the bonds between them, amping up trust, giving them extraordinary confidence in one another and their ability to understand one another. "By the time we left Europe," says Andy Farmington, "I could read emotion in the back of JT's shoe."

Of course, long-married couples can read each other's mood through tiny details in their clothing, finish each other's sentences, and predict — with a high degree of accuracy — their partner's reaction to complex events. The difference is speed. Normally, these talents arrive after years and years of matrimony. But the Red Bull Air Force trained in flow, so they went from A to B in less than a month.

It was an alchemical transformation, no doubt about it. But it was also just the warm-up round. When that month was over, the Air Force packed up their gear and boarded a plane and headed for downtown Chicago.

It was time for their trip round Suicide Corner.

SUICIDE CORNER AND SITUATIONAL AWARENESS

They dress quickly, putting on their wingsuits in the street beside the Willis Tower. A security guard lets them into the building; they cross the lobby as a pack. In the elevator, steel buttons and only three possibilities: LL2, 99, and 103. Someone, no one remembers who, punches the floor.

It's a short trip. Their skyward chariot clocks in at eighteen miles per hour, going the length of five football fields in just over a minute.

Ironically — in a testament to how good the wingsuit's glide ability has become and despite the fact that they're about to jump off the roof — the Air Force went up faster than they came down.

Out of the elevator and down a hallway. Another security guard, a fifty-foot staircase, an oversize steel door. As it cracks, a blast of wind — the way it happens up high. They pass that threshold and into a strange maze. Towering antennas, enormous fans, window-washing equipment. JT Holmes calls it "standard roof junk," as if roof junk was something encountered on a regular basis.

They walk toward the center of the building. Chicago, like a carpet, unfurls before them. The view is clear skies and fifty miles in every direction. But their gaze is already spoken for. In the southwest corner, a black ramp over the side, a pirate's plank into a yawning abyss.

What the fuck was I thinking? JT wants to know.

And that's when the adrenaline hits him. Hits all of them. A pulse-pounding wash, the thrill ride before the thrill ride. None care too much for this feeling. In fact, despite the frequency with which many dismiss these athletes as "adrenaline junkies," the term is actually one of the greatest misnomers in sport. Of the hundreds of athletes interviewed for this book, very few enjoy this rush. Most share professional kayaker Tao Berman's sentiment: "I'm the farthest thing from an adrenaline junky. I can't stand that feeling. If I'm feeling adrenaline, it means I'm feeling too much fear. It means I haven't done my homework. It means it's time to get out of my boat to reassess."

But they are all flow junkies — the difference is critical.

And chemical. The fight-or-flight response — a.k.a. the adrenaline rush — cocktails adrenaline, cortisol (the stress hormone), and norepinephrine. It's an extreme stress response. The brain switches to reactive survival autopilot. Options are limited to three: fight, flee, or freeze. Flow is the opposite: a creative problem-solving state, options wide open.

Yet there are reasons for the confusion. The two highs are linked. Risk heightens focus and flow follows focus. This means that the fight-or-flight response primes the body — chemically and psychologically — for the flow state. Athletes report moving through one to get to the other. Danny Way, for example, has a phrase he uses to remind himself of the importance of this transition. "Never a glitch on takeoff," he says. He means that when you're teetering between flow and fight-or-flight, all it takes is one errant thought to send you in the wrong direction. When Way pushes off onto the MegaRamp, he has seconds to flip this switch. If he can follow his focus into flow, he lives to ride another day. But if panic swamps the circuitry? "The greatest slams of my life took place when that happened," he says. "Almost every time, I've ended up in the hospital."

The Red Bull Air Force calms down differently; they circle up and have a quick powwow. They are a few moments from impossible. There isn't much to say.

"You good with this?"

"Yeah."

"You good with this."

"Check."

"Mike looks scared."

"I'm good."

"Sure?"

"Sure."

A few more deep breaths. A quick "This is what we trained for" reminder from JT. And then, that most fabled sound in action sport: the countdown. "Three-two-one dropping."

Going over the edge is bad; the first three seconds are worse. It takes three seconds to fall about ninety feet and accelerate to terminal velocity. The more air rushing over the wings, the more rigid they become, the more control the pilots have. "Once the wings are pressurized," says JT, "it becomes automatic, like driving a car. That's when I calm down, when my conscious mind snaps off, and I dive into the zone."

Once JT's pattern recognition system recognizes that his wing's are powered up, he can relax and — according to experiments run by Harvard cardiologist Herbert Benson — that's flow's real trigger. This so-called relaxation response floods the body with high quantities of nitric oxide (NO) — an endogenous gaseous signaling molecule. "[T]he NO," writes Benson, "counteracts the norepinephrine and other stress secretions. Simultaneously, as the NO puffs billow forth in the brain and body, the brain releases calming neurotransmitters . . . such as dopamine and endorphins. As a result of these secretions, the blood vessels dilate or open up, the heart rate decreases, the stress response fades, and inner tranquility takes over."

But that wasn't Andy Farmington's experience.

Positioned at the back of the diamond, when Farmington leapt, he encountered a blast of "dirty air" rolling off his teammates. Combined with the blast blowing up the side of the Tower, there was too much turbulence for his wings to pressurize. Instead, he dropped like a stone.

"For those first few seconds," he says, "I was looking around and thinking maybe this was a bad idea after all."

But it was too late to abort. Farmington had a choice — he could either give in to the fight-or-flight response, allowing himself to be swept away in the tide of adrenaline, cortisol, and norepinephrine, or he could use the enhanced focus these chemicals provided to redirect his attention to the problem at hand. This is where all that flow time in Switzerland came in handy.

Training in high-stress situations increases what psychologists call "situational awareness." Defined as the ability to absorb information accurately, assess it calmly, and respond appropriately, situational awareness is essentially the ability to keep cool when all hell breaks loose. Because attention and pattern recognition are so heightened by flow, training in the state radically increases situational awareness. In this case, this allowed Farmington to not fight, flight, or freeze. Instead, he held it together until he fell through the dirty air and into a cleaner pocket below. "Then my wings started to pressurize and I turned my attention to JT's shoe and we were off."

Yup, they were off — and heading straight for Suicide Corner.

In Switzerland, the team trained by proximity flying vertical cliffs roughly the size of the Willis Tower. They had a pretty good idea of what it felt like to fly in formation down a structure that size, but what they never found was a turn as tight as Suicide Corner. "There was no way to prepare for it," says Holmes, "it was a total unknown."

And it did not disappoint.

"Going round Suicide Corner felt like I was making a really sharp turn in a jet airplane," says Farmington, "except there was no airplane. The power, speed, and pressure were the same, but there was no separation — no fuselage, no cockpit — between myself and those forces."

Out of that turn and into another, this one merely ninety degrees.

By that point, Devore was so deep into the zone, he felt like someone else was flying his body. "I was just listening to the Voice," he says, "taking directions. This was a ninety-degree turn at 150 miles per hour, and my experience was this voice in my head saying, 'Oh look, you're turning again.'" Deployment was the next concern. They were using low-profile BASE rigs, with canopies extending 225 feet square. Normally, because of these space requirements, formation flyers separate before deployment. For similar reasons, they prefer large landing zones. Neither was in the offing here. "There were buildings all over the place," explains Holmes. "No outs (places to ditch in times of trouble) and we didn't have 360 degrees to work with. I tried to go long and low, Jon pulled early, and Mike and Andy had to make do with what was left in the middle."

Life and death would be measured in millimeters and milliseconds. The entire team would have to pull in short succession, one right after another, and within a two-second window. Worse, because no one knew exactly which direction they would be facing when those chutes opened, they would each immediately have to grab their steering toggles, survey the scenery, and yank. If they had failed to notice something and turned the wrong direction? "When my canopy opened," continues Devore, "there were guys floating four feet away from me."

Without flow, none of this would have been possible. The pattern recognition and information chunking that took place in Switzerland would not have led to instinctive behavior in Chicago. Muscle reaction times would have been slower, intragroup trust weaker. Neither the spotlight attention needed to know when to pull nor the future prediction required to determine which direction to turn would have been in the offing. Panic would have swamped the system and Suicide Corner would have earned its namesake.

Instead, the Air Force floated safely to the ground.

"It was the highlight of my career," says Devore, "it was our Super Bowl on the Moon."

"What an unbelievable rush," adds Swanson.

About this last part there is no debate. Flow is a rush like no other. If you want grounds for comparison, consider the current use-abuse rates for mood-altering, mind-altering, and performance-enhancing drugs: In America, over 22 percent of the population has an illicit drug problem; one out of ten take antidepressants; 26 percent of kids are on stimulants, purportedly for ADHD, anecdotally for performance enhancement. And prescription drugs? They've just surpassed car accidents as the number one cause of accidental death. Add this up and you'll find a trillion-dollar public-health crisis.

Now consider what these abused drugs do. The primary illicit drug of choice is marijuana — that triggers the release of anandamide. Antidepressants are some combination of dopamine, norepinephrine, and serotonin; tobacco and ADHD drugs affect dopamine and norepinephrine; and prescription drugs of abuse are opioids like Oxycontin — meaning they affect the endorphin system. In other words, Americans are literally killing themselves trying to achieve artificially the same sensations that flow produces naturally.

Of course, as a perfect endogenous combination of these drugs, flow is also a major rush. But unlike the dead-end highs currently plaguing public health, flow doesn't sidetrack one's life; it revitalizes it. Flow is the rush of possibility: a product of radical neurochemical, neuroelectrical, and neuroanatomical function triggering whole-body transformation. As Devore concludes: "I really think we're the next stage in human evolution."

Or, to put it another way: flow is the telephone booth where Clark Kent changes clothes, the place from where Superman emerges.

5

The Flow Shortcut

DIRTBAGS TO SAMURAI

In our quest to map flow and see how it amps up performance, there is still one component missing: performance over time. Certainly, what we learned from meeting Laird Hamilton, Danny Way, Dean Potter, and the Red Bull Air Force is that flow is the secret to Superman. Yet the Millennium Wave and Great Wall MegaRamp were deeds over and done in seconds. The Willis Tower jump lasted less than two minutes; Potter's climbing trip through Patagonia almost a month. But a month is not a year is not a career. The question here isn't about how flow helps these athletes do the impossible once; it's about them doing the impossible over and over and over again. It's about long-term mastery, not short-term success, and a question most certainly raised by the ascension of Shane McConkey.

By almost any measure McConkey did not follow the standard path toward mastery. Consider the trilogy of his "most famous" naked spread eagles. On this list, the Colorado backcountry cliff huck described earlier in this book ranks third. Second place, meanwhile, clearly belongs to the Palisades.

Located a short hike away from the top of Squaw Valley's Siberia chair, the Palisades are one of skiing's most iconic proving grounds, a nasty series of rocky faces, intense steeps, tiny chutes, and little mercy. "Dropping into some of the Palisade chutes is as abrupt as dropping a quarter into a pay phone . . . ," explains the website Tahoetopia. "Lose it in process and the rest of the ride is like being in a wave tank in physics class. You end up feeling like the Tin Man after a good thrashing by the flying monkeys."

Even when everything goes right on the Palisades, things can go wrong. In 1975, during the filming of the cult-classic ski flick *Daydreams*, Greg Beck aired 100 feet off a cliff on the Palisades (now known as Beck's Rock), nailed the landing perfectly, and still knocked himself out cold.

A few yards away from Beck's Rock sits "Extra Chute," where a fifty-foot drop gives way to a fifty-five-degree landing. In 1995, Shane McConkey was filming atop the Palisades with ski filmmaker and close friend Scott Gaffney. He had been throwing crazy backflips down Extra Chute all morning, when a stranger approached and introduced himself as a representative for a new energy-bar company, Naked Energy. The guy wanted a promotional photograph so he offered McConkey $100 to jump the cliff nude. Back then, McConkey was both a nationally ranked mogul skier and the US Extreme Skiing champion, but neither title came with paychecks worth a damn. He was still bussing tables to make ends meet. So yeah, off came the clothes and off he went, throwing the second most famous naked spread eagle in history—smack down the center of Extra Chute.

The number one Shane McConkey naked spread eagle took place a few years earlier. By then, McConkey had graduated from Burke Ski Academy in Vermont with some exceptional racing skills and dreams of becoming the next Ingemar Stenmark. Those plans were nixed when he was tossed off the US Ski Team for being too small. Afterward, he moved to Vail and was making ends meet by delivering pizzas and trying his hand at professional mogul skiing. He did pretty well on the tour, winning his first event in 1993, but not long after, at a Vail bump off, McConkey fell early on his first run. Already eliminated from competition, he decided to celebrate by tossing a backflip off the final booter. "The crowd went nuts," wrote Rob Story in *Skiing* magazine. "Ski patrol did too. They kicked him off the hill, since inverted aerials were illegal at that sphincter-puckered time."

McConkey, of course, did not take this sitting down. Or fully clothed. He snuck back onto the mountain, got back to the starting gate, stripped to the buff, streaked the race course, and, of course, threw a series of naked spread eagles along the way — the most infamous in the history of skiing. Vail, in their wisdom, banned him for life. McConkey was fine with that. He moved to Squaw Valley, and continued on his quest to have more fun than anyone — ever.

The stories are endless. McConkey threw backflips on monoskis, moonwalked on snowblades, and invented the now-legendary ski-film movie character "Saucer Boy," a Jack Daniel's swilling, gear-laden, extreme, well, saucer rider. Freeskiing pioneer Mike Douglas once described what it was like to room with the superstar: "Every morning he'd be the first up and wake me up with 'Wakey wakey, hands off snakey!' Then he'd proceed to poison the room with his farts, then he would clog the toilet with a massive coiler (that he'd be really proud of) followed by half a roll of toilet paper, then he would show off all the most disgusting things he could find on the Internet. If we were lucky, we'd go skiing or something. If we weren't, the process would just repeat all day long."

That said, when it came time to go skiing, few could equal McConkey's prowess. His skills on the snow, well, in one of Steve Winter's films, Ingrid Backstrom, herself one of the greatest skiers in the world, spoke for many when she said: "Pretty much it's always a bad idea to try to do something Shane can do." To this day, skiers use the phrase "McConkey turn" to refer to a giant, high-speed power carve, usually made in some nosebleed steep, rock-strewn, cliff-laden, downright foreboding spot that — through the radically transformative capacity of a McConkey turn — had suddenly become a playground.

Yet this does raise one additional issue — how does an undersize, washed-up racer with a penchant for practical jokes become the person that ski writer Leslie Anthony once fittingly described as "the ski world's first Superman"? In 1995, Shane McConkey was bussing tables and skiing naked for extra cash. Less than a decade later, he was a legend. But against what odds?

By the time McConkey's star really began to rise, he'd already abandoned the traditional structures of athletic excellence. He was no longer a student at Burke Academy, had been tossed out of professional ski racing, and quit the pro mogul game. Gone were all the trappings of institutionalized mastery. No more world-class coaches, world-class assistant coaches, video playback reviews, dry land skill drills, team nutritionists planning his meals, team chefs cooking his meals, or team techs tuning his gear. McConkey had jettisoned the whole deal, yet — somehow — climbed to far greater heights on his own.

This same puzzle surrounds most of the early action and adventure sports stars. Before the X Games came along, these guys were ski bums and surf burnouts and for good reason. The party never stopped. Forget about drug testing; drug-taking was almost mandatory. And the closest most got to a meal designed by a team nutritionist was a Clif Bar. Yet in less than two decades, these same rebel misfits would push the boundary of human performance to astounding heights. Hell, by the time McConkey was done, his chosen sport was barely recognizable as the same game.

Alaska is the wild frontier, skiing's ultimate proving ground. In 1990, when extreme-skiing pioneer Doug Coombs made the first descent of Python Peak, it was a very big deal, considered the "first serious descent of the era." In total, Coombs made hundreds of turns down this fifty-degree Chugach beast, because, of course, his survival was at stake. Fifty degrees is damn steep. Standing straight up, Coombs could reach out and tickle the slope. No wonder he made hundreds of turns — turns are what give skiers control.

Well, eight years later, McConkey would repeat the feat, only this time he straight-lined Python — making exactly zero turns from top to bottom and hitting speeds over sixty miles per hour along the way. Of course, this is only one example. In the past few decades, the bounds of the possible have been pushed farther and faster than ever before in history — yet the folks doing the pushing were never anyone's ideal candidates for the job. To say this community has exceeded expectations would be a considerable understatement. These folks started out dirtbags and ended up samurai. How exactly did that happen?

MOTHERS, MUSICIANS, AND MARSHMALLOWS

Over the past century, the science of expert performance has gotten rigorous and codified. Thousands and thousands of experiments have been run; plenty of conclusions reached. Three dominate. Call them:

mothers, musicians, and *marshmallows.* This famed trilogy — details in a moment — represent our best ideas about the path to mastery. Yet there's a wrench in these works: most action and adventure athletes took a radically different path.

These athletes haven't just redefined the limits of human potential; they've redefined those limits by doing the opposite of what the experts say they should have done. It's peculiar, all right. Their stratospheric success suggests that we may have completely misjudged the path toward stratospheric success. In fact, it suggests something far more radical: that if we really want to be our best, we don't just have to rethink the path toward mastery; we need to reconsider the way we live our lives.

But first, the *mothers.*

In the early 1980s, University of Chicago educational psychologist Benjamin Bloom launched the Talent Project, one of the larger and more thorough "retrospective" studies of expert performance ever undertaken. The Project examined the lives of 120 people, all under the age of thirty-five, all of whom had demonstrated the highest levels of accomplishment in one of six fields: swimming, tennis, sculpture, piano, mathematics, and research neuroscience (i.e., two artistic fields, two psychomotor, two cognitive). The question at the center of the study was: Where does prodigious talent come from, special individuals or special circumstances?

Before the study began, Bloom was convinced that talent was innate and what we call expertise (mastery) is the result of talented individuals identified early, then encouraged to blossom. Afterward, though, the data told a different story. Few of Bloom's research subjects showed any great promise as children. No Mozart concertos before the age of three; no solving for pi from the crib. Instead, the one commonality was encouragement, a lot of encouragement. In each case, there was a parent or close relative who rewarded any display of talent, and ignored or punished the opposite. Prodigies, it seemed, were made, not born. As Bloom later told reporters: "We were looking for exceptional kids, but what we found were exceptional conditions."

This was a cornerstone finding, replicated and expanded and potent. The idea settled an uneasy corner of the nature/nurture debate: it democratized expertise. Provided the right environment and the proper encouragement, it meant that everyone had a shot at perfection. It meant there were no "chosen few."

But many of the athletes involved in action and adventure sports came up the hard way. The wrong environment, little encouragement. "A lot of us were from broken homes," skateboard pioneer Duane Peters once told the *LA Times.* "We were freaks and misfits." And if home life wasn't rosy, the outside world was even less supportive. Twenty-five years ago, skateboarding was a crime; snowboarding was banned at most resorts; and surfing, to quote the always relevant *Point Break,* was "for little rubber people who don't shave yet."

Certainly, there are plenty of action and adventure athletes who came from incredibly supportive backgrounds. Bloom wasn't wrong — "mothers" matter — but too many of these super athletes came up sideways, backward, and feral for this to be the single deciding factor. Something else is going on. And that something else is where the *musicians* come into play.

In the early 1990s, Florida State psychologist Anders Ericsson performed one of the more famous studies of expertise in recent history. By surveying elite violinists at Berlin's Academy of Music — a.k.a. musicians — Ericsson found that while one's early environment was helpful, what truly distinguished excellent players from good players from average players was hours of practice. By the time they were twenty years old, expert violinists had put in 10,000 hours of "deliberate, well-structured practice." The others had not. As Malcolm Gladwell famously explained in *Outliers:* "[The] research suggests that once a musician has enough ability to get into a top music school, the thing that distinguishes one performer from another is how hard he or she works. That's it. And what's more, the people at the top don't work just harder or even much harder than everyone else. They work much, *much* harder."

But another wrench. If 10,000 hours of "deliberate, well-structured practice" is the secret sauce, consider the difference between Ericsson's definition of the term: "This type of practice is focused, programmatic, carried out over extended periods of time, guided by conscious performance monitoring, evaluated by analyses of level of expertise reached, identification of errors, and procedures directed at eliminating those errors," and Shane McConkey's goals while skiing: "What I love to do on the hill is find an interesting way to do something fun." Or, for that matter, consider his chosen sport. "If you remember the 1980s, you probably weren't skiing" was a once popular saying whose sentiment still rings true — but it's not exactly the ideal backdrop for "deliberate, well-structured practice."

Put differently, deliberate well-structure practice is a rigorous, compliance-based approach to mastery. It means you crawl before you walk. It doesn't mean Laird Hamilton surfing Pipeline at age four, or Danny Way in the deep end of the pool at the Del Mar Skate Ranch by seven. In broader terms, deliberate practice is also how we train genius these days. It's factory athletics. It's Kumon math tutoring, Baby Einstein, Suzuki violin, et al. But it's also the world McConkey walked away from that naked day at Vail. He turned his back on the factory, yet somehow still went on to become Superman.

Finally, the trouble with *marshmallows*.

In 1972, Stanford psychologist Walter Mischel performed a fairly straightforward study in delayed gratification: he offered four-year-old children a marshmallow. Either the kids could eat it immediately or, if they waited for him to return from running a short errand, they would get two marshmallows as a reward. Most kids couldn't wait. They ate the marshmallow the moment Mischel left the room. Yet a small percentage could resist temptation and, over time, this turned out to a big deal.

When interviewed fourteen years later, the kids who could wait were more self-confident, hard-working, and self-reliant. They could handle stress better and could handle tests better. Those who resisted at four ended up scoring 210 points higher on their SATs at sixteen. This may not sound like that much, but, as fellow Stanford psychologist Philip Zimbardo explains: "[That] is as large as the average difference recorded between the abilities of economically advantaged and disadvantaged children. It is larger than the difference between the abilities of children from families who parents have graduate degrees and children whose parents did not finish high school. The ability to delay gratification at four is twice as good a predictor of later SAT scores as IQ. Poor impulse control is also a better predictor of juvenile delinquency than IQ."

But there's another issue. According to psychologists, by definition, action and adventure athletes are "sensation seekers." They're impulsive pleasure junkies. Delayed gratification is not their game. Hell, in a 2009 *Outside* magazine profile of Shane McConkey, journalist Tim Sohn wrote: "Riding in a backpack as his mother skied, a three-year-old McConkey would shake the pack's support bars while making known what he wanted: 'Pow, Mommy, pow,' or 'Bump, Mommy, bump.'" Seriously, does "Pow, Mommy, pow" sound like a kid who didn't eat the marshmallow?

So what gives? How do a bunch of impulsive hedonists raised far from the storied incubators of athletic excellence end up rewriting the rule book on human potential? The short answer, of course, is flow. The long answer is where Philip Zimbardo comes back into our story.

THE IMPORTANCE OF TIME PERSPECTIVES

It started with illness. When Philip Zimbardo was five years old, he got a bad case of whooping cough and a worse case of pneumonia. This was 1939, New York. Zimbardo's family was too poor for private care, so he was sent to the charity ward of the Willard Parker Hospital for Children with Contagious Diseases. In those days before antibiotics, 63 percent of all children with whooping cough or double pneumonia did not recover. Many a friend Zimbardo made in that hospital died in that hospital. Zimbardo found that the only way he could stop himself from sinking into despair was imagination — he kept imagining better possible futures. And to considerable impact.

After Zimbardo recovered and was released, he was shocked to realize he viewed his stay in the hospital as a positive one: the time in his life that he learned to be self-reliant. "From this experience," he later wrote, "I . . . learned that the past can be psychologically remodeled to make heaven of hell. Other people learn the opposite lesson, storing and recalling only the worst of times. . . . The horrors and sheer ugliness of the past they have experienced become a permanent filter through which they view all their current experiences."

Zimbardo went on to become one of the most well-regarded psychologists of the twentieth century, author of more than fifty books, and past president of the American Psychological Association. He taught at both Yale and Stanford and was at the latter institution when Walter Mischel performed his famed marshmallow experiment. The results caught Zimbardo's attention, but not because he was interested in delayed gratification. Rather, because they seemed to confirm his childhood suspicions about time.

Zimbardo noticed two competing "time perspectives" at work in Mischel's experiment. A time perspective is the technical name for the "permanent filter" Zimbardo described. It's essentially our attitude toward time. For example, in Mischel's experiment, the kids who ate the marshmallow immediately were *present hedonists*. They lived for the now and not the later. It wasn't that they were unable to delay gratification, it's that not delaying gratification — the downstream result of being a present hedonist — was their strategy for living.

And this strategy has an upside. As individuals, Presents are creative, spontaneous, open-minded, high-energy risk takers who play sports, have hobbies, make friends easily, and find lovers often. Their lives are fun-filled and fast-paced. Unfortunately, this comes at a cost.

While Presents are often the life of the party, that's often the end of the line. Because they act without anticipating consequences, don't often learn from past failures, and are across the boards unable to resist temptation, attractions of the drugs and sex and rock-and-roll variety often derail their lives. A dominant present orientation has been correlated with mental health problems, juvenile delinquency, crime, and addictions. And when it comes to the long path toward mastery, with neither desire to plan nor long-term vision, Presents have a difficult time accumulating anything close to 10,000 hours of practice, deliberate or otherwise.

On the other hand, kids who didn't eat the marshmallow are *future oriented*, thus able to resist temptation today for a chance at a greater reward tomorrow. "Futures" have much to recommend them. In dozens and dozens of studies, they outperform Presents in most every category: they get better grades and more education, are healthier and more optimistic, make more money, solve problems more consistently, are more mindful of morality, and can make the best of failure. They are the movers and shakers in this world. Zimbardo writes:

While presents avoid work ... futures consider work a source of special pleasure. For them, tomorrow's anticipated gains and losses fuel today's decisions and actions. Gratification delayed for greater reward is always a better bet for futures, who will trade a bird in the hand for a flock in the future. Unlike their present-hedonistic peers who live in their bodies, the futures live in their minds, envisioning other selves, scenarios, rewards and successes. The success of Western civilization in the past centuries can be traced to the prevalence of the future orientation of many populations.

Obviously, Futures are more likely to achieve the 10,000 hours needed for mastery, but here too are unintentional consequences. Futures burn out. They become stressed-out workaholics. Blood pressure goes up, bowels get irritable, heart attacks increase, sex lives disintegrate, marriages fail, children become burdens, friends become memories, and the whole house of cards comes crashing down. So common is this experience that UCLA psychologist Steven Berglas has coined the term *supernova burnout* to describe the phenomenon. In other words, even when plans work out, Futures place a dangerous bet: too much delayed gratification can rob them of their motivation — which is the very thing that made them Futures in the first place.

After three decades of research, Zimbardo found that the healthiest, happiest, highest performers blend the best of both worlds. The optimal time perspective combines the energy, joy, and openness of Presents, with the strength, fortitude, and long-term vision of the Futures. But how to produce this blended perspective is the more important question.

Time perspective is possibly genetic, probably cultural, and definitely hard to shake. It is shaped by geography, religion, socioeconomic status, education, and a host of other powerful forces. It operates unconsciously and ubiquitously. But if optimal results require blending a present orientation and a future orientation, getting into flow is one of the most efficient mixing mechanisms at our disposal. Flow reorients Presents toward the future and Futures toward the present and both to considerable result.

Presents are sensation-seeking pleasure junkies. Flow releases a bevy of enormously potent feel-good neurochemicals at once, arguably the most powerful cocktail the brain can produce. It's the very sensation sensation seekers seek most.

Psychologists describe flow as "autotelic," from the Greek *auto* (self) and *telos* (goal). When something is autotelic — i.e., produces the flow high — it is its own reward. No one has to drag a surfer out of bed for overhead tubes. No one has to motivate a snowboarder on a powder day. These activities are intrinsically motivating, autotelic experiences done for their own sake. The high to end all highs.

Yet the flow high is different from all other highs — meaning it does more than just motivate. For starters, flow doesn't just happen anywhere. As we'll explore in depth in Part Two of this book, the state shows up most reliably when we're using our skills to the utmost. It requires challenge. While other hedonic pleasures — drugs, sex, gambling — make us feel good on their own, flow only shows up when we're pushing ourselves to higher and higher levels of performance. "Because flow involves meeting challenges and developing skills," explains Csikszentmihalyi in *Good Business,* "it leads to growth. It is an escape *forward* from current reality, whereas stimulants like drugs lead backward."

This is a very important point. Flow carries within it delicious possibility. In the state, we are aligned with our core passion and, because of flow's incredible impact on performance, expressing that passion to our utmost. Under normal conditions (playing chess, writing a report), this is empowering. But as author and adventurer Rob Schultheis writes in his cult classic, *Bone Games,* under life-threatening conditions (he's describing a flow state that occurred while mountaineering), it's utterly transformational: "The person I became . . . was the best possible version of myself, the person I *should have been* throughout my life. No regrets, no hesitation; there were no false moves left in me. I really believe I could have hit a mosquito in the eye with a pine needle at thirty paces; I couldn't miss because there was no such thing as a miss. It didn't matter whether I fell or not, because I couldn't fall, any more than two plus two can equal three."

When doing what we most love transforms us into the best possible version of ourselves *and* that version hints at even greater future possibilities, the urge to explore those possibilities becomes feverish compulsion. Intrinsic motivation goes through the roof. Thus flow becomes an alternative path to mastery, sans the misery. Forget 10,000 hours of delayed gratification. Flow junkies turn instant gratification into their North Star—putting in far more hours of "practice time" by gleefully harnessing their hedonic impulse. In other words, when it comes to time perspectives, flow allows Presents to achieve Futures' results.

On the other side of this coin, flow pulls Futures into the present. Because there is no time in the zone, there's no way to worry about tomorrow. There's literally no tomorrow. Flow provides Futures with blissful release from all that endless striving. And since the release is autotelic, Futures who find themselves in flow don't need to find new ways to slog toward the future. The state is intrinsically motivating so the slogging takes care of itself.

For similar reasons, the flow path presents an alternative to the standard Futures' mothers-marshmallows-musicians approach to mastery. For starters, mothers aren't required on the flow path. No one had to encourage McConkey to ski. Skiing produces flow and flow is autotelic. It was all the motivation he required.

The marshmallow experiment, meanwhile, highlights the power of willpower. If kids can't develop the inner strength to resist temptation, they can't master themselves, let alone anything else. This makes life tricky for action and adventure athletes who, by definition, are marshmallow-eating, sensation-seeking hedonists ("thrill and adventure seeking" is one of the four categories used by psychologists to delineate sensation seekers). But once the sensation seekers jump on the flow path, they don't need to delay gratification to achieve success—gratification becomes their path to success. "I'm doing what I love," explains McConkey. "And if you're doing what you want to do all the time, then you're happy. You're not going to work everyday wishing you were doing something else. I get up and go to work everyday and I'm stoked. That does not suck."

The lesson of the musicians, meanwhile, is that 10,000 hours of deliberate practice is the only sure way to acquire real expertise. But are we certain? A quick shorthand for learning is the more emotionally powerful an experience, the more chance the details of that experience get moved from short-term storage into long-term memory. Both flow and high-risk situations produce extremely powerful emotional experiences. "As a result," says high-performance sports psychologist Michael Gervais, "athletes in flow in death-facing situations likely gather more relevant data and code it more efficiently. Having these experiences frequently could significantly shorten the learning curve toward expertise."

Already, this has been proven correct in less extreme circumstances. In 2007, South Korean researchers looking at e-learning (electronic games, Web-based learning tools, and electronic tutoring) discovered a significant correlation between flow and positive learning attitudes and outcomes. In 2011, neuroscientists with the United States' Defense Advanced Research Projects Agency (DARPA) found that military snipers trained in flow decreased the time it took to acquire their targets by a factor of 2.3. Similar research run with amateur (i.e., nonmilitary) snipers found that flow cut the time it took to teach novices to shoot like experts by 50 percent. This means that flow doesn't just provide a joyful, self-directed path toward mastery — it literally shortens the path.

SEEING LINES

When Philip Zimbardo said that the success of Western civilization has been based upon a future orientated time perspective, he was describing the "struggle now, salvation later" hypothesis of the Protestant work ethic. This ethic is among the reasons the mothers, marshmallows, and musicians ideas have become so wildly popular: they confirm what we already want to believe. We have traded the now for the later and in collectively making this switch may have missed a vital point: it doesn't need to be so hard. With passion and play as the gateway to performance and possibility, we no longer have to mistrust ourselves. We can harness our hedonic impulse, using moments of spontaneous joy to shorten our path to mastery. Which, of course, is exactly what Shane McConkey did.

You want more proof? Then let's turn back the clock to the mid-1990s, take a trip to Squaw Valley, California, and ride the Broken Arrow chairlift. Beneath us sits some of the steepest, strangest terrain on the mountain. It's Salvador Dalí strange. The landscape appears, as author Dr. Rob Gaffney explains in *Squallywood* (his epic guide to Squaw's gnarliest lines), "to have been made by wet sand passing through a closed fist." In the winter, when snow starts to pile up between these formations, all sorts of deadly possibilities appear: tight chutes, boulder drops, big multistage cliffs. Among them is the line now known as "Sacrifice" — though calling it a "line" is being generous.

A steep headwall funnels into a tiny chute that ends at a granite boulder that overhangs a snowfield that gives way to a series of medium-sized cliffs that funnel into a really big cliff at the bottom. Sacrifice isn't a ski run: it's a trip to the morgue.

Shane McConkey wasn't so sure. He too had been eyeing Sacrifice for a while. Instead of rocks and death, he noticed that there was a tiny patch of snow above each cliff. So could he hop and pop and connect those dots? It was a tricky question. To make the entrance he'd need speed, enough to suck up his legs and sail over that boulder. And then things got interesting: a hard left midair, land on a dime, immediately leap right, zigzag a twenty-five-footer, then stomp the landing and straight-line off the monster air. Finding an interesting way to do something fun was McConkey's modus operandi. Sacrifice was his kind of fun.

"Shane loved trying to find the hardest way down the mountain," says Scott Gaffney. "It was almost a compulsion: Seek out impossible spots and dream up ways to navigate further. In that way he was literally a visionary — he just saw things other people didn't."

Some of this talent was inherited. Shane's father, Jim McConkey, was a legend in his own right. According to his official Canadian Ski Museum biography, "'McConk,' as he was affectionately known, preferred what was then the strictly unconventional. His 'gelandi jumping' and acrobatics on skis were the precursors to freestyle aerials and the freestyle movement generally. He sought out and reveled in difficult conditions: broken crust, ice, and the infamous 'mashed potatoes' . . . in order to improve his skills. Thought to be nearly impossible to ski, he was the first to conquer the gullies at both Alta and Snowbird."

Shane was born in British Columbia, and his parents divorced when he was four. His mother, Glenn, relocated to Santa Cruz, California, with Shane in tow. The parting was bitter and father and son rarely saw each other afterward. "They barely had a cup of coffee together before Shane was thirty," continues Gaffney, "but Shane idolized his father. He was a huge influence. Shane wanted to be just like him."

In trying to be like his father — and possibly because sensation seeking has a genetic component — Shane's perspective shifted. He started reading the mountain differently, seeing lines that others couldn't. He also started skiing those lines. Of course, this produced flow, which upped his performance, which made other lines possible. "Once Shane decided a line was possible," says professional skier-skydiver JT Holmes, one of McConkey's closest friends, "he felt that it had to be done. But he also felt he was one of the best skiers in the world, so if anyone was going to do it, he should be the one. That was the way his mind worked. That was Shane being logical."

In 1998, Shane's logic led him to Sacrifice. He nailed the line perfectly. Scott Gaffney filmed it — viewable in *Something About McConkey* — and the hop-and-drop ski technique known as "billy goating" was born. As billy-goating required new skills, it led Shane farther down the flow path, which led to even more skills, which opened up new possibilities, which drove him forward still. "During his big-mountain competition days," wrote Micah Abrams in one of that era's preeminent ski magazines, *Freeze*, "McConkey would routinely point out lines that snaked through rock faces and across gut-churning cliffs to his fellow competitors. More often than not, he was met with blank stares or rolled eyes, to which he would respond empathically: 'Dude, it's totally doable!' Then he would go do it, and then he would win."

Along these lines, Olympic gold medalist skier Jonny Mosley tells a story about the first time he went to British Columbia to film a ski movie with McConkey: "In one particular scene Shane skied a thirteen-stager where he lost his ski on one of the twenty-foot cliffs in the middle of this exposed line. He snapped it back on and shredded the rest. It was at this point that I reconsidered my thoughts of getting into the business where Shane had made his name."

And this is sort of where skydiving comes in.

McConkey began tossing himself out of airplanes in 1995. By 1999 he'd become a proficient-enough BASE jumper to begin considering his childhood dream — reenacting the ski-off-a-cliff-and-deploy-a-parachute-to-evade-the-bad-guys scene from *The Spy Who Loved Me*. It took a few years to work out the technical details, but in 2003 he went Bond off a 400-footer in Lover's Leap, California. Most people thought it was a stunt. McConkey claimed it was the way forward: evolution, progression, what was next. No one believed him. In 2004 he ski-BASE'd off the 13,025-foot Eiger in Switzerland.

Then they started to believe him.

For McConkey, ski-BASE gave him a way to start seeing really different lines. He has a phrase for aesthetically enticing terrain that had forever been off-limits because of gargantuan cliffs at the run's end: "closeout lines." With ski-BASE, these closeout lines were finally open for business. "My whole vision," he says, "is that there are these impossible lines that no one would ever ski because they end in death cliffs. With parachutes, you can ski them. Those lines are totally doable now."

Ski-BASE is definitely not the kind of result that shows up on the compliance-based path to mastery. McConkey did not spend his adult life trying to shave four seconds off his time in the giant slalom. Instead, he saw lines and pursued flow and, as legendary skater Tony Hawk once told reporters, changed the world: "Shane brought everyone hope. It was like a new day and what can we do with it? What are we going to explore? How far can we take this?"

So how far can *we* take this? It's a good question, with the "we" being the most important part. Flow, as Csikszentmihalyi discovered, is ubiquitous. This means that all the superpowers detailed in this first section of the book—the fluid brain-wave control exhibited by Laird Hamilton, the deep relationship to the Voice enjoyed by Dean Potter, the near-telepathic prowess of the Red Bull Air Force, and the accelerated path to mastery trod by Shane McConkey—are available to any and all. This is who we are and how we're wired. Flow is our birthright. But what do we do with that knowledge? As always, that part is up to us.

PART TWO

FLOW HACKER NATION

listen: there's a hell of a good universe next door; let's go.

— E. E. CUMMINGS

6

Outer Flow

DOUG AMMONS AND THE STIKINE

It was one of the most dangerous experiments ever run, and it was run in silence. Doug Ammons told no one ahead of time. The editor of several different science journals, Ammons did not tell his colleagues. He did not tell his wife, or his children, or his friends. Definitely not his friends. "They would have told me I was committing suicide," recounts Ammons, "that I was on a death trip. They wouldn't have understood."

How could they understand? This wasn't about dissecting frogs or sequencing DNA or even splitting the atom. This was about actual transformation. Ammons wanted to transform himself into a drop of water. He was betting his life on the possibility.

Ammons is a true polymath. He holds degrees in math, physics, and psychology, is a classical guitarist, black belt in karate, successful businessman, acclaimed author, respected philosopher, and, without question, one of the most revered kayakers in history. In 2000, *Outside* made a list of the ten greatest adventurers since 1900, with their major criterion being "their achievements permanently altered the landscape of adventure." Ammons is number seven.

Whitewater-wise, his achievements include over fifty first descents, a sizable number of solo expeditions, and a few, um, more peculiar trips. On a number of occasions, Ammons has paddled Class V (expert only) rivers without a paddle, or hand-paddling as they call it. Many people think of hand-paddling as a stunt, and solo-paddling — especially on a big river — as suicide. To Ammons, as he explains in his book *Whitewater Philosophy,* both are a form of research: "Perhaps the most beautiful experience in kayaking is flow. There isn't any other sport that demands such intimacy with nature, moving in harmony with the power and intricacy of the river, and whitewater kayaking is the preeminent flow sport. When you paddle, well, there is the feeling that you are pouring yourself right into and through the river, with no distractions at all, you can weave yourself right into the current. Soloing is the open door for understanding how close to the river you can be."

Ammons's desire for river intimacy is rooted in an even bigger desire: the deep ache to participate in the fundamental components of creation: elemental powers, eons of time. "Adventure sports form a modern Tao," he once told reporters, "allowing us to take part in the very forces that sculpted and shaped the world around us." And it was this desire for primal participation that first drew Ammons to the wilds of upper British Columbia, to one of the last great secrets, to the Grand Canyon of the Stikine.

The Stikine has been described as one of the world's forgotten wonders, but it's unlikely to become a tourist attraction anytime soon. The weather is cold and gray on a good day, downright mean on a bad. The surrounding wilderness covers an area twice the size of France, with a human population numbering in the low thousands. Grizzly bears, meanwhile, are everywhere.

Yet the wildlife and wildlands are just sideshow attractions. The canyon is the real show: a vast gorge carved by a ferocious torrent, some sixty miles of colossal Class V+ whitewater: twenty-five "Holy Mother of God" rapids, hundreds of smaller tortures, and a reputation as the Mount Everest of expedition kayaking.

In his essay "A Brief History of the Stikine," Ammons agrees:

> This is not a normal river run, not even by the standards of highly experienced class V kayakers. The rapids are dominated by compressional turbulence, incredibly large holes, closed out features,

and monstrous slabs of water that you stick to like fly paper as you try to make your moves. It's an ominous and spectacular canyon, over 1,000 feet deep and in some places so narrow that a helicopter can barely slip through. You are exposed to rockfall while scouting and even in your boat. It isn't the Zambezi, there is no warmth in the glacial water or the typically blustery fall weather. The flow is between 8,000 and 20,000 cfs at low water and levels can change as much as ten feet in a day. Many sections are from 60 to over 120 feet per mile, and as any big water paddler knows, when you combine steep and narrow with lots of water, you're talking the real shit. Attempts are made at low water in the early fall, and there's the very real possibility of a freeze or snow, which has happened to two different teams. For 70 percent of the canyon, it is very difficult or utterly impossible to climb out, with vertical walls on both sides rising straight out of the river. If you do have to bail and climb out, as has happened to eight teams, it is easy to get lost up on the plateau and entirely possible to get killed by the wildlife. . . . This isn't California. It's the goddamned Canadian wilderness.

It was paddler Rob Lesser who first spotted the Stikine on a trip up to Alaska. This was 1977. He charted a plane for an overflight. The walls were so steep, the canyon so deep, there wasn't much to see. What he saw looked foreboding. Lesser labeled rapids "Killer Falls I" and "Killer II" and the like. And he liked. Four years later, Lesser returned with a team of exceptionally skilled kayakers and a helicopter for support. They managed about 60 percent of the canyon. One member of their team, John Wasson, nearly drowned along the way. They named the rapid after him (Wasson's Hole); they named another the Hole That Ate Chicago. It was just that kind of river.

Lesser came back in 1985, this time with legendary boaters Bob McDougall and Lars Holbeck, and another helicopter. The chopper ferried supplies, abetted portages, and served as a security blanket should things go sideways. But there was no sideways. The trio pulled it off, completing a milestone first descent down the whole of the Stikine.

In 1989, Lesser and McDougall returned, with Doug Ammons as their third. This time no helicopter. The team was attempting the first self-supported expedition through the canyon. It was a big bet. Without a chopper in tow, if they got into trouble, the closest help was easily a mountain range away.

This being the Stikine, they quickly got into trouble.

Seven miles into the trip was Entry Falls, the first of the river's major rapids. Doug McDougall went first, trying a conservative sneaker route around the boil. So much for conservative. He got swallowed, smashed, slammed, cartwheeled, washing-machined, window-shaded, and then — arguably the worst deathtrap a kayaker can encounter — pinned beneath an undercut rock. About to black out, McDougall saw a glimmer of light, clawed upward, got swept sideways, slapped a handhold, and, somehow, managed to propel himself into an eddy. His kayak was long gone.

"When he was done puking water," recounts Ammons, "he had a simple choice. He could swim the horrifying rapids below — which would probably kill him — or scale the sheer canyon wall. He was barefoot. The wall was nearly 500 feet tall and completely rotten. It didn't matter. He climbed."

The climb took hours — the very worst Ammons can remember. It's been twenty-five years, and he still has nightmares. McDougall was his best friend and sure to die. It was a gruesome ordeal, but somehow he didn't die. Still, that was it for McDougall; he never paddled big water again.

The same cannot be said for Ammons. The following year, he came back to the Stikine with a different crew. Again, passage was not easy. Rocks the size of basketballs were pulling free from the walls and raining down on their boats. Scouting lines required serious climbing skills and considerable imagination. "A lot of the time the closest you can get to a rapid is 300 feet above it," says Ammons. "From that height, fifteen-foot waves look tiny. The only way to solve the puzzle is to astral project yourself down onto the river, lock that image into your mind, and hope you can remember all the different pieces when it counts."

Despite the difficulties, the second time turned out to be the charm. Top to bottom in three days. The first self-supported trip down the Stikine. In paddling lore, the trip was the rough equivalent of Reinhold Messner summiting Everest without supplemental oxygen.

For Ammons, though, it wasn't enough. The rawness of the canyon, the power of the river, the primal forces on such broad display. "It spoke to me, the place, the river, it was like a mirror trying to show me something fundamental about myself, something I desperately needed to know."

Which was about the time Doug Ammons started considering a solo expedition down the Stikine.

"Soloing requires huge commitment. You can't rely on your partners or ask their opinion, or even take solace from their presence. There's no support. You can only reach inside yourself for answers. There's a purity there, a stripped-down clarity that demands only one thing — belonging. To me, that's the essence of good paddling: belonging to the place. Being a part of it, merging into it. To be a drop of water on the Stikine — that's what I wanted. That's when the truth would come out."

THE FLOW LANDSCAPE

We'll return to the truth a little later; first, a deeper look at the broader view. Up to now, this book has focused on extreme athletes doing extreme acts and perhaps it's all a little too extreme. But remember the reason: action and adventure sport athletes have used flow to accelerate performance faster and farther than almost any other group of people in history. Taking a look at how far they've come gives us a sense of the possible. It provides a benchmark. Yet this doesn't mean these athletes have cornered the market on flow.

Far from it.

There are a great number of on-ramps into flow, with action and adventure sports being only one of them. For writers, poets, painters, sculptors, dancers, musicians, composers, etc., creativity is their frequent gateway. Scientists and engineers often feel the same. Endurance athletes, meanwhile, can ride pain and exhaustion into the zone. Runner's high is the fabled name for this experience, but it also shows up in swimming, cycling, rowing, hiking, cross-country skiing, and almost any other activity where suffering long distances is a factor.

In the world of philanthropy, *helper's high* is the term for an altruism-triggered flow state, literally brought on by the act of helping another. Originally discovered in the 1990s by Big Brother/Big Sister founder Allan Luks in those involved in front-line, hands-on altruism (like volunteering in a soup kitchen), helper's high has since turned up in a far wider range of do-gooder activities (like bidding at a charity auction). There's even a milder flashback version — when people recall their good deeds, a helper's high afterglow can arise.

Technology offers even more examples. Video-game players get into flow so frequently that Csikszentmihalyi's ideas have become the most widely accepted theoretical framework for explaining the lure of the joystick. Studies have shown that the amount of flow generated by a video game directly correlates to everything from player engagement to overall product success. In fact, as Dr. Erik Gregory, the executive director of the Media Psychology Research Center, wrote in 2007: "Placing players in flow is the key to video gaming's universal appeal."

Meanwhile, for Internet surfers, researchers have found flow the secret ingredient to almost every aspect of online experience. Both website slipperiness (the ease with which we enter and exit an online experience) and website stickiness (how certain sites hold our attention) are influenced by the state. Researchers at Vanderbilt University have found that from the marketing side of this coin, online flow experiences attract customers, mitigate price sensitivity, and positively influence subsequent buying behaviors.

And technology users are only half of this picture, as technology creators have also harnessed this power. "At its best, writing code happens in a state of 'flow'" reads a line in Oracle's *Developer Insight Series*. And it's not just Oracle employees who feel this way. So important has flow become to software development that industry analysts and authors Tom DeMarco and Timothy Lister argue that time-based accounting (paying people for hours worked) needs to be replaced by flow-based accounting (paying people for the amount of time they spend in flow at work), writing: "The phenomena of flow and immersion give us a more realistic way to model how time is applied to a development task. What matters is not the amount of time you're *present*, but the amount of time that you're *working at your full potential*. An hour in flow really accomplishes something, but ten six-minute work periods sandwiched between eleven interruptions won't accomplish anything."

Nor is it just coders. As University of California, Berkeley, biophysicist and one of the Internet's original architects, Reese Jones, points out: "All of the basic activities that led to today's high-tech revolution — circuit design, software design, network design — require laser-focused attention and produce flow, and doing any of these tasks well is just not possible without the state." So if you're looking for a non-athletic example of the kind of revolution that occurs when a group of people begin harnessing flow on a regular basis, Silicon Valley is not a bad place to start.

But to return to where we started: with flow accessible and important in so many different domains, why does this book focuses primarily on action and adventure athletes? Simple: in all these other domains flow is a luxury; in extreme sports, it is a core requirement. In fact, even though flow is consistently associated with all elite-level athletic success, it's actually rather elusive in traditional sports. Ken Ravizza, a psychologist at California State University at Fullerton, who examined instances of flow in bat-and-ball and track-and-field sports (and who calls flow by Maslow's name, "peak experiences"), explains: "The peak experience in sport is a rare personal moment that remains etched in the athlete's consciousness. It serves as reminder of the great intrinsic satisfaction that sport participation can provide. Peak experiences during an athlete's career are relatively rare but their intensity acts as a standard, or qualitative reference point, for subjectively evaluating future performance."

Again, this is not the case with action and adventure sports. Take a 2000 study run on kayakers on the Class V Cheat Canyon in West Virginia. While the subjects included everyone from novice to professional paddlers — meaning it wasn't just extreme athletes involved — researchers found "every individual is likely to experience flow at least once while paddling the Cheat Canyon or, in the case of daily studies, at least once a day." The point is this: if we want *more* flow in our lives, the best place to start that investigation is with the people with the *most* flow in their lives.

And that is exactly where we're going next. Part One of this book concerned itself with the so-called "characteristics of flow," what an individual experiences in the zone. With this stage set, we can now turn our attention to the "conditions for flow" — the circumstances that speed entrance into the state. *Flow triggers* is the term we'll be using to describe these circumstances and, over the next four chapters, we'll be examining four varieties: external triggers, internal triggers, social triggers, and creative triggers. But at the heart of all are three critical questions: How have these athletes managed to produce flow so consistently? What are the conditions that led to their success? And how can we bridge the gap between the extreme and the mainstream, importing these conditions into our daily lives?

HACKING FLOW

It wasn't intentional, that's the first thing to know. Certainly, action and adventure athletes have found flow more frequently than most, but much of their success has been accidental.

Take *external triggers,* our starting point. These are qualities in the environment that drive people deeper into the zone. One tamer example comes from office design. In recent years, as the production of flow has been deemed critical to the success of organizations, organizations have reacted by trying to design environments that produce more flow. As flow requires focus, one of the first changes suggested by experts was the removal of cubicle farms, those open office plans that permit constant interruption. "These interruptions ... move us out of 'flow' and increase research-and-design cycle times and costs dramatically," writes Greylock Partners venture capitalist James Slavet on Forbes.com. "Studies have shown that each time a flow state is disrupted it takes fifteen minutes to get back into flow, if you can get back at all."

Yet if focus is the goal, then rearranging office furniture is the long way around. Action and adventure athletes cheat this process with fundamental biology. Evolution hardwired humans to pay attention to certain stimuli more than others and, as these athletes have discovered, nothing catches our attention quite like danger.

Humans evolved in an era of immediacy, where threats were always of the tiger-in-the-bush variety. Immediate threats require immediate responses, and this fact has shaped our brain more than any other. Consider information processing. Every second, our senses gather way more data than we can actually handle. As a result, much of what the brain does is tease apart the critical from the casual. Since nothing is more critical than survival, the first stop most of this incoming information makes is our danger detector: the amygdala.

An almond-shaped sliver of the temporal lobe, the amygdala is responsible for primal emotions like hate, anger, and fear. It's our early warning system, an organ always on high alert. With most incoming sensory information heading there, when there's danger lurking in the environment, we don't have to rely on artificial forces like office design to drive attention. Merely by plying their trade in a "high consequence" environment — with high consequence being the first of the external triggers we'll be examining — extreme athletes rely on risk to drive focus, the requisite first step toward producing flow.

Another way to think about this is "hacking." The term comes from electronics, wherein hackers were originally found (the word has since taken on darker connotations), those interested in tinkering with technology in an attempt to improve performance. In this case, instead of hacking "external" technologies like computers and telephones, our focus is on hacking "internal" technologies — our own psychology and neurology. As such, we'll be using *flow hack* and *flow hacker* to refer to any action that helps propel people into flow, and anyone performing such an action, respectively. In these terms, extreme athletes use risk as a "flow hack" because flow follows focus and consequences catch our attention.

But consequences do more than catch our attention: they also drive neurochemistry. As risk increases, so do norepinephrine and dopamine, the feel-good chemicals the brain uses to amplify focus and enhance performance. Because norepinephrine and dopamine feel *really* good, playing with this trigger often produces long-lasting effects: risk takers are transformed into risk seekers. "There was a rush," Doug Ammons once wrote, "and for that moment we couldn't tell the difference between joy and the grab in our throat, but we knew without saying that it was a new path. And from that point on nothing seemed the same."

Once danger becomes its own reward, risk moves from a threat to be avoided to a challenge to be risen toward. An entirely new relationship with fear begins to develop. When risk is a challenge, fear becomes a compass — literally pointing people in the direction they need to go next (i.e., the direction that produces more flow). "If you're interested in mastery," says University of Cambridge, England, neuropsychologist Barbara Sahakian, "you have to learn this lesson. To really achieve anything, you have to be able to tolerate and enjoy risk. It has to become a challenge to look forward to. In all fields, to make exceptional discoveries you need risk — you're just never going to have a breakthrough without it."

When these athletes actually take a risk (putting themselves in a high-consequence situation rather than a high-risk environment), an even bigger neurochemical response is facilitated. Risk taking itself releases another big squirt of dopamine, further enhancing performance and increasing pattern recognition. Once the pattern-recognition system lights onto the proper response (i.e., identifies the chunk that will save the athlete's hide in this particular situation), even more dopamine is released and the cascade continues.

As we know these facts, we also know a bit about hacking the "high consequence" flow trigger. For starters, risk is always relative. While some danger must be courted for flow, confrontations with mortality are not required. In fact, even physical risk itself is optional. A shy man need only cross the room to say hello to an attractive woman to trigger this rush. In casual conversation, merely telling someone the truth can serve the same purpose. "To reach flow," explains Harvard psychiatrist Ned Hallowell, "one must be willing to take risks. The lover must lay bare his soul and risk rejection and humiliation to enter this state. The athlete must be willing to risk physical harm, even loss of life, to enter this state. The artist must be willing to be scorned and despised by critics and the public and still push on. And the average person — you and me — must be willing to fail, look foolish, and fall flat on our faces should we wish to enter this state."

What all of this adds up to is options. Certainly, risk is needed for flow, but if you don't want to take physical risks, take mental risks. Take social risks. Emotional risks. Creative risks. Especially creative risks. The application of imagination — one *very* shorthand definition of creativity — is all about mental chance taking. And the risk is real. Loss of respect, loss of resources, loss of time — the consequences of betting on a bad idea can certainly threaten survival.

Yet, if we're going to hack flow by trading mental risks for physical risks — and especially if we want the same kind of accelerated performance seen today in extreme athletes — then our commitment to the process better be ferocious. Why? Because today's action and adventure athletes aren't just occasionally pulling the high-consequence flow trigger; they're squeezing hard and all the time.

Action and adventure sports are packed with do-or-die moments. Traditional athletics, in contrast, are cushioned by the artifice of the game. In basketball, the only time one can launch a game-winning buzzer beater — the riskiest shot — is in the last seconds of play. And the worst thing that can happen if that shot goes wide? Being benched for the next game. But action and adventure sports have an unflinching referee: the laws of physics. A surfer who doesn't commit completely to every inch of a big wave ends up begging for mercy at the bottom of the impact zone.

Thus, if we want the accelerated performance of these athletes, we need their ferocious commitment as well. More than that, we need to understand that risk is only the first of our external triggers, and flow hackers have plenty more choices available. In fact, it was these additional choices that Ammons was counting on to help him survive the Stikine.

RICH ENVIRONMENT, DEEP EMBODIMENT

It's not easy to get to the Stikine. Start in Washington, and head north. Drive 600 miles of empty gravel road, not a soul in sight. Plenty of time to think. In the fall of 1992, Doug Ammons drove those miles alone — so what was he thinking? "No one knew where I was or what I was doing," he says. "I was thinking, if this went wrong, they would never find my body."

Ammons didn't care. He'd come for the consequences. He knew how to leverage risk to access flow and — critical for this mission — believed he could remain in the state for a very long time. "I had no choice," he says. "The Stikine is three days' worth of relentless. It runs Class V between rapids. Portaging requires big wall climbing and rappelling. Scouting requires heightened awareness and really good problem-solving skills. None of this is possible without flow. You can't control this river, you can't muscle through it, you have to become part of it, you have to flow with it."

Ammons was betting his life on the ability to summon and maintain one of the most elusive states on earth, a hefty wager to say the least. Yet he could place this bet with confidence because he wasn't only relying on risk to trigger flow. He was also depending on two other external triggers — "rich environment" and "deep embodiment" — to keep him in the state.

A "rich environment" is a combination platter of novelty, unpredictability, and complexity — three elements that catch and hold our attention much like risk. Novelty means both danger and opportunity. To our forbearers, a strange scent in the wind could be prey or predator, but either way it paid to pay attention. Unpredictability means we don't know what happens next, thus we pay extra attention to what happens next. Complexity, when there's lots of salient information coming at us at once, does more of the same.

In fact, most of us have some familiarity with complexity triggering flow. If you've ever stood before a vast canyon and felt awe — well, awe is a state of total absorption and the front end of flow. When sucked in by the incomprehensible complexity of geologic timescales and epic beauty, reality pauses, if only for a moment. And in this moment, we taste the pinpoint focus, loss of self-consciousness, and time dilation that are deep zone companions.

Action and adventure athletes taste these experiences so often because nature is jam-packed with novelty, unpredictability, and complexity. Rivers are living entities. Same with the mountains and the waves. The Alaskan snowpack morphs on a moment-to-moment basis; the swells of Teahupoo lurch to their own rhythms. In places where anything can happen, a wandering mind is a dangerous mind; thus rich environments automatically tighten focus and drive flow.

And for those of us who want to take advantage of this fact, yet have no interest in action and adventure sports? Simple: Seek out complexity, especially in nature. Go stare at the night sky. Walk in the woods. If you can't find big nature, contemplate the small. The reasons there are so many clichés about universes inside of dewdrops is because there are universes inside of dewdrops. No dew to contemplate? Use technology to induce awe: surf your city with Google Earth or go see an IMAX movie.

Next, up novelty and unpredictability. Normally, we go out of our way to avoid both. We rely on old habits, we cherish our routines. And why not? Automatic pilot is efficient. Routines save the brain energy and who hasn't driven to work without remembering the trip? Yet vary the route next time. Brush your teeth with the wrong hand. These against-the-grain tricks increase novelty and unpredictability, demanding focus and pattern recognition, and both are the real goal.

"You don't need a giant wave or a big-mountain to trigger these responses," says neuroscientist and director of the Krasnow Institute for Advanced Study at George Mason University, James Olds. "The brain's reaction isn't dependent on real, external information. It's reacting to a constellation of inputs from the sensory system. If you can light up that same constellation—say replace the novelty found in a natural environment with new routines in your daily life—you'll get the dopamine and norepinephrine. This is why the flow hack of the twenty-second century is going to be a button on your augmented cognition device that lights up this same constellation." Olds, by the way, practices what he preaches, driving a different route home from work every day.

The last external flow trigger, "deep embodiment," is a kind of full-body awareness. Humans have sensory inputs all over the place; 50 percent of our nerve endings are in our hands, feet, and face. We have as many neurons in the gut and heart as in the brain. We also have proprioception to detect position in space, and vestibular awareness for balance. Deep embodiment means paying attention to all of these sensory inputs at once.

More inputs means more information. Way more information. The brain can't process this deluge consciously. Too slow. Too inefficient. In many situations, too dangerous. When critical data arrives via fire hose, there's no time for neurotic debate. "[T]asks that require real-time sensorimotor integration are best handled by the implicit system," explained Arne Dietrich in a 2011 paper for *Neuroscience and Biobehavioral Reviews*. "Explicit interference into the execution of these kinds of tasks tends to decrease their effectiveness." Deep embodiment, then, is the transient hypofrontality fast track and thus another reason action and adventure athletes have found flow so frequently.

"Action and adventure sports demand deep embodiment," says Ammons. "Especially kayaking. Big rivers accelerate you in every direction at once. This puts the vestibular system into overdrive. This isn't just your mind paying more attention — suddenly your entire body is paying attention. When this happens, it's outside our conscious capabilities. There are no words. Our language becomes that of the river. All the features of the river speak to you and you to them through motion. There is tension, threat, there is joy and release, and overall, a deep, deep sense of flow. You are literally part of the flow of the world."

If we want to pull the deep embodiment trigger in less extreme environments, then we simply have to learn to pay attention to all these input streams. This isn't hard. Zen walking meditation teaches an open-senses/all-senses awareness. Balance and agility training (like playing hopscotch or running ladder drills) enhance proprioception and vestibular awareness. Yoga, tai chi, and just about every martial art blend both together. And if technology is more your speed, there are video games for both Xbox's Kinect and Nintendo's Wii that do the same.

Ammons, meanwhile, was counting on all of these external triggers to survive the Stikine. He knew all three would be present the moment his boat hit the water. No longer on land (deep embodiment), alone in one of the largest and most isolated wildernesses on the planet (rich environment), and closing in on Entry Falls, the first major rapid and the place Bob McDougall almost died (high consequence). Without question, he was primed for flow.

THE PARADOX OF CONTROL

Yet it wasn't until "Wicked Wanda," the Stikine's third major rapid, that Ammons felt the state's full embrace. A steep ramp, an evil hole, a pummeling wave-train run-out — Wanda's is wicked all right. Ammons got spun upside down somewhere between the ramp and the hole. It could have been a disaster; it was a blessing in disguise. When he rolled to right himself, he rolled right into flow. "Up to that point," he says, "it was taking everything to hold it together. I was so far out there. Totally alone. The intimidation factor was keeping me out of flow. But rolling required deep embodiment and that did the trick. Halfway through the roll, I just snapped into the state."

Just in time. Located a few rapids downstream was Wasson's — what legendary kayaker Gerry Moffat calls a "million-dollar hole." "Meaning," he says, "most people wouldn't paddle it for a million dollars." But there's no retreat. Wasson's is surrounded by vertical cliffs, so portaging, hiking upstream, or climbing out are impossible. It's do or die.

For Ammons, it was almost die.

"Wasson's has two big disaster features that have to be avoided," he says. "But there was no line. The right side and the center were North Shore impact zones — just incredibly violent. Everything was punching left, pushing into the main hole. No matter what I did, I was 99 percent sure I would be annihilated."

Ammons was out of options; he let himself get swallowed. "It was the most unbelievable sensation, this thing I knew was impossible, that just couldn't work, I got to watch myself piece it together. I could feel all of the river's reactions and could feel myself melding with them. My goal was to do this inconceivable thing, to be a drop of water. Surviving Wasson's was proof I had done it. From that point on, I knew the impossible was possible."

The sensation Ammons is describing is the "paradox of control," another of flow's defining characteristics. The paradox is real power in places we should have none. It's that sense of controlling the uncontrollable familiar to day traders and emergency-room surgeons, only here taken to its farthest extreme.

What creates this feeling is a two-part contradiction. Part one: Flow is exceptionally pleasurable, but mostly in retrospect. "It is this absence of ... emotion, of almost any kind of conscious awareness of one's state, that is at the heart of flow," writes University of Pennsylvania psychologist Martin Seligman. "Consciousness and emotion are there to correct your trajectory; when what you are doing is seamlessly perfect, you don't need them." Part two: You may be unemotional, but you're not asleep. In the throes of the paradox, you're fully aware of the ass you're kicking — just not entirely certain you deserve all the credit.

Ammons agrees: "There aren't any words to describe this feeling.

Too frequently, athletes fall back on clichés and machismo. They paddle something hard and when someone puts a microphone in their face, all they can come up with is 'I tamed that bitch.' But when you're actually in those moments, if you're going to survive, nobody is arrogant. You have to be humble and open to access this control. Of course, since most people's knowledge of action and adventure sports comes from energy drink ads and 'blending with the environment' doesn't really move product, we're sold this 'extreme dude' lie instead."

But the extreme dude lie is hiding a potent flow hack: humility. "When you're arrogant and egotistical," says Dr. Olds, "you're shutting out complexity, novelty, and unpredictability to preserve a distorted self-image. Any incoming information that could lead to self-doubt is stamped out. It's a massive data reduction. Humility moves in the other direction, it opens us up and increases incoming information. As a result, there is more opportunity for pattern recognition, more dopamine, and less need for judgmental metacognition."

Ammons stayed humble and stayed in the zone. He survived Wasson's and went on to survive the Stikine. For those keeping score, he made only two portages along the way: one around V-Drive, a death-trap rapid that would remain unrunnable until 2001 (when the river shifted a boulder) and the upper half of Site Zed, which — with help from near-perfect conditions and a sizable support team — was finally run in 2012.

Yet, despite the magnitude of his accomplishment, it would be a very long time before anyone heard the tale. Besides his wife and two close friends, Ammons told no one for eighteen years. Since then, other than a short essay and a few incidental mentions, this is the first time many details have seen print. He's also refused to profit from the experience, turning down a long list of film deals and sponsorship opportunities. In fact, in the history of action and adventure sports, the Stikine solo may be the greatest story never told and one of the few times someone has pulled off the impossible and flat out refused to use it for personal gain. Humility matters.

On a final note, it's been over two decades — but no one has yet to repeat Ammon's solo.

7

Inner Flow

MANDY-RAE CRUICKSHANK AND THE NOW

Mandy-Rae Cruickshank never intended to become a superhero. She grew up shy in the suburbs of Alberta, Canada. She was *exceptionally* shy. Way too timid to give book reports in school, she failed projects rather than face fears. During lunch or recess, even when all her friends were together, she was too bashful to go over and say hello. The only place Mandy-Rae ever felt comfortable was the water. While her aquatic passion blossomed into competitive synchronized swimming in high school, her coach made a point of telling her parents that she had no future in the sport, lacking, apparently, the requisite drive to take things to the Olympic level. "By the time I got out of high school," says Cruikshank, "it was pretty clear to me and to most who knew me that I was never going to do anything groundbreaking."

On her way to never, and capitalizing on her passion for water, Cruikshank opened a scuba shop in Vancouver. She soon became friendly with another dive-operation owner, Kirk Krack, and he introduced her to the ancient sport of free diving. Arguably the simplest athletic pursuit in the world, free diving — or diving without a breathing apparatus (i.e., scuba tanks) — requires only a body and a breath. Divers suck in nearly as much air as possible, then descend into the depths of the ocean. Sometimes they use fins; sometimes they go barefoot. Occasionally, weights are involved. And every now and again, the big blue is traded for the shallow end of the pool and divers compete in "static apnea"—essentially hanging limp in the water to see who can hold their breath the longest.

There are dangers, of course. When outside pressure crushes inside airspaces, the results can be exceptionally painful. Eardrums rupture with regularity. The biggest threat is blacking out, which can happen because of low oxygen, high carbon dioxide, loss of blood pressure, or several other factors. It's for all of these reasons that, as Alec Wilkinson explained in the pages of *The New Yorker,* "[Free diving] is frequently described as the world's second most dangerous sport, after jumping off skyscrapers with parachutes."

Krack, himself, discovered free diving accidentally. His early expertise was in mixed-gas deep scuba, but in the late 1980s, while running a dive shop in the Caymans, he had taken to "skin diving" (as the term *free diving* didn't yet exist) on his days off. With a little practice, he found himself capable of holding his breath long enough to play around at depths of sixty to 100 feet. The real change occurred in 1997, when Pipin Ferreras, then one of the few professional free divers in the world, decided to set a new world record in the Caymans and asked Krack—whose dive shop owned all the necessary equipment—to help him out.

"I had zero free diving technique at the time," recounts Krack, "but I watched Pipin prepare for his dive and he started by doing pull downs—descending about thirty feet, hanging out for a while, then popping back up. He did this a few times. Back then, all I did was dive as deep as possible right away. Using my technique, after a few hours, I found that the length of time I could hold my breath increased considerably. When I tried doing Pipin's pull downs, I got the kinds of breath-holds that used to take hours to achieve, in minutes."

Krack had uncovered a technique for triggering the mammalian diving reflex, a reflex that optimizes respiration and, like dolphins, whales, and some birds, allows us to operate underwater for extended periods of time. Here's how it works: When the nerves of the human face come in contact with water, our heartbeat begins to slow (10 to 30 percent in amateurs; up to 50 percent in professionals). A slower heart rate requires less oxygen, leaving more left over for other organs. Next, as pressure from depth increases, blood leaves our extremities—first fingers and toes, next hands and feet, finally arms and legs — and surrounds the heart and brain. Lastly, during deeper dives, organs and circulatory walls allow blood plasma and water to pass through them, preventing the chest cavity from collapsing inward with the massive pressure increase.

While the mammalian diving reflex was first discovered by navy scientists back in the 1960s, so small were free diving circles, it remained a well-kept secret until here in the twenty-first century. But Krack got obsessed. He learned everything he could about the reflex, built training programs around the ideas, then opened Performance Freediving International. He taught folks about peak inhalations (filling all pulmonary airspaces) and packing (taking in tiny sips of air after the lungs have been filled, which, if done wrong, can lead to broken ribs, punctured tracheas, and quick blackouts) and breath-ups (a way to lower heart rate, increase blood oxygen, and dispel carbon dioxide). He got very good at this teaching. By the time he was getting to know Cruikshank, Krack had already coached both Brett Leemaster and Tanya Streeter to world records.

Krack and Cruikshank soon found themselves romantically intertwined (they're now married with children) and this proved a boon for Mandy-Rae's training. The mammalian diving reflex is inhibited by stress, so being comfortable in the water is a considerable advantage when trying to learn the technique. Cruikshank was a natural. Even more important was her ability to equalize at depth. "I had never been below thirty-six meters before," she recounts, "but in early 2000 I got a chance to go deep on a tandem 'no-limits' dive (no limits means she was towed downward by a weighted sled and relied on an air bag to return her to the surface). That's how I found out I had no trouble equalizing at 100 meters. When Kirk realized this, he decided we were going for a world record."

Thus, in the Caymans and roughly eighteen months after first taking up free diving, Mandy-Rae took a very short boat ride out to the competition area — really nothing more than a square of ocean marked off by buoys — grabbed hold of that weighted sled once again, and let herself be dragged to depth. If only it were that easy. Sure, in no limits, the sled and the air bag do all the work, but that turns the trip into a purely mental game. "Physically," says Cruickshank, "all that's required is you hang on and go for a ride. Mentally, it's like playing chess against yourself. Its will and technique versus panic and pressure. It's about forcing the mind to stop thinking. It's about flow. If you can't get into flow, if you can't melt into the water, become part of the water, then you can't freedive — there's just no other way to go deep."

This mental game is especially hard for Cruickshank, a self-described "head case." "From the moment I get out of bed to the moment I go to sleep," says Cruickshank, "my brain never turns off. So, when I dive, it's really important that I don't let myself get consumed. But Kirk showed me I could do the impossible. That changed something inside of me. I became compelled. I had a reason to win the fight against my brain. I had to find out what else was possible. I had to find out if I was capable of doing something no one else in the world could do, something nobody had ever done before."

Turns out, she could.

On September 23, 2001, Cruikshank set her first world record, a 136-meter "no limits" descent. The following year, she set a second world record for a 6:16 static apnea breath-hold. A year after that it was no-fins "constant ballast" — divers descend and ascend with weights and under their own power — world record of forty-one meters. And she was just getting warmed up.

In total, Cruickshank set seven world records in seven years, including her March 24, 2004, constant ballast (this time with fins) breakthrough of seventy-eight meters. "That was the one people will always remember," says Krack. "She beat the previous record by ten meters. It was a huge jump. One of the largest single jumps in the history of the sport." Cruickshank explains it differently: "I'm just an ordinary woman who learned she was capable of extraordinary things."

INTERNAL FLOW TRIGGERS

The question raised by Mandy-Rae Cruickshank is fairly straightforward: How did she learn she was capable of extraordinary? Turns out, she didn't learn *how* to do anything. Mandy-Rae learned *when* — when she was capable of extraordinary. This made all the difference.

Mandy-Rae took up an activity that demanded she live in the now. Not metaphorically. Not in some groovy hippie way. Quite simply: 300 feet underwater, there's *no way* to be elsewhere. When she says, "It's really important to not let myself get consumed," she means, when diving, not thinking about the future (where she could run out of air) or the past (where a poor decision made her use up too much air) is survival. Instead, Cruickshank has trained herself to keep attention right here, right now—which is the only time flow can show up and the only time *we're* capable of extraordinary.

Yet the here and now isn't seen much these days. In our always-on, hyperconnected world, there are endless reasons to be elsewhere. Every time we answer an e-mail or return a text or check our Facebook page, we are there and not here. And just as frequently, we are then and not now. With inboxes piling up, today's luncheon, tonight's parent-teacher conference, tomorrow's deadlines, the report due next week, the performance review right after that, well, no wonder we can't live in the moment.

Instead, as Douglas Rushkoff writes in *Present Shock*, "[W]e tend to exist in a distracted present, where forces on the periphery are magnified and those immediately before us are ignored. Our ability to plan—much less follow through on it—is undermined by our need to be able to improvise our way through any number of external impacts that stand to derail us at any moment. Instead of finding a stable foothold in the here and now, we end up reacting to an ever-present assault of simultaneous impulses and commands."

Not only is the *distracted present* a miserable place to be, it's also the worst kind of self-handicapping. Study after study shows that we're terrible multitaskers. By trying to improve performance by being everywhere and everywhen, we end up nowhere and never. The sad truth is that our lives are pulling us in every direction save the one where we're most effective.

Worse, as anyone who ever attempted meditation has quickly discovered, changing this tendency is not easy. Using the mind to silence the mind is a long-term endeavor. Tibetan Buddhist meditators—who have arguably self-selected for this ability—can spend over two decades learning to wield it reliably. Yet Mandy-Rae's ascension didn't take decades. It didn't even take years. She went absolute beginner to world record holder in eighteen months, and why? She took a shortcut into the now.

Just as flow states have external triggers, conditions in the *outer environment* that create more flow, they also have internal triggers, conditions in our *inner environment* that create more flow. Internal triggers are psychological strategies that drive attention into the now. Back in the 1970s, Csikszentmihalyi identified "clear goals," "immediate feedback," and "the challenge/skill ratio" as the three most critical. Let's take a closer look.

"Clear goals that define immediate success" is how this first trigger is typically described. Generally, the thinking's been that clear goals help identify our task (so we know what to do) and align that task with belief (so we know why we're doing it). But the most important piece, as University of Illinois cognitive scientist Daniel Simons discovered, is how clear goals impact attention.

In 2003, Simons showed a short film of basketball players passing a ball around a court to his students, and asked them to count the passes. When the film was over, he had one question: "How many people saw the gorilla?" As it happened, midway through the clip, a guy in a gorilla costume walked to the middle of the circle of basketball players, beat his chest a few times, then walked off. As it happened, most of the students didn't see the gorilla.

Simon's "invisible gorilla experiment" has since been repeated dozens of times — most recently with radiologists looking at radiological screens and a cartoon gorilla — and always with the same result. Not many people see the gorilla. In the radiologist's version (a 2012 study run at Brigham and Woman's Hospital in Boston), 83 percent of doctors tested failed to spot the animal. The point is this: when the brain is charged with a clear goal, focus narrows considerably, the unimportant is disregarded, and the now is all that's left.

Just as important, in the now, there's no past or future and a lot less room for self — which are the three intruders most likely to yank us to the then. This also tells us something about emphasis. Philip Zimbardo pointed out that Western society is dominated by Futures — i.e., those well-trained to strive for goals. Thus, when considering "clear goals," most have a tendency to skip over the adjective (clear) to get to the noun (goals). When told to set clear goals, we immediately visualize ourselves on the Olympic podium, the Academy Award stage, or the Fortune 500 list saying, "I've been picturing this moment since I was fifteen," and think that's the point.

It's not the point.

Those podium moments can pull us out of the present. Even if success is seconds away, it's still a future event subject to hopes, fears, and all sorts of now-crushing distraction. Think of the long list of infamous sporting chokes: the dropped pass in the final seconds of the Super Bowl; the missed putt at the end of the Augusta Masters. In those moments, the gravity of the goal pulled the participants out of the now; when, ironically, the now was all they needed to win.

If creating more flow is our aim, then the emphasis falls on "clear" and not "goals." Clarity gives us certainty. We know what to do and we know where to focus our attention while doing it. When goals are clear, metacognition is replaced by in-the-moment cognition, and the self stays out of the picture.

"When I dive constant ballast," says Mandy-Rae Cruickshank, "I don't think about breaking a record, I can't ever think about the whole dive. It's too overwhelming. I have to chunk it down, create tiny, clear goals. I go through kick cycles. The Voice (the voice of intuition) keeps count. I want to pay attention through one cycle, then the next, then the next. Keep the count, that's my only goal. If I keep the count, I can stay in flow the whole dive."

Applying this idea in our daily life means breaking tasks into bite-size chunks and setting goals accordingly. A writer, for example, is better off trying to pen three great paragraphs at a time — the equivalent of moving through Mandy-Rae's kick cycles — rather than attempting one great chapter. Think challenging, yet manageable — just enough stimulation to shortcut attention into the now, not enough stress to pull you back out again.

Immediate feedback, our next internal trigger, is another shortcut into the now. The term refers to a direct, in-the-moment coupling between cause and effect. The smaller the gap between input and output, the more we know how we're doing and how to do it better. If we can't course correct in real time, we start looking for clues to better performance — things we did in the past, things we've seen other people do, things that can pull us out of the moment. When feedback is immediate, the information we require is always close at hand. Attention doesn't have to wander; the conscious mind need not get involved.

Of course, for action and adventure athletes, getting the information they require is automatic. As National Outdoor Leadership School (NOLS) founder Paul Petzoldt once said: "In the mountains, feedback is instant." Same with the rivers, rocks, and oceans. In these environments, the laws of physics deliver instantaneous, unmediated feedback. No judges, no scorecards, no review in the *New York Times*. Just cause and effect. Either Mandy-Rae holds her breath at depth, or she blacks out trying.

This automatic feedback is another reason extreme athletes have found flow so frequently, but what if we're interested in pulling this trigger without help from the laws of physics? No mystery here. Tighten feedback loops. Put mechanisms in place so attention doesn't have to wander. Ask for more input. How much input? Well, forget quarterly reviews. Think daily reviews. Studies have found that in professions with less direct feedback loops— stock analysis, psychiatry, and medicine — even the best get worse over time. Surgeons, by contrast, are the only class of physician that improve the longer they're out of medical school. Why? Mess up on the table and someone dies. That's immediate feedback.

And that brings us to the "challenge/skill ratio," the last of our internal flow triggers, and arguably the most important. The idea behind this trigger is that attention is most engaged (i.e., in the now) when there's a very specific relationship between the difficulty of a task and our ability to perform that task. If the challenge is too great, fear swamps the system. If the challenge is too easy, we stop paying attention. Flow appears near the emotional midpoint between boredom and anxiety, in what scientists call the *flow channel* — the spot where the task is hard enough to make us stretch but not hard enough to make us snap.

How hard is that? Answers vary, but the general thinking is about 4 percent. That's it. That's the sweet spot. If you want to trigger flow, the challenge should be 4 percent greater than the skills. In technical terms, the sweet spot is the end result of what's known as the Yerkes-Dobson law— the fact that increased stress leads to increased performance up to a certain intensity, beyond which performance levels off or declines. In real-world terms, it's not much at all.

In most situations, we blow by 4 percent without even noticing. But this is not the case in extreme sports. In the big waves, big rivers, and big-mountains, a half degree of difficulty can mean the difference between home for dinner and never home again. Under these conditions, the desire for improvement keeps athletes from understepping, and the need for survival from overstepping.

This sweet spot keeps attention locked in the present. When the challenge is firmly within the boundaries of known skills — meaning I've done it before and am fairly certain I can do so again — the outcome is predetermined. We're interested, not riveted. But when we don't know what's going to happen next, we pay more attention to the next. Uncertainty is our rocket ride into the now.

It's also for this reason that uncertainty causes the brain to release dopamine. A lot of dopamine. When anything can happen, survival could be at stake. Dopamine heightens attention and pattern recognition — two things that are absolutely essential to dealing with the unknown. Of course, being dopamine, this is all exceptionally pleasurable. Or, as Stanford neurologist Robert Sapolsky likes to say: "*maybe* (meaning uncertainty) is addictive like nothing else out there."

And maybe is also the only road to impossible. This is why the challenge/skill ratio is so important. If we want to achieve the kinds of accelerated performance we're seeing in action and adventure sports, then it's 4 percent plus 4 percent plus 4 percent, day after day, week after week, months into years into careers. This is the road to real magic. Follow this path long enough, and not only does impossible becomes possible, it becomes what's next — like eating breakfast, like another a day at the office.

Miles Daisher, one of the best BASE jumpers in the world (who we'll get to know later), explains: "Ever since you were a little kid, you always have a dream about what you can accomplish. As soon as you get close to that dream, there's another. There's always a desire to keep learning, to keep evolving. Here's the line. Let's tickle it a bit. And then you figure out that's not actually the line. The impossible is actually a little farther out, so let's go over there and tickle it again. You do this for long enough and you just get used to it."

And for you and me, this is all very good news. A feel-good sweet spot for flow that only requires a 4 percent increase in effort? Seriously, who can't push 4 percent further than the last time around? Or, for that matter, clarify goals or tighten feedback loops? It's not too difficult to keep flow's internal triggers in mind when you're chugging through your daily routine. Unlike flow's external triggers — which are admittedly harder to pull without being an action and adventure sport athlete — these internal triggers are strategies accessible to any and all. In fact, the only real problem is how deceptively ordinary these strategies appear.

Don't be fooled.

Despite the ordinary, as Mandy-Rae discovered, pull these triggers frequently enough and results get extraordinary in a hurry.

MINDSET AND THE FLOW CYCLE

In the middle 2000s, Stanford psychologist Carol Dweck got to know racecar driving coach Ross Bentley. Considered one of the best in the business, Bentley built his career around mental preparedness. He believed that winning was all about flow, but the nature of the sport made this especially difficult. With races lasting for hours, errors are inevitable. The key is being able to make a mistake and not let it ruin concentration. Faster drivers are those who can stay in the zone no matter what. Dweck suspected mindset played a role in this ability. Bentley suspected she was right.

Mindset refers to our feelings toward basic qualities like intelligence and athletic talent. After more than thirty years of research, Dweck found that most of us have one of two basic mindsets. Those who have "fixed mindsets" believe abilities like intelligence and athletic talent are innate and unchangeable — i.e., fixed at birth. Those with "growth mindsets" believe abilities are gained through dedication and hard work, that natural-born talents are merely starting points for a much longer learning process. When Kirk Krack taught Mandy-Rae she was capable of the impossible — and she got curious to find out what else was possible — that's having a growth mindset. And it's this same mindset that Bentley and Dweck suspected was responsible for the flow states of winning racecar drivers.

In 2007, to see if their suspicions were right, Dweck and Bentley recruited forty top drivers, then tested them on mindset before, during, and after every race of the season. The results were significant. They found that drivers with growth mindsets were able to enter flow more quickly and stay there no matter what went wrong during the race. Across the board, they were the winning drivers.

What's more important is why.

The short answer is that a growth mindset is one of the secrets to maximizing the total amount of flow in your life. The longer answer starts with the challenge/skill ratio. If you consistently overestimate or underestimate your abilities, then tuning that ratio is like playing darts handcuffed and blindfolded. To find 4 percent, you need accurate self-knowledge — and this is tricky for fixed mindsetters.

"When you think about it," Dweck writes in her book *Mindset,* "this makes sense. If, like those with the growth mindset, you believe you can develop yourself, then you're open to accurate information about your current abilities, even if it's unflattering. What's more, if you're oriented toward learning, you need accurate information about your current abilities in order to learn effectively. However, if everything is either good news or bad news — as it is with fixed-mindset people — distortion almost inevitably enters the picture. Some outcomes are magnified, others are explained away, and before you know it, you don't know yourself at all."

The absence of self-knowledge makes it harder to tune the challenge/skill ratio. Equally vexing, if the resulting feedback is unflattering, fixed mindsetters tend to distort the bad news — making it even tougher to remain dialed in.

A growth mindset moves us in the other direction. Self-knowledge accumulates over time. Finding flow becomes less a quest than a habit. "It's a job to continuously find flow," says Mike Horn, arguably the greatest living adventurer (among other accomplishments, Horn and a companion became the first to hike to the North Pole during the winter). "You have to train your body to prepare for the state, you have to train your mind to prepare for the state. You have to know yourself, and your limits, know exactly what you're afraid of and exactly how hard to push past it. That's serious work. But get it right and not only does it become easier to find flow once, it becomes easier to find it again and again."

In other words, finding 4 percent not only helps create more flow in the moment, it helps create more flow over the long haul. And when it comes to flow — the haul is far longer than most suppose.

There are two common misconceptions about flow. The first is that the state works like a light switch — on or off. You're either in flow or out. Yet flow is not binary. The state is just one *step* in a four-part flow cycle. It's impossible to experience flow without moving through this entire cycle. And this brings us to the second critical misconception: that flow always feels flowy.

The first step in the flow cycle is known as "struggle." Herbert Benson, the Harvard cardiologist who did much of the foundational research on this cycle, chose that name for a reason. Struggle is a loading phase: we are overloading the brain with information. "For a business-person," writes Benson in his book *The Breakout Principle*, "this may be concentrated problem analysis or fact gathering. The serious athlete may engage in extensive and demanding physical training. The person on a spiritual quest may plunge into concentrated study . . . or intense prayer, meditation, or soul searching."

A profound chemical change takes place during struggle. To amp up focus and alertness, stress hormones like cortisol, adrenaline, and norepinephrine are pumped into the system. Tension rises. Frustration as well. Our problems seem unsolvable, our effort unsustainable, and the whole situation feels as far from flow as one could get.

How we handle these negative feelings is critical. In struggle, we're using the conscious mind to identify patterns, then repeating those patterns enough times that they become chunks. Until that happens, we are awkward and uncomfortable. To move through struggle takes a leap of faith that the effort will really result in skill acquisition. By definition, this demands a growth mindset.

The next stage in the cycle is "release." To move out of struggle and into flow, you must first pass through this second stage. Release means to take your mind off the problem, to, as Benson says, "completely sever prior thought and emotional patterns." If you've been cramming for a test all day, go for a walk. If you've been trying to master double black-diamond ski slopes, take a few runs down the blues. If the innovation team has been pulling all-nighters for a week, send them out for dinner and a movie. The method is unimportant. The message is relaxation. The moment this occurs, another chemical change follows: nitric oxide floods the system. This endogenous gaseous signaling molecule causes stress hormones to decline and feel-good neurochemicals like dopamine and endorphins to rise in their place.

Norwegian skier and BASE jumper Karina Hollekim has a great story about release. In 2002, after meeting Shane McConkey, she decided to become the first woman to give ski-BASE a try. This was nothing she approached casually. After two years of serious preparation, Hollekim decided she was finally ready. The jump took place at Lover's Leap, off the exact same cliff that McConkey had first ski-BASE'd. "I was really nervous," she says. "But Shane was a great mentor. He knew I was ready, knew I had the skills, knew that the best thing he could do was take my mind off things. So he tagged along and brought his mother and a huge bag of fireworks. On top of the cliff, he lit off this rocket packed with tiny plastic skydivers. It exploded, then started raining down flaming skydivers. It was so funny. I remember rolling around in the grass laughing. And that did the trick. I relaxed and let my training take over. It made for a great jump. Just right into the zone."

And the zone, the flow state itself, is the third stage in this cycle. Struggle gives way to release gives way to flow — hallelujah.

Afterward, we move into the fourth and final step in the cycle: "recovery." Flow is an extremely expensive state for the body to produce and maintain. It requires a lot of energy and a lot of neurochemistry and both take a little while to replenish. This is some of what goes on in recovery. More important, memory consolidation is taking place. Information is moving from short-term holding into long-term storage. Here, to borrow the gamer's phrase, we are "leveling up," or, as Benson prefers, "returning to a new normal."

But just like struggle, recovery is another cycle step that doesn't feel flowy. Handling the massive delta between the world-at-your-feet sensation that comes with flow and the utterly ordinary, all-too-human reality that shows up afterward is not always pleasant. There's no more feel-good neurochemistry, no more superhuman powers. It can take a considerable amount of resilience to navigate recovery; here too a growth mindset makes a difference.

"If you don't believe developmental learning is possible," says Jamie Wheal, high-performance expert and executive director of the Flow Genome Project, "then it's hard to see flow as the result of something you did differently. Or could do again, or do better with more practice. After experiencing flow, the person with a fixed mindset wants to take unilateral credit for the amazing performance that came with the state. That's the basis of their self-esteem. If I can do that, then I must be that — all the time. But we know that flow is a transitory state — it comes, and it goes. So when it leaves, the same person who took all of the credit for its presence is left with all of the blame for its absence. For someone with a fixed mindset, that's often too much to tolerate. At the expense of health and relationships, they start seeking the high all the time; or they self-handicap their performance with substance abuse, poor training, reckless decisions — so they've got the easy out of 'Well, I wasn't really trying.'" And for fixed mindsetters, this isn't where problems end. To find flow again, the entire cycle needs to restart. This means moving from recovery back into struggle. But if you're stressed out about not being in flow during recovery, then getting fired up for serious frustration of struggle becomes a much harder task. This is also where action and adventure athletes have another advantage — recovery comes built in.

Most of these sports are weather dependent. A big-wave surfer needs big waves; snowboarders prefer deep powder; kayakers want specific water levels to run rivers. These "epic conditions" do not show up every day. In this world, when the big storm blows in, everyone takes advantage. Then the storm passes, and it's time to relax. This built-in lag time creates space for rejuvenation. It allows athletes to build up reserves during recovery and prepare for next round of struggle.

And this too doesn't happen much anymore. In today's world, rarely do we give ourselves permission to recover; rarely does anyone else. Finish one project and there are always a dozen more deadlines to be met. In fact, in most of our lives, the reward for having a high-flow experience and pulling off something challenging at work is usually more work, more responsibilities, and less time to meet them all. Yet if we want to flow from cycle to cycle, we need to take full advantage of recovery to regroup and recharge. In short, on this path, you have to go slow to go fast.

Equally important, as we'll see in the next section, sometimes you don't just have to go slow to go fast — sometimes you have to go sideways.

LATERALIZATION

Ian Walsh was born May 10, 1983, on Maui, Hawaii, and started surfing not long after he could walk. Blessed by geography and timing, Walsh grew up down the block from Jaws, the big-wave mecca of the tow-surf movement. As he was hitting puberty, the movement was hitting its stride. Forty-foot waves, fifty-foot waves, sixty-foot waves — Walsh had a front-row seat. "I grew up watching the greatest show on earth," he says.

Then he joined the show.

At sixteen, Walsh towed into Jaws for the first time. At twenty-one, he towed into a proper seventy-footer at Jaws and earned a nomination for Wave of the Year in Billabong's XXL Awards. A few years later, Shane Dorian, one of the greatest surfers in history, asked Walsh to become his tow partner. With Dorian as his mentor, Walsh's big-wave knowledge expanded exponentially, as did his time on the waves. Pretty soon, and not unlike Shane McConkey, Walsh too started "seeing lines."

"People always said Jaws was impossible to paddle when it got big, but I started noticing these tiny windows of opportunity, places on the wave that looked steep enough, if you could position yourself just right, paddling — just maybe — seemed possible."

So Walsh began studying pictures of the break, trying to confirm his suspicions. He started talking the idea through with friends and spending more time at heavy paddle spots like Maverick's and Todos Santos. He also tried to get ready mentally. The only way to paddle Jaws is to use gravity to accomplish what strength cannot. "It's a different kind of commitment," says Walsh. "With a Jet Ski you hold the line and get pulled into a wave and that can be a gut-check moment. But with paddling, you have to hang up on the ledge, then wait until the wave's about to break before you can get in."

Horrific wipeouts were bound to occur. Two- and three-wave hold-downs likely. This was the real problem. Walsh might have been an extraordinary surfer, but he was a damn ordinary breath holder. "I was really bad at it," he says. "I never told anyone, it was my secret, but when I started thinking about paddling big waves, I maxed out at a thirty- to forty-second breath-hold. That can be a one wave hold-down at Jaws."

This also meant that two and three wave hold-downs — which would come from paddling Jaws — were too far outside his comfort zone. This is the critical detail. Walsh's philosophy is: "It's not how good you are; it's how good you want to be." He has a growth mind-set. He also had a lifetime's worth of experience with flow and knew exactly how far he could use the state to stretch performance — but multiwave wipeouts were more than he could handle. They pushed the challenge level too high. So instead of trying to muscle through, Walsh took an entirely different tack — he "lateralized."

In technical terms, Walsh began looking outside his domain of expertise for help surmounting his problem. In nontechnical terms, on a 2008 flight to Hawaii, he opened up his in-flight magazine and saw pictures of a woman swimming with dolphins. The article was about Mandy-Rae Cruikshank and Kirk Krack and their work at Performance Freediving International. Walsh read the article and learned that there were techniques that could increase his breath-holding capabilities. Free diving, he decided, might give him the confidence boost he needed to mentally prepare to paddle Jaws.

In October of 2010, Walsh spent a few weeks with Freedive International. Before he showed up, his best deep dive was twenty-five feet, and his best breath-hold forty seconds. How fast did he improve? After a day with Krack, Walsh pulled off a 100-foot descent and a 3:30 breath-hold. After a few weeks, he set his personal best at 120 feet and a 4:40 hold. Four months later, when winter storms sent heavy swells toward Jaws, Walsh was ready.

On February 8, 2011, alongside fellow big-wave riders Greg Long and Mark Healy, he rode a Jet Ski out to the lineup. The waves were colossal: fifty feet, maybe fifty-five. The wind nuking. The surf so choppy it took forty-five minutes to anchor, but this was an entirely new problem for him. In all his years at Jaws, Walsh had never set an anchor, as he'd always needed the Jet Ski to ride waves.

Anchoring wasn't the only issue. Surfers use landmarks to triangulate their takeoff spots. Pick a point too far outside and the waves will pass you by. Pick one too close and you can accidentally find yourself in the impact zone. The launch point for tow-in surfing was 150 feet beyond where Walsh thought the paddle spot should be, but nobody paddled Jaws on monster days, so where the paddle spot should be took a little while to determine.

Then he determined.

As soon as Walsh lined up properly, a set darkened the horizon, a behemoth bearing down. He spun his board and started paddling. He kept paddling. His goal was takeoff as late as possible, let the wave jack all the way up before popping to his feet.

But when he finally popped, nothing happened. The wave was standing straight up, but Walsh was hung up on the ledge, perched above the chasm. "I was really late," he says. "When I jumped to my feet the wave already looked beyond vertical. The wind was ripping up the face with so much force that I had to grab the edge of my board with my right hand just to try to keep myself in it."

Grabbing the edge did the trick. With his weight forward, the nose dipped and the board followed. He dropped straight down, a ferocious drop, full of free fall and bounce — down, down, down, board chattering, nose bobbing, Mach speed. At the last instant, Walsh stabilized and took control. He dove deep into his bottom turn, then a few quick cuts to get into position for the tube. The curtain closed. Walsh spent a few seconds inside the barrel, got spit out and tossed from his board. By then, it didn't matter — the ride was his.

In those few moments, Walsh inverted a century of surf wisdom and did the impossible. He'd paddled into a wave so off-limits to paddlers that the entirely new sport of tow surfing had been invented to erase that problem. More incredible, there hasn't been a big-wave tow day at Jaws since. Paddling is now the way surfers catch big waves. Walsh shifted the paradigm.

And certainly, lateralization isn't the only way to shift paradigms, but on the flow path, it's often the only way forward. Sooner or later, there's always a Jaws: a mental hurdle we can't clear, a decision too dangerous to attack head on. In those situations, sideways is forward. Plus, these days, sideways is often the way life works. "Careers are a jungle gym, not a ladder," wrote Facebook COO Sheryl Sandberg in her book *Lean In,* and she's not wrong. Statistics vary, but today, the average person changes jobs seven times between ages eighteen and forty. Most important, there's momentum on the flow path. Lateralization allows you to hold on to that thrust no matter the circumstances.

Momentum over time — that's the invisible kung fu.

And that's also what athletes mean by the term *progression*. Walsh had been surfing at Jaws since he was a kid. There had been days, weeks, months, and years of 4 percent plus 4 percent plus 4 percent, of pushing himself into ten-foot, twenty-foot, thirty-foot surf, of continuously testing limits, of lateralizing, of nearly dying, of driving past injury and fear, of honing skills, getting stronger, getting smarter — a self-taught, near graduate-level education in hydrodynamics, meteorology, body mechanics, and flow.

Of course, most of us don't think about these facts. We can't see progression or feel momentum. It's invisible kung fu. Instead, when we see a surfer riding Jaws, the tableau is neurologically unfathomable. The brain's pattern-recognition system is built to lump like with like, but when in most of our lives have we put ourselves in the path of Godzilla? There are no grounds for comparison. So we look at Jaws and feel fear, dread, and awe — because that's what evolution designed us to feel. But that's not what Ian Walsh felt.

"Mostly," he says, "it felt like another day at the office."

8

The We of Flow

MARK POWELL AND CAMP 4

Not everything comes easily for flow junkies who use action and adventure sports to get their fix. These athletes face issues. The first is environmental. Not only are these sports seasonal — an issue for any addict — but even in season, no matter the sport, certain weather conditions produce more flow than others. In skiing, for example, both the radical novelty of floating in powder and the deep embodiment that results are fast flow triggers. Thus, when it's dumping outside, skiers don't want to be inside, trapped at a desk job. Worse, epic terrain is usually far from town, so getting from that desk job to the mountains in time for the storm requires even more freedom and flexibility.

Training is the next concern. Flow is found at the far edge of our abilities. Athletes have to stay in tip-top shape to continue pushing up the challenge level and accessing the state. While some cross-training is always possible, there's no real substitute for hours on the hill (on a bike, in a kayak, etc.). Yet this means even more time away from jobs and families and similar, traditional commitments.

Societal attitudes are also problematic. Hedonism has a bad name and telling people you're addicted to an altered state where self vanishes and time slows down rarely elicits the best of reactions. "We'll come back from a day of skiing and talk about dumb stuff," says professional skier, climber, mountaineer, director, and photographer Jimmy

Chin. "'I had this rad line through the trees' or 'Did you see me hit that cliff?' What we don't say is 'I got into that amazing headspace again, and I fucking felt like God.'"

The final issue is the whopper, both the puzzle that action and adventure athletes have spent the past half century trying to solve and the point where all of this comes together: how to make a living amid all this flow hunting.

It was a man named Mark Powell who first solved these issues. As a child, Powell loved climbing stories, but he never really gave the sport a try. That changed in 1954. A stint in the air force convinced him life was short, so he took a job in Fresno to be near the mountains, then hooked up with a local chapter of the Sierra Club for a weekend in Yosemite. Unfortunately, Powell was also a chubby chain-smoker, horribly out of shape. On his first trip to the Valley, he was essentially hauled to the top of Lower Cathedral Spire.

Powell's embarrassment became motivation. Over the course of a winter, he became a fitness fanatic, shed forty pounds, and quickly morphed into one of Yosemite's nimbler rock rats. It was a spectacular transformation, but it gave him peculiar ideas. Back then, Yosemite climbing was a short-term affair—duck in, climb hard, duck out—squeezed between real-world responsibilities. Definitely not an end in itself. People saw rock climbing as training for mountaineering—those long weekends in the Valley were preparation for big-mountain multiweek assaults. As Steve Roper explains in his classic Yosemite biography, *Camp 4*, Powell changed all this:

> He knew that a person who didn't mind a little hardship had no need of a full-time job. Life was cheap in the Valley; one didn't have to pay camp fees, didn't need any shelter besides a flimsy tent, and didn't even think of suits and ties. One had no real need for a car, or insurance policies, or haircuts. If one cooked in camp, in lieu of grabbing a burger at nearby Yosemite Lodge, a dollar a day would suffice. Those who worked in the winter and saved even a few hundred dollars might have six months a year in which to play. The best incentive for a long-term visit, sensed early by Powell, was that by climbing four or five times a week one could get into magnificent shape, something that weekenders couldn't.

Thus Powell moved into Yosemite, becoming its first full-time resident. He set up camp in Camp 4, a then-unpopular tent site with two clear assets: year round working toilets and huge boulders. The toilets were useful for obvious reasons. The boulders came in handy for training purposes, and to hide behind, should the rangers come around after camping permits had expired.

And his plan paid off. After moving in, Powell went on a tear, putting up an astounding twenty-one first ascents, including four Yosemite classics, in roughly twenty-two months. Other climbers soon took notice. "Powell distinguished himself on each climb as stronger, faster and bolder," wrote Joseph Taylor in *Pilgrims of the Vertical*. "He pushed mates and built an aggressive style of rushing routes without much reconnoitering. He also showed how living in Yosemite could transform an aspirant into an elite. . . . By dedicating himself to the pursuit of excellence, Powell changed the sport."

Innovation breeds imitation. Pretty soon, other climbers were moving into Yosemite. What began as a subset of another sport (climbing as training for mountaineering) became a subculture in its own right. Pretty soon, Camp 4 became a scene — often described as Beatnik culture gone vertical — yet that's only part of the picture. Take the poetry-spouting, hepcat-talking, drug-taking, nature-loving, antiestablishment stance of standard Beatnik culture, then add in enormous quantities of life-threatening risk and an addictive, quasi-mystical state that allowed climbers to survive those risks. Camp 4 denizens weren't just playing bongos and smoking pot; they were teaming up to put up first ascents on Yosemite's biggest walls and redefining human possibility in the process.

These early Camp 4 residents chased an altered state into an alternative lifestyle and their weirdo plan worked — their incredible success on the walls was the proof. Want more proof? Powell's innovation spread like wildfire.

Over on the North Shore of Oahu, at the same time Camp 4 was being established, Greg Noll and a handful of California transplants were creating a big-wave surfing community all their own. Pretty soon, there were skaters in Dogtown, windsurfers at Hood River, freeskiers in Jackson Hole, mountain bikers in Marin, downhill mountain bikers on Mount Fromme — this list is long. Why has there been near-exponential growth in ultimate human performance these past few decades? Because action and adventure sports athletes discovered that one of the easiest ways to find flow is to band together to chase the state.

KEITH SAWYER AND GROUP FLOW

Why is "together" such an effective strategy? For starters, the obvious. Humans are a social species. We're competitive, cooperative, sexually attracted, and all the rest. These are all exceptionally powerful motivators. As a result, when other people are present, we pay more attention to the present. Companionship drives focus into the now — it's arguably the simplest flow hack in the world.

And the not so obvious? Well, that's where Keith Sawyer comes into our story. A professor of psychology, education, and business at the Washington University in St. Louis, Sawyer got interested in this question via the group dynamics of improvisational jazz. Since early childhood, Sawyer played piano. By the time he was a teenager, he was playing in groups. That's when he first noticed it. "When you play in ensembles there's a shift that can occur," he says. "It's an incredible sensation. The group finds its groove. Creativity goes through the roof. Performance soars. Suddenly everyone can anticipate what the other person is going to do before they do it. It's an emergent property; a whole is greater than the sum of its parts effect."

Sawyer really wanted to understand this effect, but took a little while getting around to it. He came out of MIT with a degree in computer science, spent a few years in the business world, but eventually his old interest won out. In 1990, Sawyer began a University of Chicago doctoral program in psychology under Mihaly Csikszentmihalyi. His fascination with group dynamics soon led him to the literature of high performance, where he discovered a problem: "All the studies that had been run on high performance were about solo performers. There was this huge gap in what led to high performance in groups. Almost no one had done work on the topic."

Yet Sawyer's partnership with Csikszentmihalyi proved fortuitous. In his 1990 book *Flow*, Csikszentmihalyi described a peculiar phenomenon that arose in groups: "Surgeons say that during a difficult operation they have the sensation that the entire operating team is a single organism, moved by the same purpose; they describe it as a 'ballet' in which the individual is subordinated to the group performance, and all involved share in the feeling of harmony and power."

Csikszentmihalyi suspected this feeling was the by-product of individual members of the group being in flow. Sawyer thought something more dynamic was going on. In *Group Genius,* he explains it this way: "My years of playing piano in jazz ensembles convinced me that what happened in any one person's mind could never explain what made one night's performance shine and another a dud. At any second during a performance, an almost invisible musical exchange could take the piece in a new direction; later, no one could remember who was responsible for what. In jazz, the group has the ideas, not the individual musicians."

Sawyer took a field biologist's approach to decoding this dynamic: heading out into the world to videotape incredible creative groups engaged in improvisational performance. His studies ran the gamut, from improv-theater performers to earthquake-relief workers. He developed a technique known as "interaction analysis," a research tool that allowed him to chart the real-time conversational turns that make collaboration possible. After fifteen years of research, Sawyer realized that Csikszentmihalyi hadn't taken things far enough. "When performance peaks in groups," he says, "this isn't just about individuals in flow — it's the group entering the state together, a collective merger of action and awareness, a 'group flow.'"

We've already seen group flow in action. When the Red Bull Air Force flew around Suicide Corner, it was this shared state that helped them survive the trip. But Sawyer discovered it's not just action and adventure athletes having this experience. Everywhere people gather, group flow can arise. If you've ever sung with a church choir, played in a band, played a team sport, taken part in a play, taken part in a brainstorming session, gone dancing, gone to a rock concert, joined a startup, joined a drum circle, done improvisational anything — those highlight moments forever seared in your memory: that too is group flow in action.

And forget the highlights. Ever been so sucked into a great conversation that hours passed like seconds? So have plenty of others. Csikszentmihalyi discovered the most commonly reported instances of flow are those of group flow showing up when people are having a conversation — especially, for reasons we'll get to, if those conversations happen at work.

And wherever group flow shows up, it leaves its mark. The same pleasure chemicals behind individual flow also arrive with the group variation — only we seem to like them more. In comparison studies run by St. Bonaventure University psychologist Charles Walker, "solitary flow" (what Doug Ammons experienced on the Stikine) was measured against "coactive flow" (this comes from individual activities done in groups, like surfers sharing a break) was measured against "interactive flow" (where interaction is inherent to the activity, like rock climbing with a partner). Walker discovered that the more social an activity, the higher "flow enjoyment" — the level of joy experienced in flow — was for participants.

Higher enjoyment correlates to higher motivation, of course, but these same chemicals also enhance performance and improve social bonding (more on this in a moment). As a result, in group flow, spontaneity, cooperation, communication, creativity, productivity, and overall performance all go through the roof. "In a study of more than 300 professionals at a strategy consulting firm, a government agency, and a petrochemical company," writes Sawyer, ". . . the people who participated in group flow were the highest performers."

And the better news: Group flow is eminently hackable. In fact, in Yosemite, this is exactly what happened. By banding together to chase flow, those climbers turned life in Camp 4 into one giant group flow trigger.

The best news? If we want similar results, moving to the Valley is optional.

GROUP FLOW TRIGGERS

As of late, we've been tracking a trail of triggers. We've seen how to tune external triggers, altering environmental conditions to get more flow, and how to tweak internal triggers, altering psychological conditions to get more flow. But Sawyer also discovered that flow states have social triggers — ten in particular — which are ways to alter social conditions to produce more group flow.

A number of these social triggers are already familiar. The first three — *serious concentration; shared, clear goals; good communication* (i.e., lots of immediate feedback) — are the collective versions of individual preconditions identified by Csikszentmihalyi. Two more — *equal participation* and an *element of risk* (mental, physical, whatever) — are self-explanatory given what we already know about flow. The remaining five require a little more information.

Familiarity, our next trigger, means the group has a common language, a shared knowledge base, and a communication style based on unspoken understandings. It means everybody is always on the same page, and, when novel insights arise, momentum is not lost due to the need for lengthy explanation.

Then there's *blending egos* — which is the collective version of the same sort of humility that allowed Doug Ammons to merge with the Stikine. When egos have been blended, no one's hogging the spotlight and everyone's thoroughly involved.

A *sense of control* combines autonomy (being free to do what you want) and competence (being good at what you do). It's about getting to choose your own challenges and having the necessary skills to surmount them.

Close listening occurs when we're fully engaged in the here and now. In conversation, this isn't about thinking about what witty thing to say next, or what cutting sarcasm came last. Rather, it's generating real-time, unplanned responses to the dialogue as it unfolds.

Always say yes, our final trigger, means interactions should be additive more than argumentative. The goal here is the momentum, togetherness, and innovation that comes from ceaselessly amplifying each other's ideas and actions. It's a trigger based on the first rule of improv comedy. If I open a sketch with, "Hey, there's a blue elephant in the bathroom," then "No, there's not," is the wrong response. With the denial, the scene goes nowhere. But if the reply is affirmative instead — "Yeah, sorry, there was no more space in the cereal cupboard" — well then that story goes someplace interesting.

In the case of those early Yosemite climbers, their story went someplace interesting because Camp 4 was chockablock with social triggers. Concentration and risk are baked into rock climbing, and, if climbing teams are going to be successful, close listening, shared goals, ego blending, and good communication must be as well. A sense of control and equal participation are also key. It's not nearly as much fun to go into the vertical world with someone with significantly lesser or greater abilities (i.e., no equal participation, loss of control), so perfect partners are consistently sought; but with people living far apart and climbing occasionally, they are much harder to find. In Camp 4, population density solved this issue. Meanwhile, familiarity and always say yes—our two final contenders—emerge from finding that perfect partner and climbing with them repeatedly, something far more likely to happen when folks are living side by side in Yosemite, rather than spread around California.

It was mostly unintentional, but these ten triggers turned Camp 4 itself into a giant group flow hack. But if you're interested in similar results, there's no need to take up rock climbing. Turns out social triggers are relatively easy to pull, and we've already seen proof. Why does group flow show up most frequently in work conversations? Because they tend to involve shared goals, carry an element of risk (because there's money involved in work), include familiar partners, and require more concentration. How easy is it to produce group flow? Merely chatting on the job can be enough to put you in the state.

And even pulling a few triggers can bring big results. The government-owned Swedish transportation company Green Cargo instituted lengthy monthly meetings (akin to personal coaching sessions) to sharply increase the amount of feedback employees received. The result: they saw such a boost in performance, the company turned a profit for the very first time in its 120-year history.

Unfortunately, not every company is this innovative. As Sawyer points out in *Group Genius:* "It can be hard to find this kind of experience in large corporations, which tend to reward closing up communication, narrowing the channels, and minimizing risk. That's why people who seek out group flow often join startups or work for themselves. Serial entrepreneurs keep starting new business as much for the flow experience, as for the additional success."

Of course, becoming a serial entrepreneur, going into business for yourself, or moving into Camp 4—these are all high-risk decisions. Not a surprise, right? We already know that the flow path is no place for the timid. But does this mean we'll have to unearth a wellspring of hidden courage to continually access this state? Most certainly. Yet this is not quite as difficult as it seems. Turns out there's hidden leverage available, both a secret balm to make you braver and one of the best flow hacks yet discovered: community.

SOCIAL SUPPORT

Why did Powell's innovation spread like wildfire? It held people together. Why did it hold people together? Because there are extraordinarily powerful social bonding neurochemicals at the heart of both flow and group flow: dopamine and norepinephrine, which underpin romantic love, and endorphins, which enhance maternal bonding in children and social bonding in adults. When these chemicals start showing up in places like Camp 4, they unite the tribe—and often in unusual ways.

Just as flow is democratic—anyone can experience the state—group flow is egalitarian: anyone, regardless of class, race, religion, sex, politics, or whatever, can share the experience. Neurochemicals bond regardless of background. It's why it's not unusual to find a posse of, say, Jackson Hole skiers containing a couple of hippies, a redneck lunatic, a conservative millionaire, and a stay-at-home mom. Group flow is a social unifier and social leveler, creating what cultural anthropologists call "communitas"—that deep solidarity and togetherness that results from shared transcendent experiences.

This solidarity is useful. People feel different on the other side of flow: stronger, more confident, more capable. Yet the surreal nature of the experience—time dilation, vanishing of self—can make the transformation difficult to trust. If you don't believe you're really capable of doing what you just did, your chances of doing so again go down considerably. Group flow changes this equation. "When you know you're sharing that heightened awareness with others," says Jimmy Chin, "it makes it more real. If someone else is experiencing the same thing, you can look at one another and say: 'Did that happen? Did you feel that too?' That matters. It's proof, but proof you can't really talk about, proof that there aren't words for, like a big, shared secret."

More acceleration comes from the social support that solidarity provides. Finding flow is not easy. Finding it repeatedly tougher still. The struggle phase can drag endlessly on, the urge to give up growing stronger as that last memory of flow grows dimmer. But collective momentum fights hard against the individual inertia. In any action and adventure community, when one member's in struggle, another's in flow — and probably using that state to do something amazing.

Amazing energizes. Whether it's cooperative excitement or competitive jealousy, one person's triumph becomes another's motivation. This creates a flywheel effect: the group itself gains momentum. In his book *Camp 4*, Steve Roper gives a fabulous example:

> Two of Camp 4's boulders loomed above all others. Columbia Boulder, the biggest, stood near the center of camp, and it had no easy routes. . . . One route, the Robbin's Pullup (named after legendary climber Royal Robbins), especially intrigued us. Robbins had done the route back in the mid-fifties but had been unable to repeat it, and no one else had either. The fifteen-foot problem overhung crazily on its lower part; a lieback/pinch-grip pullup was the only real hold to start out with, but it would obviously take superhuman strength to make the move. One day in 1960 . . . a fellow named Harry Daley, an occasional partner of Robbins, strode over to the problem. We giggled behind his back, for Daley was hardly the strongest among us. He placed both hands on the pinch-grip and tentatively plastered a foot on a microhold. So far, so good. We'd all gone this far. We smiled condescendingly. Then, incredibly, he pulled upward and lunged for an edge far above. He gripped this and levitated upward. He'd made it. We stood with mouths open before bursting into a cheer. Then, even more incredibly, three or four of us scampered up the problem as if we've been doing it for years. A psychological barrier had been broken. Robbins heard about the feat within hours, and strode over and did it on his first try.

Beyond breaking psychological barriers, social support systems also helped climbers overcome tactical barriers. In Yosemite, one person's mishap became everyone's map. Strong ties maximize information sharing. Mental training tips, physical training tips, performance tips, flow-hacking tips, etc. — all were passed around and preserved. Before collectives like Camp 4 were established, information could take years to circulate through the culture. Once action and adventure sports athletes began to build communities, a knowledge base accrued, technical languages developed, technological development accelerated. But what truly changed the game was a technological development unlike any other: an innovation accelerant, barrier-breaking training tool, and ultimate flow hack all rolled into one: the suddenly affordable video-cassette recorder.

STACY PERALTA AND *THE SEARCH FOR ANIMAL CHIN*

The affordable VCR arrived in the mid-1970s, then standard wars of the VHS versus beta variety and Supreme Court decisions of the copyright infringement variety kept the machines away from the masses for over a decade. But once they did arrive, change came quickly. The 10 percent of American households who owned VCRs in 1983 blossomed to 30 percent by 1985. Historians feel 1986 was the turning point, the year video-rental sales eclipsed movie-ticket sales and the moment the technology truly exploded. And with his résumé of perfect timing, there was Stacy Peralta, ready to ride that wave.

Peralta is a force. By age fifteen, he was skating for the Zephyr Skate Team — making him an original Z-Boy (as in *Dogtown and Z-Boys*) — by twenty-one, an entrepreneur. In 1978, he teamed up with enigmatic engineer and skateboard designer George Powell to found Powell-Peralta, a company that would dominate the skate market throughout the 1980s. At the root of that domination was the Bones Brigade, the Powell-Peralta skate team, arguably the most famous in the history of the sport. In the mid-'80s, Peralta began making movies to market the team. By 1987, he'd gotten good at it. That year, Peralta released *The Search for Animal Chin*. That year, North American VCR penetration passed 50 percent. The combination proved potent.

Historically, as Matthew Malady pointed out in a 2011 article for *Slate*, it's hard to understate the impact of the *Chin*:

Twenty-five years ago, back when ESPN still devoted a sizable chunk of its production budget to *Scholastic Sports America,* skateboarding-phenom-turned-entrepreneur Stacy Peralta produced, directed, and filmed something called *The Search for Animal Chin.* The film, which combines skate footage with a road-trip narrative starring a crew of professional skateboarders known as the Bones Brigade, forever changed the sport by transforming skaters into movie stars. It also functioned as a coming out party for a precocious towheaded string bean by the name of Tony Hawk and, in the process, paved the way for the extreme-sports explosion that eventually begat the X Games . . .

For members of the skate community, *Animal Chin* was an announcement of arrival. Skaters, like almost every other group of action and adventure athletes, were a scattered subculture. There was a movement brewing, for sure, but in the days before MTV made it okay to look weird in the suburbs, no one really knew how strong. *Animal Chin* united this tribe. With VCRs suddenly everywhere, the message — essentially have fun while skating — went wide.

The tricks went wider.

Before the availability of cheap VCRs, the fragmented nature of the action and adventure sports world acted like a brake on innovation. With communities isolated from one another and magazines the only available messenger — and the difficulty of dissecting dynamic moves through static images — novelty spread slowly. When someone in California developed a new trick, years could pass before skaters in Wisconsin were throwing them consistently. The VCR changed the game. Flicks like *Chin* became training tools, with guys like Tony Hawk and Rodney Mullen as de facto professors. Skaters could rewind and rewatch. They could pause. In other words, in action and adventure sports, the arrival of the VCR marked the moment innovation became open sourced.

The VCR became the ultimate flow hack. If a skater in Jersey got into a flow state and did something amazing, a group of skaters in Boston would try to leverage group flow to improve that trick. For beginners, the videos were ways to learn your ABCs. For experts, it was game on. Skaters no longer had to wonder how good the best in the world really were, or how good they needed to be to take their place. Those films set the gnar high bar — now everyone could try to clear it.

"You can't really describe the impact these movies had on performance," says Joe Donnelly, longtime action and adventure sports journalist and former editor in chief of the pioneering snowboarding magazine *Stick*. "They lit a fuse. On the sport's side, there was immediate progression: bigger ramps, bigger drops, more extreme lines, more technical tricks. But the films also progressed the culture. They married the athletic, the artistic, and the outlandish. The culture itself became more extreme and a whole new world of possibilities opened up."

And for the rest of us, well, we've come a ways since the VCR. Any smartphone or tablet computer opens these same possibilities up to everyone. Want some Animal Chin in your own life? Join an online community. Watch videos. Read stuff. Get smarter. Try stuff. Get into flow. Use flow to do something amazing. Post videos. Teach others how you did it. And repeat. That's what action and adventure athletes did, that's one of the main reasons they went so far so fast.

And this tells us something important. We tend to think of guys like Dean Potter and Shane McConkey as lone-wolf mavericks, but Potter passed so much time in Camp 4 that he earned himself a nickname: "Mayor of the Dirtbags." And McConkey spent most of his career in Squaw where, as JT Holmes explains, "even tough guy pros like me can't go into the 7-Eleven and brag. There are so many great athletes in this community, there's a pretty good chance that the girl behind the counter did something radder than me last weekend."

Potter, McConkey, Holmes, and every other athlete in this book got farther faster because they packed their lives with flow triggers and flowed in packs. They leveraged powerful neurobiology to build tighter communities, leveraged those communities to drive innovation, then open-sourced innovation to much larger communities and collectively rode the reverberations into the history books. The lone-wolf maverick is a myth. When it comes to becoming Superman, we really are in this together.

9

The Flow of Imagination

THE EVOLUTION OF THE DOUBLE SKI BASE

They pulled the RV up to the side of the bridge and the Primal Crew got to work. Miles Daisher, then twenty-three years old, climbed on top of the vehicle, grabbed a two-by-twelve, and strapped it down. Half of the plank was still on the roof; the other half became a crude diving board, jutting into the darkness and over the river, a long 120 feet below. Someone else set up the bungees, a couple of folks grabbed walkie-talkies and went to spot for cops, and the newbie — this guy named Shane McConkey — stood to the side and watched.

Welcome to the early 1990s, McConkey's very first night in Squaw Valley. At the time, bungee jumping was a nascent sport, underground and illegal. But McConkey had friends in the Primal Crew — a bunch of guys like Daisher, ski bums who worked for Primal Instinct, then one of the few bungee operations in the world willing to take paying clients on clandestine bridge jumps. This was McConkey's "Welcome to Tahoe" party.

The Primal Crew lived in the Primal House, an infamous Squaw crash pad. There was a trampoline in the living room. There were always parties. The online travel magazine *Matador Network* once asked the question "Ever wonder where Red Bull athletes come from?" Their answer: "Back in the mid-1990s, there was a house in Squaw Valley, California. They called it the Primal House."

But all of this was still to come. First there was the small matter of that nighttime stealth mission off the bridge at Angel's Camp. Daisher went first. He took a few confident steps toward the end of the diving board, bounced once, and — because he wanted the new guy to understand — threw his best trick.

"I didn't know Shane McConkey," says Daisher. "I had no idea he was a pro skier. With his long hair, I just thought he was another hippie from Colorado. So, you know, I had to let him know who he was dealing with. I threw a 'wild turkey.'"

There is nothing easy about throwing a wild turkey: a front one-and-half flip into a half twist into as many backflips as one can execute before the bungee pulls taut. Daisher learned how to add the twist to the front flips by jumping off diving boards into swimming pools. It's how the trick got its name. "The only time I was willing to try it," says Daisher, "was after two shots of Wild Turkey."

That night at Angel's Camp, Daisher aced it. Didn't get tangled in the ropes, got off three and a half backflips, just perfect. Afterward, McConkey sidled over and asked how he'd done it. Daisher didn't take him seriously. "I was like, yeah, right, this hippie is gonna pull off a wild turkey. I gave him like two lines of explanation — mostly rope-management stuff — and walked away."

Turns out, the damn hippie had mad skills. McConkey climbed up on the roof of the RV, bounced off the diving board, and nailed the trick on his first try.

"Afterward," says Daisher, "it was on."

It was on all right. McConkey moved into the Primal House and tacked a two-dollar bill to his wall. That was always the bet. "We spent all our time trying to think up new bungee tricks," said Daisher, "stuff no one had ever done before. It was always about pushing the envelope and pushing our creativity and 'I bet you that two-dollar bill that I can do that!'"

One of the things Daisher and McConkey learned to do was skydive. Another Primal House denizen, Frank "The Gambler" Gambalie, taught them. A security-systems designer by trade, Gambalie started bungee jumping to let off steam. Pretty soon, he had a second job with Primal Instinct. One day, as he was setting up a bridge jump, a couple of guys wearing parachutes showed up, walked over to the railing, and

hopped off. It was the first time Gambalie had ever seen BASE jumping. It wouldn't be the last.

While most skydivers put in a minimum of 200 airplane leaps before attempting a BASE jump, the Gambler gave it a go after twelve.
He never looked back. Gambalie went on to set a number of BASE records, including the longest free fall — twenty-six seconds, off the Troll
Wall in Norway — and also found ways to put his security training to
good use. For "insurance" reasons, jumping off buildings is frowned
upon, so he would dress as a technician to sneak past security, then
use his knowledge of locks and alarms to get to the launch site. These
tactics helped him become the first to leap off New York's Chrysler
Building, wherein, after hiding in the building all night, Gambalie got
off a 5 A.M. launch, silently floated to the ground, then cemented his
legend by hailing a cab to flee the scene.

In 1998, the Gambler began teaching both McConkey and Daisher
to BASE jump. By 1999 the lessons were over. In June of that year,
Gambalie leapt off of Yosemite's El Cap, landed safely in the meadow
below, and was immediately greeted by two rangers. BASE jumping is
against the law in all national parks, and Yosemite's rangers are particularly zealous. Fearing arrest and a $5,000 fine, Gambalie fled toward
the Merced River, dumped his chute on the bank, then dove in. The
cold water sapped his strength, the current did the rest. Divers didn't
recover his body for twenty-eight days.

Both Daisher and McConkey took his passing hard, but action and
adventure athletes have a different relationship with death. "When
Frank died," recounts Daisher, "everybody told us it was time to stop
BASE jumping. But that's not what Frank would have wanted. He believed in doing what you love and we weren't going back. After he died,
I quit my job and moved to the Drop Zone (a Tahoe-area skydiving
operation). I lived in a tent and packed chutes. Shane and I spent all
our time trying to piece together Frank's knowledge. I would tell him
something Frank had taught me, and he would tell me something
Frank had taught him, and pretty soon another two-dollar bet was
born."

In Gambalie's honor, Daisher and McConkey created the "Plunge
to Your Death Camp." Future Red Bull Air Force member JT Holmes

was one of the first to attend, along the way becoming one of the few to learn to BASE jump before learning to skydive. Afterward, Holmes was just as committed to his new sport as McConkey and Daisher. And this led to even more two-dollar bets.

There was "skyaking," which is skydiving in a kayak into a river. There was a bicycle jump — when Daisher road a mountain bike out of an airplane. Ski-BASE emerged from this period as well, then wingsuit ski-BASE. "That was a big deal," Holmes says. "Wingsuit ski-BASE jumping didn't come from a Bond film; it came from our imagination. No one had done it before. So when Shane had to try it out for the first time, yeah, we were all pretty nervous."

Then Holmes invented a new way to attach a parachute to another parachute — which meant they could deploy one chute, cut it away, and deploy the next. "We had this idea about a double ski-BASE," says Daisher, "where you would jump off a cliff and deploy your chute, then land on a hanging snowfield, cut away that chute, rip these amazing turns in a place no one had ever been before, leap off a giant cliff at the end, deploy that second parachute, and land somewhere far below."

In March 2009, the double ski-BASE was pitched to Red Bull (who sponsor all three athletes). Daisher was elsewhere, but Holmes and McConkey got backing to fly to Italy's Dolomites range and make the attempt. It was by far the farthest anyone had ever taken either of these sports; it was so far beyond imagination that even today most people still can't wrap their heads around the idea — but that's probably because they're looking in the wrong direction.

Jimmy Chin explains: "When people think about action and adventure sport athletes the first thing — often the only thing — they think about is the physical risk involved. But I've gotten to know and work with an extremely diverse group of these athletes — from new school freeskiers through grizzled 8,000-meter-peak mountaineering veterans — and I've come to one conclusion about everyone, myself included. The greatest athletes aren't interested in the greatest risks. I mean, sometimes they're taken, sometimes not, but those physical risks are a by-product of a much deeper desire to take creative risks. Don't be fooled by the danger. In action and adventure sports, creativity is always the point."

CREATIVE TRIGGERS

Why is creativity the point? Turns out, this is one of the trickier questions we have to answer. Obviously, the reason has plenty to do with flow, but the relationship between flow and creativity is complicated and not completely understood. Moreover, every time someone makes a list of skills needed in the twenty-first century, creativity tops it. The quality most desirable in a CEO? According to a global survey conducted by IBM of 1,500 top executives in sixty countries: creativity. What about the skills our children need to thrive in the future? According to the Partnership for 21st Century Skills—a collection of 250 researchers at sixty institutions—creativity is again the answer. So if ever there was a critical yet overused term in need of clarification, this is it.

Let's start with a standard working definition of *creativity*. There are plenty to choose from but "the process of developing original ideas that have value" is arguably the most common, so we'll go with that. The first thing to know about coming up with original, valuable ideas is how deeply this process scares us. Every time we have a creative insight and share it with the world, we come up against some very primal terrors: fear of failure, fear of the unknown, fear of social ridicule, fear of loss of resources (time, money, access, etc.). There's significant risk involved in every step of this process.

Drilling down deeper, beyond the risk taking involved in idea generation, there's a second mechanism at work: pattern recognition. When Apple cofounder Steve Jobs said, "Creativity is just connecting things," he wasn't wrong. When coming up with a new idea, we always have to find patterns—i.e., Jobs's connection between things—that we haven't seen before. At a fundamental level, then, coming up with original, valuable ideas always requires risk taking and pattern recognition—and this means dopamine.

Dopamine is the pleasure chemical released whenever we take a risk or identify a pattern. We feel this inrush as excitement, engagement, and curiosity. But dopamine does more than just stimulate our emotions and increase our motivation—it also tightens focus, drives us into the now, and, thus, speeds entrance into flow. What all of this means is that the creative act (one that requires risk taking and pattern recognition) is itself an exceptionally potent flow trigger.

"When you're concentrating on something that matters," explains Harvard psychologist Ned Hallowell, "when you can't proceed on automatic pilot, that's when flow shows up. That's creativity to a T. Once you've thrown out the rule book and begun making creative decisions, the risk involved tightens focus and triggers a neurobiological cascade — it sweeps you right into flow."

Even better, the flow state itself acts like a force multiplier for creativity. In flow, beyond this neurochemical reaction, there are also neuroanatomical and neuroelectrical changes taking place. Neuroanatomically, with large swatches of the prefrontal cortex deactivated, our inner critic is shut off and our inner monologue rendered silent. As a result, we're more receptive to novel experiences (the building blocks of new ideas) and much less inhibited (thus more likely to present those new ideas to the world). This is why, for example, in studies run by University of Pennsylvania psychologist Sharon Thompson-Schill, when transient hypofrontality was artificially induced and subjects were presented with creative problems to solve, the hypofrontal subjects came up with more novel insights in far shorter time frames than control subjects.

Neuroelectrically, flow's baseline brain-wave pattern of low alpha/high theta also boosts creativity. Alpha means we're calm, confident, and content (thus more willing to take risks) and that the lines of communication between the subconscious mind and the conscious mind are wide open (thus more chances for pattern recognition and novel insight). Theta, meanwhile, is a relaxed state where the brain can move from notion to notion without much internal resistance — like what happens when you're about to fall asleep — and has long been associated with intuition and idea generation.

If we put this all together, what we find is a powerful reciprocity: creativity triggers flow; then flow enhances creativity. But equally important to our story is how action and adventure athletes have taken advantage of this reciprocity. Part of this is simply the nature of these sports. "When you're out skiing or skating with your friends," explains Micah Abrams, "if you see your friend do something mind-bending, there's a natural inclination to immediately want to try it, to immediately want to add to it. Everyone builds off each other. It's competition and creativity and rolled into one." Or, as Miles Daisher explained: "It was always about pushing the envelope and pushing our creativity and 'I bet you that two-dollar bill that I can do that!'"

Of course, creative one-upsmanship has been a part of action and adventure sports for a very long time. What changed — the key factor that allowed these athletes to take such complete advantage of this flow trigger and, arguably, the fundamental alteration that lit the fuse on the accelerated progression at the heart of this book — was the turbo-boost known as the "freeride movement."

The movement dates back to the 1980s, when snowboarding was still a banned sport at most resorts. The original freeriders were snow-boarders who got around this ban by taking their show into the back-country — where they were *free* from resort rules and *free* to interpret that terrain any way they wanted. This freedom, of course, translated into far greater opportunities for creativity, which triggered more flow, which further enhanced creativity, which supercharged the rate of innovation, jacked up performance, and — when captured on cellu-loid — looked like such ridiculous fun that everyone wanted in on the action.

Shane McConkey included. In the 1990s, McConkey borrowed the term *free* to apply to skiing. He also extended its meaning. "Shane desperately wanted to get away from the popularized word 'extreme,'" says Scott Gaffney. "It was overused and did not define the kind of skiing he felt he enjoyed most. So he coined the term 'freeskiing.' That's where it originated. Now, the 'free' prefix is used in all kinds of action sports — e.g., freesurfing and freeriding (meaning on a mountain bike), when people are performing outside of competition."

More important, freeriding tilted the value structure of action and adventure sports. It overemphasized self-expression. It de-emphasized winning. And especially de-emphasized the idea of a solitary winner. As long as freeriders were seeing interesting lines and riding those lines in interesting ways, they were winning. No longer was the fastest person down the mountain the best athlete on the mountain. To really win, you had be creative. "Creativity became the way athletes judged success," continues Jimmy Chin. "Did I pick a cool line? Did it look stylish? Was I innovative? Did I add anything to the conversation? It's why so many of these guys now see themselves as artists as much as athletes. Freeriding changed the culture."

And because all of these creative freeriding choices triggered flow, this cultural change was reinforced. Over and again. What began as an individual value became a societal virtue. These days, imagination and innovation form the basis for how these athletes are judged, and judge themselves. It's also how they get paid. You don't just need to be better, stronger, faster to get a part in an action and adventure sports movie — you need to be all those things and still show us something new. Most important, you need fierce commitment to vision — you need to be willing to bet your ass on your idea.

Think about this for a moment. While all creative types take risks for their ideas, very few are willing to go as far as action and adventure athletes. When Daisher dreamed up skyaking — if that little insight had been a bad one? Or when Holmes invented the technology that opened the door for the double ski BASE? Or when McConkey tried out wingsuit ski-BASE for the first time? All of these acts required a level of commitment to creativity not often seen in society.

By way of comparison, consider entrepreneurship. Starting a company is considered one of the riskiest and most creative acts in business. We celebrate the risk taking of entrepreneurs, we lionize their unwavering commitment to innovation. Well, Danny Way's Mega-Ramp was an innovation that cost more than $500,000 to build— or roughly what it takes to get a startup off the ground — and Way didn't just have to raise that cash (i.e., convince his sponsors to pony up), he also had to be the first guy down the results. Or the strapped crew, with their invention of tow surfing. How many organizations do their product research at Jaws? At Teahupoo? At Maverick's? Because this is the other half of the creativity story. It's not merely that action and adventure athletes take advantage of this flow trigger. It's that they have made creativity so core to the culture that the culture is willing to die for their creativity.

You want more proof? A few days before McConkey and Holmes left for Italy to attempt the double ski-BASE for the first time, McConkey was hanging with Daisher, back in California. "He was giving me a lecture," says Daisher. "He was saying: 'What we do for a living? We both have families. You need to tighten up your ends. You have to have a will.'"

THE FALL OF SUPERMAN

Shane McConkey and JT Holmes arrived in Italy for their shot at the double ski-BASE on March 25, 2009. After a few days scouting locations, a day spent nailing a ski-BASE (single, not double) off the 8,612-foot Sossongher, and a couple more lost to bad weather, they took the cable car to the top of the Sass Pordoi, a 9,685-foot mountain in the Dolomites.

The view from the top is one of the best in the range. There's a restaurant up there and a nice lookout spot. McConkey and Holmes had a cup of coffee at the former, then spent some time at the latter, hunting a suitable location for the double ski-BASE. They found one too, just perfect, but decided to save that fun for another day. Instead, the Sass Pordoi also features a gorgeous, 2,000-foot cliff that McConkey had ski-BASE'd the previous summer. That day—if the damn wind would ever die down—he wanted to give wingsuit ski-BASE a try.

The damn wind finally died down. McConkey and Holmes hiked out to the cliff and roped down to a spot below the edge. From there, McConkey threw rocks and started counting. He counted ten, maybe twelve seconds before impact. Plenty of time, he figured, for everything that needed to be done on the way down.

Still, the launch would be critical. McConkey and Holmes built a big jump at the cliff's edge, but the snow was crappy, so they started over. The second time was the charm. With the kicker dialed, they climbed into their flight gear and snapped into their skis. Holmes went first. He pointed his boards toward the cliff, made a few quick turns, then nailed a perfect double backflip into the abyss. McConkey was left alone on the side of the mountain. He had a Go Pro camera on his head and was wired for sound. "Oh yeah," he said into the microphone, "here we go, another wingsuit ski-BASE."

Then he exhaled deeply, just once, and pointed his tips toward the edge.

It was a fantastic takeoff. He hit the jump perfectly, sailed off the Sass Pordoi, and did what he could not back in Crested Butte so many years before: a perfect double backflip.

It was the last time something in his life went right.

It's impossible to steer a wingsuit with skis on, so McConkey had invented a release system — really just a strap to yank on that unlatched his bindings. But when he yanked, only his right ski popped off. It then got tangled with his left. He reached down to manually release the binding, but the move flipped him upside down — which meant he could neither see the ground approaching nor deploy his parachute for fear of further entanglement. Some people, including Daisher, believe you should throw the chute anyway, but McConkey had long argued for the need to release the skis first, get into a stable position for flight, and then throw the chute. He did, in fact, manage to release his ski and get into a stable position. "It was an amazing recovery," Holmes said afterward, "but he was already too late."

McConkey died on impact. He left behind a wife, a three-year-old daughter, and a fifteen-year legacy that, despite the startling rate of progression in these sports, will most likely remain unmatched for some time. As former *Powder* magazine managing editor Leslie Anthony wrote in *White Planet,* "The ski world's superman was gone." The double ski-BASE remains, though, the chapter yet unwritten. Holmes says it's only a matter of time, and if he doesn't do it, someone else will. That's the tradition. That's how these things get done. That's really why McConkey was considered a genius. He did what all geniuses do: He shifted the paradigm. He opened our eyes. He gave his life so that, maybe, we could reinvent ours.

PART THREE

TIME TO RISE

We are the ones that we've been waiting for.

— ALICE WALKER

10

The Dark Side of Flow

JEREMY JONES

As a rule, most mountain men are, well, mountains. Big guys, head to toe. They tend toward thickness, with the extra weight needed to not shake apart when the temperatures drop below zero. They tend toward tallness, as winter mountaineering demands trail blazing through deep snow and those of lesser stature end up swallowed while post-holing. They are not, as a rule, five-foot-seven and 145 pounds. Then again, when has Jeremy Jones — ten times voted *Snowboard* Big-mountain Rider of the Year — ever followed the rules?

As a child in Vermont, back when snowboarding was still banned at most resorts, he spent the majority of his time alone, dragging his board up backyard hills, riding down, and repeating. He barged onto the circuit back before it was a circuit, a story his O'Neil biography (one of Jones's sponsors) sums up nicely:

> Without the sponsors and support today's athletes may take for granted, Jones started competing at fourteen and though averaging about thirty-five contests a season, he didn't stay in a hotel until he was twenty. One winter he ate more than 300 peanut butter and jelly sandwiches and graduated high school $10,000 in debt. He'd lose fifteen pounds each winter and one season got so sick, he gave his sponsors an ultimatum: either they up their support or he'd have to

walk away. He saw all of it though, as an initiation. "You have to earn your deal," he reasons, "the better the job, the harder the initiation."

Yet, despite the grueling nature of his initiation, Jones walked away from the job. On his way to his very first pro competition, he stopped to visit his brothers in Jackson Hole, Wyoming, and took a sharp left turn. Instead of becoming a world champion racer, Jones decided he'd rather wash dishes for the chance to freeride Jackson every day.

Jackson Hole is not your average ski mountain. The in-bounds terrain is the most ferocious in the Lower 48, the out-of-bounds terrain harsher still. Point of fact: the first three extreme ski contests held in Alaska were all won by Jackson Hole skiers. It was also Jackson Hole skiers and snowboarders who pioneered Alaska as the mecca of winter sports filmmaking. In fact, it was Jeremy's brothers, Todd and Steve Jones, alongside Dirk Collins and Corey Gavitt, who cofounded the extreme-sports filmmaking company, Teton Gravity Research (TGR), and did much of that pioneering.

Along similar lines, while Jackson introduced Jeremy to the possibilities of big-mountain riding, it was Alaska that sealed the deal. In 1998, the first year TGR was making films in the far north, Jeremy flew up for a visit. "Alaska was a different planet," he recalls. "On that first trip, I was as scared as I've ever been, riding the biggest lines of my life, making the fastest turns of my life and afterward I'd realize I hadn't come close to hitting my limits — that I could have gone even bigger, even faster. The rules were different up there. It's like we'd found a place that had the best snow, totally unexplored, and, by the way, there's less gravity too."

Over the next decade, Jeremy became part of a group of snowboarders, skiers, and filmmakers who established Alaska as snow sports' ultimate proving ground. "It was brain-scrambling," he says. "Things that were impossible in the morning were possible by the evening. Literally. Rules that were adhered to vehemently, rules that had been in place since the beginning of winter sports, rules like don't do this because you'll die, were changing on a daily, sometimes hourly, basis."

It was also the beginning of the end. Different people have different gateways into flow. Jeremy favors a rich environment. Novelty, complexity, and unpredictability are his favorite triggers. Unfortunately, in Alaska, choppers are only allowed to fly in certain permitted areas. Within a few years all of Valdez had been explored. Then the athletes and filmmakers moved to Haines and opened up another frontier. Within a few more years, every inch of Haines had also been explored. It was a serious problem for Jeremy.

"I would find myself at the top of these amazing lines," he says, "except I had ridden them five times before. In that kind of familiar territory, to get the buzz I wanted, I was having to red-line sixty-degree chutes. Over big cliffs. Chasing avalanches. Really, really out there. And that was all I was doing: flying to the top of mountains, pushing farther out onto that edge. I just knew, it was only a matter of time before something went really, really wrong."

Jones also knew that the bureaucratic boundary only applied to helicopters—if he was willing to hike for his turns, he could go as uncharted as desired. But uncharted meant self-sufficiency. It meant fortitude. And with storms that can last for weeks, it also meant that rescue and resupply were nonexistent possibilities. Plus, his new plan involved climbing up the peaks he wanted to snowboard down—an idea that would compound the already significant dangers of big-mountain snowboarding with the long list of catastrophes that come with high alpine mountaineering.

"There's an upside and a downside," explains Jeremy. "The downside is that to make the climb I have to spend three hours like a sitting duck. Avalanches, of course. But one tiny snowball that knocks free at the top of a couloir can become the size of a refrigerator by the time it reaches the bottom. I need all of my senses peaking to survive—and that's the upside. Climbing drives me right into the zone. This makes a big difference on the way down. I notice everything—the blind roll-over suddenly isn't blind. Snow stability and where the fractures are and unlike helicopter riding—when you get to the top and have only a few seconds to get into the zone before dropping in—I know I'll be in there on my descent. If I climbed to the top successfully, that's 95 percent of what I'm worried about. When I take off down my line, I know I'm already peaking, which means I can push my limits that much further."

Jones envisioned what came to be called the "Deeper" experiment—being dropped off by a plane, far outside the helicopter permit zone.

He wanted to spend a month in remote Alaska, just a small crew living out of tents, climbing for all of their turns. It would not be easy. He knew he would need a post-graduate level education in snow science, meteorology, and mountaineering to prepare. He'd have to convince his sponsors — who were then making bank on helicopter scenes in Alaska — that the much slower process of snowboard-mountaineering would entice their audiences. And he needed a team — athletes, filmmakers, guides, etc. — willing to roll some damn uncertain dice.

It took four years to put the expedition together. By the early spring of 2009, he was finally ready. TGR had agreed to make his trip into a movie; his sponsors had agreed to foot the bill, and athletes like Travis Rice and Jonaven Moore had agreed to roll those dice. The plan was to fly to Haines, then head into Glacier Bay National Park. They would use a small plane to hunt a high cirque rising from a flat plain (where they could set up camp far outside avalanche range), pack two weeks' worth of supplies, and get dropped off. Two weeks later the plane would fly back and make a second supply drop. In the interim, they would take expedition snowboarding farther than ever before.

Big surprise — little went according to plan.

Jeremy had lived in Jackson Hole for a few years, but later migrated to the Tahoe area. Shane McConkey had become one of his best friends. Their wives were close. Their children played together. One day after arriving in Alaska, four years after he began planning the Deeper trip, Jeremy's phone rang — Shane had died in Italy. "I flew home. Shane's wife and daughters moved in with me and my wife for a couple of weeks. But I couldn't stay. All these people were depending on me. Four days later, I had to fly back to Alaska and start the trip."

Jones returned to Alaska just as the weather cleared. They used that window to location scout, eventually finding a suitable base camp some sixty miles outside of Haines. They had two days to set up that camp before Jeremy flew back to Tahoe for Shane's funeral. A day after that he was back in Alaska. "It was heavy," he says. "Deeper had been my dream for years, but after the funeral, at four-thirty in the morning, when I'm driving to the airport, the very last thing I wanted to do was head back into the mountains."

Heavier was the weather that followed Jones back to camp. A ten-day storm blew in, bringing temperatures of twenty below. Jones, stuck in a tent, had plenty of time to think about everything that had just happened. "It raised the proverbial question: Why do we do this? But I got to see up close the incredibly powerful effect Shane had on people. Most people are so afraid of dying they never live. Shane lived his life to the fullest. He lived thousands of lifetimes and changed thousands of lives. The world needs more people like Shane. And that was exactly why I was on this expedition — to push into uncharted territory, to try to experience life to the fullest, to bring a little of that back to the rest of the world."

On the eleventh day, just as they were about to run out of food, the storm cleared. Blue skies and big mountains. Before the storm, Travis Rice had started building a massive jump over a huge crevasse gap. As soon as the sun returned, he finished the project and kicked off the show. Sixty miles from nowhere, no rescue available, Rice threw an eighty-foot, cork backside 720 over the gap. From that moment on, no one looked back.

They stayed in the backcountry a month in total, along the way pushing snowboard mountaineering farther than anyone had taken it before. Throughout the whole expedition, Jeremy carried a portion of Shane's ashes. He also named a peak after him. "It's a really ascetic line," says Jeremy. "I knew that once people saw it, they would want to come ride it, and they would get that same feeling that I got, that Shane got, and when they left, they would bring a little bit of that back to the world."

THE PITFALLS AND THE PATH

In Parts One and Two of this book, we've examined the state of flow and the cutting edge of flow hacking. We've built a bridge between the extreme and the mainstream — seeing what action and adventure athletes are doing to reliably reproduce this state and how to start applying this information in our own lives. But this merely marks the beginning of a much longer trek. Thus Part Three of this book is devoted to seeing where this trail goes — it's a look at our future in flow.

For starters, our focus here is the immediate future. Our immediate future. Once you begin applying the techniques described in this book, you'll immediately start producing more flow in your life — which also means you need to be prepared for the ramifications. Flow is an alternative path toward mastery, but, like any path, not without its pitfalls. There's a serious dark side to flow, and this chapter provides a map to that minefield.

The state of flow, like the path that bears its name, is volatile, unpredictable, and all-consuming. Flow *feels* like the meaning of life for good reason. The neurochemicals that underpin the state are among the most addictive drugs on earth. Equally powerful is the psychological draw. Scientists who study human motivation have lately learned that after basic survival needs have been met, the combination of autonomy (the desire to direct your own life), mastery (the desire to learn, explore, and be creative), and purpose (the desire to matter, to contribute to the world) are our most powerful intrinsic drivers — the three things that motivate us most. All three are deeply woven through the fabric of flow. Thus toying with flow involves tinkering with primal biology: addictive neurochemistry, potent psychology, and hardwired evolutionary behaviors. Seriously, what could go wrong?

And that's part of the problem — even when everything goes right, things go wrong. Walking this path demands constantly increasing the challenges we face. We are climbing a ladder of escalating risk — with this ladder being the first of the dangers encountered on the flow path.

Continuously pushing on the challenge/skill ratio means it's scary here, and it's going to get scarier. Sooner or later, if we stay on this path long enough, pushing past one's comfort zone is going to require exceeding traditional margins for safety. As a working artist this could mean moving beyond popular tastes (see first bee-bop, later free jazz musicians, early impressionist painters, auteur filmmakers, etc.) and risking, in many cases, one's livelihood. For action and adventure athletes, of course, the consequences can be much more severe.

Take Jeremy Jones's trajectory. He chased flow from a racing career into big-mountain riding into the helicopter whirl of Alaska — upping the danger level with every step. And when helicopters proved insufficient, he decided to add mountaineering into the mix. If measuring simply by the size of the body count, on the list of ways to get dead in the extreme, mountaineering wins no contest. Seriously, if he keeps it up, what are the chances Jeremy Jones dies of natural causes?

And while there's clearly an order-of-magnitude difference between them, beyond the physical risks, Jones's relentless commitment to the path jeopardized his financial future as well. When he first took up snowboarding it was barely a sport, let alone one with a future. He devoted his teenage years to sleeping in cars and hoping an actual industry would emerge. And once it did emerge, he walked away. At the time Jones switched from competitive riding to big-mountain riding, the rest of the snowboard world was solely interested in halfpipes and flippy tricks — neither of which were then part of the big-mountain landscape. And when Jones decided to start snowboard-mountaineering, heli-riding was where all the sponsorship dollars were lodged. At each of these steps, and plenty of others in between, Jones chanced his career.

And these types of decisions are not too unusual on this path. All or nothing tends to be the kind of commitment flow demands — and it demands it of everyone. If you embark down this road, the requisite risk taking will continuously back you into uncomfortable corners. It's almost ironic. How many self-help books have been written about living with passion and purpose (i.e., traveling the flow path); yet how few actually mention the dangers involved.

Equally insidious is how flow prepares us to handle these dangers. In the state, our skills are peaking, our inner critic shut down, and our ability to feel fear significantly dampened. "I felt I could not be hurt . . . ," wrote Brazilian soccer star Pelé in his autobiography, *My Life and the Beautiful Game.* "Perhaps it was merely confidence, but I have felt confident many times before without that strange feeling of invincibility." And while Pelé's correct, there's a serious catch — flow makes you feel invincible, right up to the moment you're not. After all, Shane McConkey was the closest thing to Superman the world has yet seen and he didn't beat those odds.

Nor is he alone. "The joy I get from skiing, that's worth dying for," said C. R. Johnson — not long before he died skiing. Canadian freestyle skier and four-time X Games champ Sarah Burke is now sorely missed. So are Arne Backstrom, Caleb Moore, Jeremy Lusk, Ryan Hawks, Aaron Robinson, Kip Garre, Antoine Montant, and many more. ESPN called 2011 the "grimmest year in [action] sports' collective history," and then explained why: "[T]he action-sports community averaged one pro athlete death every three weeks." The year 2013 — while not yet in the books — is starting to look grimmer than 2011.

Does this mean we have to be willing to face mortality to chase flow? Not exactly. Flow forces you to evaluate life through a different lens. It gives you reason to live — but live this way long enough and those reasons become more important than dying. This is what the self-help books don't tell you. Fully alive and deeply committed is a risky business. Once you strip away the platitudes, a life of passion and purpose will always cost, as T. S. Eliot reminds us, "Not less than everything."

THE DARK SIDE, THE BLISS JUNKIES, AND THE QUESTION OF CONTROL

Almost everything we've just covered, however dangerous, falls under the category of that which can go wrong when *almost* everything goes right. This is what happens when we begin finding flow with regularity. But the state is unpredictable and there are no guarantees. A great many discover flow accidentally — having no idea how they got there or how to return. Still others, even those who once had easy access to the zone, may suddenly find themselves cut off from the source, trapped in a struggle phase without end. In either case, once flow becomes a lock without a key, the ramifications are soul-sucking to say the least.

"No question about it," says Flow Genome Project executive director Jamie Wheal, "there's a dark night of the flow. In Christian mystical traditions, once you've experienced the grace of God, the 'dark night of the soul' describes the incredible pain of its absence. The same is true for flow. An enormous gap sits between the ecstasy of the zone and the all-too-familiar daily toil waiting for us on the other end. If you've glimpsed this state, but can't get back there — that lack can become unbearable."

Even those familiar with flow can go through long stretches where the state becomes inaccessible. The struggle can last weeks, months, occasionally years. As climber Dean Potter explains, these periods are true trial by fire: "When I feel that really draining side of not being able to enter into the flow, it's horrible. I feel helpless, lethargic, restless, disturbed. The positive here is I hate that feeling so much it makes me more focused. I take all the necessary steps to get out of it as soon as I can. Sometimes, though, I end up sunk in a really bad place. True depression, trapped for quite some time. But even here there's an upside. At those times, doing anything hurts so much, I can only do what truly inspires me. Otherwise, I have no power. This allows me to lock onto ideas that are authentically mine — so the dark side of flow, for all its torment, keeps me being exactly who I am."

Potter, at least, has the ability to find his way to the other side. What about the college lacrosse star who graduates into a job as an accountant, much needed to feed her family, but not a territory nearly as rich in flow triggers as competitive, high-contact sports? The one-time drummer now working as a stockbroker? The mother of three who used to do some sculpture when she was younger but now has no time for herself? As professional big-wave surfer turned filmmaker, cattle rancher, and Patagonia Ocean Ambassador Chris Malloy pointed out in an e-mail to me, sometimes being cut off from the source simply means growing older:

> I hope you talk a little about how utterly fucked we can become when we get too old or broken or smart to keep it up. Not all of us experience a happy life after doing this shit for a couple of decades. I bet there are some PTSD similarities. It's funny, I read Sebastian Jungers's *War* and I learned something: The guys coming home are all screwed up, not because they saw people die as much as they missed the rush. I would never put myself in the same category as those fighting men, but it can be hard to get excited again. Ever. And that feeling sucks.

And the dark night of flow is an issue that society has not made particularly easy to handle. How many people have stopped playing guitar, writing poetry, or painting watercolors — activities packed with flow triggers — because these are also activities that do not squarely fit into culturally acceptable responsibility categories like "career" or "children"? How many, now grown up and done with childish things, have put away the surfboard, the skateboard, the whatever? How many have made the mistake of conflating the value of the vehicle that leads us to an experience (the surfboard, etc.) with the value of the experience itself (the flow state)?

What's painfully ironic here is that flow is a radical and alternative path to mastery *only* because we have decided that play— an activity fundamental to survival, tied to the greatest neurochemical rewards the brain can produce, and flat out necessary for achieving peak performance, creative brilliance, and overall life satisfaction — is a waste of time for adults. If we are hunting the highest version of ourselves, then we need to turn work into play and not the other way round. Unless we invert this equation, much of our capacity for intrinsic motivation starts to shut down. We lose touch with our passion and become less than what we could be and that feeling never really goes away.

The dark night of the flow happens when people glimpse the state and can't get back there, but another issue arises when people are getting into flow, yet misinterpreting its meaning. The automatic nature of the state — how every decision, every action, leads seamlessly to the next — lays a different kind of trap: it can turn flow junkies into bliss junkies. "Bliss junkies are people who think the magical ease of the flow state is the goal," says Wheal. "When they confront the difficulty of the day to day, they'd rather reach for a pill or a new lover or another meditation retreat than get down to hard work. The idea being, if it was all so easy, clear, and effortless in flow, then why not wait for the next wave to hit? Not being in flow becomes an excuse to stay listless and undermotivated."

We don't have to look far for examples. Think of rave culture or the new age movement or just about any holdover hippie community or — for that matter — almost every ski or surf town in the world. And when listless and undermotivated, bliss junkies often turn to drugs, alcohol, gambling, sex, and other high-risk behaviors to mask the pain of flow's loss or to hasten its return.

And these issues are only part of this picture. In this accounting of flow's dark side, the categories we've so far examined — the escalating ladder of risk, the dark night of the flow, and the meaning miscalculations of the bliss junky — are all personal and psychological, but there are also cultural issues to consider, namely, the questions of whether flow can be corrupted or controlled.

Neither question is easy to answer. Corruption is problematic because flow increases empathy and social bonding, but that doesn't mean pickup artists or pickpockets can't co-opt the state to further their craft. Along similar lines, no one knows if flow can be used to train super soldiers, but the US Defense Department seems committed to finding out. Most of the high-performance scientists in this book work with both athletes and the military. Red Bull, for example, has teamed up with the Navy SEALs. DARPA funds flow research (the aforementioned sniper study). Whether this is a good thing or a bad thing depends on one's trust in government and feelings for nation-states, but it doesn't take much to imagine how this experiment could go wrong.

On a slightly different scale, society likes to pay for performance and flow definitely improves performance. In action and adventure sports, for example, flow's escalating ladder of risk — once cause for marginalization — now supports an entire industry. And these supporters want footage. Thus athletes on a heli-ski film shoot (who used their ability to get into flow to get that job) can't back away from a run just because they're not feeling the flow — not if they want to continue to have a career.

These economic pressures are pushing people past their challenge/skill sweet spot and with the expected results. Squaw Valley psychiatrist Dr. Robb Gaffney (Scott's brother, who McConkey once called the best "nonpro" skier in the world) recently told NBC Sports, "All my friends who have been lost were the best at what they did. Worldwide. And yet we still lost them. . . . I do see corporate sponsorship as a big player here. They're making a lot of money. They've tapped into a reward center in the brain, the thrill-seekers are going for it, the culture's enthralled with it. It's a money-making machine."

Now, certainly, not all of us face such dire consequences in our chosen professions, but this doesn't solve the problem. Even in less extreme work lives, once we start accessing flow with regularity, performance will dramatically improve and new expectations will follow. Those added expectations will push the difficulty level up a few notches, and this extra psychological burden can easily send us past the challenge/skill sweet spot, rendering us unable to access the very state we need to meet those new expectations.

The second issue here is whether flow can be controlled. Doubtful. In technological terms, a "disruptive technology" is any innovation that creates a new market and new values and eventually displaces an old market and older values. Cars replacing horse-drawn carriages is the classic example. Flow is also a very disruptive technology. Unlike the automobile, it's not a disruptive "external" technology, but a disruptive "internal" technology, operating in the psychological rather than the physical world. This does not make it any less potent. The athletes in this book harnessed the state to displace traditional markets (today, top jocks are just as likely to skateboard as play football), alter our value system (our societal tolerance for and reward of high-risk behavior has seriously increased), and reshape culture (a $750 billion lifestyle industry). Thus the rub: Flow, like all technologies, remains morally neutral. It can be used for good or ill or both at the same time.

In esoteric terms, flow's tendency toward disruption is the reason it could be considered a "left-hand path." A "right-hand path" is a path of orthodoxy. It's cut, dry, and filled with "thou shalt nots." On a right-hand path, we follow the rules and do what we're told and no questions asked. This may sound dull, but right-hand paths have a very long history of keeping us safe. A "left-hand path," meanwhile, is an ecstatic path and mostly gray. It's little guidance and less security. Lao Tzu, founder of Taoism, warned that a left-hand path is best never begun, and once begun, must absolutely be finished.

But how to finish such a path? We have a vast gap in our knowledge. Our society has spent centuries waging war against torment. When we are depressed, we know how to fight for happiness. When we are ill, we have guidebooks toward health. When we are loveless, jobless, hopeless, not smart enough, not skilled enough, not good enough, we now have colossal industries and institutions designed to teach us to strive and seek. We have become really good at negotiating with darkness, for certain, but how much do we really know about the light?

How much do we really know about true happiness? Burning creativity? Unbridled ecstasy? As children we are taught *not* to play with fire, not *how* to play with fire. On the flow path, we are drawn forward by fire; by powerful hedonic instincts; by our deep need for autonomy, mastery, and purpose deeply fulfilled; by dizzyingly feel-good neurochemistry; by a spectrum of joy beyond common ken; by the undeniable presence of our most authentic selves; by a cognitive imperative to make meaning from experience; by the search engine that is evolution and *its* need for innovation; and by the simplest of truths: life is long and we're all scared and, in flow, at least for a little while, we're not.

TRAVIS RICE AND THE ART OF FLIGHT

A few years after *Deeper,* Travis Rice embarked on his own film project, the appropriately named *Art of Flight.* While Jeremy Jones's goal in *Deeper* had been the far frontier of snowboarding exploration, in *Flight* Rice wanted to showcase the far frontier of athletic performance — the very cutting edge of snowboarding possibility. Of course, Jones joined him for part of the trip. Of course, they went to hunt for spines.

A very short history of paradigm shifts in big-mountain riding. Early days: lots of turns, just trying to survive the steeps. Next phase: turns are for sissies, straight-lining the steeps. Then cliffs get added into the mix; big cliffs soon follow. Next athletes started doing park tricks off cliffs, then off big cliffs. And then, for good measure, spines entered the picture.

A "cirque" is a naturally formed concave amphitheater, carved by glaciers, found atop mountains. These steep slopes are dotted with protrusions — huge cliffs, knobby rollovers, bus-size boulders. Snow piles up on these protrusions, forming near-vertical, knife-edge columns, thousands of feet tall — these are spines.

And for flow junkies, spines are irresistible.

"It's full-body snowboarding," explains Jones. "The snow is so deep you need to use your arms and chest to swim, and your legs to ride. They also collapse underfoot, so you're riding mini-avalanches and dodging slough slides. Spines have blind rollovers, so you can't see below. Or to the side. Every time the midline is crossed, it's a leap into the abyss. Plus, there's no way to stop and every move is amplified by complicated forces. A tiny hop can easily become a twenty-foot ollie. It's the absolute edge of chaos. But the easiest way to live in the moment is to put yourself in a situation where there's no other choice. Spines demand that, they hurl you deep into the zone."

Jones and Rice went spine hunting in the Selkirk Mountains, outside of Revelstoke, British Columbia. Time schedules being what they were, they only had a few days together. And their first morning turned out to be frustrating. The weather was iffy, the visibility poor. They searched for hours and hours and still nothing to ride. A decision was made to park the helicopter on a mountaintop and regroup. Then a small miracle: no sooner had they landed than a break in the clouds, and off in the distance, a spine wall.

They flew to the top of the wall and climbed out. That's when one of the guides glanced across the valley and realized they were standing on the peak exactly opposite from where snowboarding legend Craig Kelly died. This struck everyone as more than a coincidence.

"Kelly was the pioneer," explains Rice. "He tore apart the fabric of how things were done in snowboarding. He was the first guy to prove you could make a living riding in the backcountry. He did all these absolutely incredible things and then decided to become a Canadian Certified Mountain Guide, which is the highest level of certification, and the hardest to get in the world. For decades, it's been a skier's-only club, but Craig was trying to become the first guide certified on a snowboard. He died on an avalanche certification trip. Fast-forward eight years, and we're standing on this giant face directly across where he died. It was powerful."

And there's an important truth hidden in that power. Action and adventure athletes have found a way to turn the worst thing that can happen on the flow path into another reason to move forward. Frank Gambalie died and Shane McConkey and Miles Daisher honored his memory by diving deeper into skydiving; Shane McConkey died and Jeremy Jones carried his ashes into the uncharted unknown. There's long tradition here — the tradition of honoring someone who has died trying to live their life to the fullest by, in turn, living your own life to the fullest.

Of course, there's a little more to the tradition than this. For starters, as Rice points out, every death brings a lesson: "Action and adventure athletes lead different kinds of lives. There aren't exactly playbooks. So the best athletes try really hard to learn from each other's mistakes, especially the fatal ones. I just lost a friend in Japan — the party got him. That was one kind of wake-up call. Craig's death was another.

There the lesson was even more complicated. The people he was with had the very best knowledge of snow science in the world — but he still died. So, sometimes, the more you know, the less you know. Sometimes, not knowing makes you more hesitant and that can help keep you alive."

Equally important is the metaphysical. "I've had incredibly profound experiences doing what I do," explains Rice. "And I'm a very different person because of it. I didn't come from a religious background. Growing up, everything was proof-driven. If you couldn't see it, couldn't experience it, it didn't exist. But I've had experiences that bitch-slapped me out of this lower-order mentality. My need for proof — I've been given it. Now, if you want to tell me that God doesn't exist, well, now you have to prove that to me."

And by proof, Rice is talking about the experience of oneness that arrives in deep flow. "At the root of all fear is separation" he says. "That's especially true for mortal fears. But in flow, that's gone completely. It's the most comforting truth — that there's no separation, no death. So when you talk about the tradition of honoring fallen comrades by pushing harder, we'll most of us have had these spiritual experiences, so part of that tradition involves this other invisible legacy — this shared exploration of the mystery."

So what does this all mean? It means that beyond pushing on physical limits, these athletes are also pushing on more nebulous boundaries. It means that at the center of the action and adventure brotherhood there's a bit of a mystery cult. It means, as it always has, that if you want to probe the mystery, sacrifice is required.

In simpler terms, these athletes have taken the radical step of turning mortality into motivation and have fundamentally rearranged their lives and their values to accommodate this change. In the last chapter, we saw hints of this shift with athletes willing to bet their asses on an idea. Here — in perhaps the surest sign of a culture of innovation — we're seeing a social extension of this same principle: when innovation leads to death, powerful tradition ensures that death leads to more innovation.

Is there a lesson here for the rest of us? Of course. There's no way to avoid the dark side of flow. Athletes hit walls, writers run into writer's block; executives overcommit and burn out. And the key that Rice and others have found is to embrace that suffering, to move through it, and to keep moving. This means learning to use the bad to fuel the good. The way Dean Potter leveraged the pain of flow's absence to drive himself closer to his most authentic self is a small example, the way the entire action and adventure community honors the dead with the death-defying a larger one.

And this is exactly what happened that day in British Columbia. Travis Rice and Jeremy Jones rode in tribute to Craig Kelly's memory. It was quite a tribute. First, Jones nailed one of the better spine rides of his career; then Rice changed the game.

The spine that Rice picked out included everything that Jones's choice featured: blind rollovers, tight chutes, huge slough, crazy exposure, and big drops, but it also included some acrobatics. Two-thirds of the way down, doing fifty-mile-per-hour hop-turns down the pointy edge of ridiculous, Rice launched off a sixty-foot cliff, spun a perfect backside 180, then landed atop another spine. It was straight out of a video game, our first glimpse of the next frontier. Watching from the bottom of the run, Jones just shook his head. "You've got to be kidding me," he said. "That is the future and the future is now."

11

The Flow of Next

In the last chapter, we took a hard look at the difficulties involved in pursuing the flow path, in this one our interest is in examining the inverse: the reasons to persevere. And the very best reason? No surprise. It's what happens when we do.

For most people, flow hacking is an esoteric pursuit. But these days, in action and adventure sports, it's become standard operating procedure. In this world, learning how to access the zone is treated like learning to read or ride a bike — it's information so fundamental it's being passed down between generations. So taking a closer look at the next generation of action and adventure athletes gives us a look at what might actually be possible for all of us, if we can make flow central to culture.

This next generation of athletes makes for an unusual case study. The extremists who came before them — the Shane McConkey–Danny Way–Laird Hamilton generation who inform the majority this book — all started out as part of a marginalized subculture with little societal support and almost no knowledge of flow. Every pinnacle they climbed, they climbed the hard way.

The athletes we're about to meet have had an almost opposite experience. They're the only generation in history to have been raised in a flow-hacking tradition, a high-flow environment, and a culture where using flow to push past impossible is par for the course. They are, to borrow the Silicon Valley term, *fast followers*. And by examining how fast and how far these followers have come, we can better gauge what just might be possible for ourselves and our children.

Even better, we are now at the front edge of a high-tech, high-performance revolution. While the athletes of the last generation had to make up their training regimens as they went along, today's practitioners are benefiting from an inrush of techniques and technologies that make accessing flow and using the state to accelerate progression far easier than ever before. Right now, these tools are mainly available to elite performers — like the next-generation athletes described in this chapter — but this too is starting to change. Thus, taking a look at these tools, seeing both where they're at today and where they'll be tomorrow, gives us another barometer for our own future potential and yet another reason to persevere.

TOM SCHAAR AND THE CHILDREN OF THE REVOLUTION

If there was a moment in time when the accelerated progression in action and adventure sports first pierced public consciousness, it was June 27, 1999. The X Games were in San Francisco, more than 275,000 people in attendance and another 55 million watching on TV. This was also the first full professional sporting event broadcast live on the Internet, so between traditional audiences, net viewers, and those who watched Web videos after the fact — a figure arguably over a 100 million — this moment marked a historic anomaly: one of the few times that so many got to see impossible become possible.

The impossible in question took place during the final round of skateboarding's Best Trick competition. Tony Hawk was squaring off against Bob Burnquist, Bucky Lasek, Colin McKay, and Andy Macdonald. On his first run, Hawk landed a varial 720 — meaning he rode up the ramp backward, launched into the air, spun around twice, then flipped his board 180 degrees, landing forward with his board now facing backward. It was a hell of a trick, perhaps not enough to win — everyone was throwing down hard that night — but all Hawk had prepared. The fact that he nailed it on his first run left him fifteen minutes of contest time to try whatever the hell he wanted. And what he wanted was the 900.

The 900 was the great impossible of skate: two and a half rotations. It required massive amplitude and dizzying commitment. The landing's mostly blind, the falls terrifying. Hawk had then been chasing the trick for thirteen painful years. Never had he pulled one off. Nor had anyone else (though Danny Way came exceptionally close in 1989). And honestly, at the X Games, Hawk didn't think he was going to break that losing streak, but with the crowd all amped up, his original intention was to just put on a show.

It was a show, all right. Hawk missed on his first attempt, but something was different — the spins felt more solid than ever before — and he made a decision: either he nailed the trick or ended the night in the hospital. "Everything blanked out except the 9," Hawk later wrote in his autobiography *Occupation: Skateboarder*. "The announcer's voice occasionally drifted into my head, telling me my time was up, that this was my last try, but there was no way I was about to stop when the 9s felt that good. . . . I don't recall walking up the ramp after each attempt. All I thought about was getting a good look in the middle of the spin so I could spot a landing. I'd just drop in, spin, fall, get up, and walk up the ramp over and over again. Everyone else had stopped skating. I remember thinking since the time limit was up I wasn't going to win the best trick with the 9, but it wasn't about the contest."

As the saying goes: the twelfth time was the charm. Hawk, finally, nailed the 900. While he didn't exactly stomp the landing — he came down in a squat, nearly dragging his back hand on the ramp — he'd pulled it off all the same. The crowd went nuts. The real world as well. Major papers ran headlines featuring Hawk's name. Every skater on the planet heard the news or, that is, almost every skater. Tom Schaar didn't hear the news. Then again, when Tony landed his nine, Tom wasn't yet born.

Schaar was born three months later, on September 14, 1999, a tow-headed kid from Malibu, California. He started skating by the time he was five years old. By the time he was nine, he was attempting 540s (one and a half rotations). This alone is unfathomable. For an entire generation of skaters, the 540 was the dividing line. "I remember thinking," explains Rodney Mullens in *Bones Brigade*, about the first time he saw the trick, "that right there, that was neck-breaking material." And once Mike McGill landed that first 540, all other pros faced a hard choice: either learn the move or quit the game. More than a few retired. Tom Schaar, though, learned the move in under a year, landing his first 540 at just ten years old.

Schaar landed his first 720 at age ten as well. That was also the year he rode down the MegaRamp for the first time. The MegaRamp gave him ideas. With all that height, with all that speed, maybe, he thought, he should give the 900 a try. It was a slightly ridiculous notion. Only six other people beside Hawk had landed the trick. Schaar was twelve years old when he decided to give it a try. Three months later he had the move down — and he was still only twelve years old.

This was about the time Schaar started thinking about the 1080 — a full three rotations, a trick no one else in the world had ever done. He decided to start working on it at Woodward, the California-based action sports camp for kids and one of only two places in the world that houses a publicly accessible MegaRamp. Schaar is five-one and ninety-four pounds — essentially the Kate Moss of skateboarding, only shorter — and the Woodward ramp proved too big for his needs. The gap jump was giving him too much speed, and he was sailing too high out of the quarterpipe for the spins to be controllable. Red Bull stepped in next. They paid for a new section of ramp, turning the gap into a rollover and allowing Schaar to dampen acceleration. That was all it took. In March 2012, and on only his fifth try, Tom Schaar landed the world's first 1080. Afterward, he told reporters: "I can't believe I can do something Tony Hawk can't." He was still only twelve years old.

Schaar's success turned him into a rock star. It also earned him an invitation to the 2012 X Games Asia, where he used the 1080 to beat out eleven-time X Games gold medalist Bob Burnquist in the Big Air finals, becoming (still at twelve) the youngest X Games gold medalist in history. He was also invited to compete against the far stiffer competition at the 2012 Summer X Games North America. Making this tale that much stranger, Schaar wasn't the only one in his age bracket to receive such an invitation. "There are about ten of us really young kids doing the contests," he explains. "It's crazy. We get to skate with these people we always looked up to."

And they get to beat them too. At Summer X, Schaar himself placed sixth, but fifteen-year-old Mitchie Brusco (in his second X Games competition) took home Big Air silver with a 720 jump over the gap and 900 off the quarterpipe. And how did he pull off two of skating's hardest tricks on the biggest stage in the sport?

"I try not to think about anything," Brusco said in a post-victory interview, "I just try to let my body do the work. My body knows how to do it better than my brain so I kind of just let it take over." Which is to say, this new generation of action and adventure athletes are already a generation of flow hackers. Even Schaar, at twelve, is starting to understand the concepts: "When I'm trying a trick," he says, "I try to block everything else out. I just try to stay calm and focused on what I'm doing." This may not sound like much, but many of the athletes interviewed for this book talk about not starting to experiment with the mental game until later in their career, and usually only after being forced in that direction by injury.

It comes down to cultural learning. Danny Way, Laird Hamilton, Dean Potter, Shane McConkey, Mandy Rae Cruickshank, Jeremy Jones, Doug Ammons — these athletes were pioneers. Trailblazers into the impossible. Tom Schaar and his fellow youngsters are the children of this revolution. Schaar was born into a world where the 900 was a done deal; he was eight years old when Danny Way jumped the Great Wall of China on a MegaRamp. As a result, both his baseline for reality and his spectrum for possibility are a quantum leap forward from almost anything anyone born in the twentieth century can imagine.

This matters.

Flow is a creation engine: it helps us pluck an idea out of imagination and bring it fully formed into the world. Tom Schaar dreamed up the 1080, then used flow to pull that vision out of his subconscious and into a material existence. There is a deep interrelationship here. Our limits are governed by flow's ability to amplify performance as much as by imagination's ability to dream up that performance. So asking the question "Where do our limits lie?" is another way of asking, "How far can we stretch our imagination?"

Here in the twenty-first century, pretty far indeed.

THE ROGER BANNISTER EFFECT

No one really knows exactly when the four-minute mile first seemed possible. Certainly, in 1923, when Finnish runner Paavo Numi clocked a 4:10.4, it wasn't beyond the pale. Yet eight years passed before anyone sliced a second from Numi's time, and it took ten more for the next three to fall. By 1942, runners had cut it down to 4:04.6; then 4:02.6 by 1943. Two years later, Swedish miler Gunder Hagg clocked 4:01.4 and impossible seemed within reach. A good tailwind, a better track surface, slicing one tick off the time — it was bound to happen.

But nothing happened.

Not in 1946. Or 1947. Or 1948. The issue, turns out, wasn't merely physical. It was mental. "Most people considered running four laps of the track in four minutes to be beyond the limits of human speed," explains Neal Bascomb in *The Perfect Mile*. "It was foolhardy and possibly dangerous to attempt. Some thought that rather than a lifetime of glory, honor and fortune, a hearse would be waiting for the first person to accomplish that feat."

It was Englishman Roger Bannister who — *nine* years after Hagg's near miss — finally broke this mental barrier and accomplished the feat, running 3:59.4 on May 6, 1954. And when we retell this tale, this is typically the point where the story stops, yet two months after Bannister did the impossible and lived, Australian John Landy did it again and then some — cutting 1.4 seconds off Bannister's time with 3:58 flat. Within five years two other runners had bested that mark; within ten the first sub-four mile had been run by a high school student. Think about this for a moment. Thirty years of collective running effort were required to do the impossible, yet it took less than a month for someone to better the feat? And less than a decade for five more people — including a teenager — to do the same?

How did this happen? The physical challenge didn't get any easier. Running a sub-four-minute mile still required running a sub-four-minute mile. All that changed was thought, assumption, the mental frame built around the challenge. Every athlete interviewed for this book agrees: after something has been done once, it becomes considerably easier to repeat. Yet why is this so? What is it, exactly, about learning that the impossible is possible that makes it suddenly possible?

It's a two part question. The first part concerns the relationship between imagination and physical possibility, what could be called the "Roger Bannister effect." The second part concerns, and especially when discussing this younger generation of extreme athletes, all the other forces amplifying this relationship. We'll take them one at a time.

"If you want to understand the Bannister effect," says high-performance psychologist Michael Gervais, "you have to understand that the brain tells stories. When most hear about an impossible feat — the sub-four-minute mile; the MegaRamp 1080 — our first reaction is: 'Not real, no way, not possible.' But we have a strong need to make meaning out of experience and this new reality forces us to change our story. We move to, 'That's crazy, far out, unreal.' Pretty soon, we accept this new reality and shift our paradigm further and this engages imagination. We start imagining the impossible as possible. What does impossible feel like, sound like, look like. And then we start to be able to see ourselves doing the impossible — that's the secret. There is an extremely tight link between our visual system and our physiology: once we can actually see ourselves doing the impossible, our chances of pulling it off increase significantly."

It was Harvard physiologist Edmund Jacobson who first discovered this link. Back in the 1930s, Jacobson found that imagining oneself lifting an object triggered corresponding electrical activity in the muscles involved in the lift. Between then and now dozens and dozens of studies have born this out, repeatedly finding strong correlations between mental rehearsal — i.e., visualization — and better performance. Everything from giving a speech to running a business meeting to spinning a 1080 are all significantly enhanced by the practice.

We also know that the benefits extend beyond the psychological (increased confidence and motivation) and into the physiological. In 2004, for example, Cleveland Clinic physiologist Guang Yue wanted to know if merely thinking about lifting weights was enough to increase strength. Study subjects were divided into four groups. One group tried to strengthen their finger muscles with physical exercise; one tried to strengthen their finger muscles by only visualizing the exercise; another tried to increase arm strength through visualization; while the last group did nothing at all. The trial lasted twelve weeks. When it was over, those who did nothing saw no gains. The group that relied on physical training saw the greatest increase in strength — at 53 percent. But it's the mental groups where things got curious. Folks who did no physical training but merely imagined their fingers going through precise exercise motions saw a 35 percent increase in strength, while the ones who visualized arm exercises saw a 13.5 percent increase in strength. How tightly are imagination and physiology coupled? Strength is among the most baseline of all performance measures and we humans can get stronger simply by thinking hard about it.

Probably the biggest insight arrived a few years before Yue's experiment, when neuroscientists found no difference between performing an action and merely imagining oneself performing that action — the same neuronal circuits fire in either case. This means that visualization impacts a slew of cognitive processes — motor control, memory, attention, perception, planning — essentially accelerating chunking by shortening the time it takes us to learn new patterns. Since the first stage of the flow cycle — the struggle stage — involves exactly this learning process, visualization is an essential flow hack: it shortens struggle.

Visualization also firms up aims and objectives, further amplifying flow. With an image of perfect performance fixed in our mind, the intrinsic system knows what needs to happens, keeping the extrinsic system from getting too involved. Similarly, when attempting something that's never been done before, we're much more likely to keep fear at bay and stay in the challenge/skill sweet spot if we've mentally rehearsed an action ahead of time.

What all this means is that learning the impossible is possible augments our ability to see ourselves doing the impossible, which triggers a systemic change in the body and the brain, which closes the gap between fantasy and reality. It also makes us significantly more flow prone. So when we do actually execute on our vision — i.e., attempt the impossible — we're far more likely to find ourselves in the zone during that attempt and far more likely to perform properly as a result.

So what does this have to do with today's extreme athletes? Plenty. Not only have the children of this revolution been born into a world where the foundational imaginal work has already been done — Tom Schaar didn't have to dream up the MegaRamp before he threw that 1080 — they've also benefited from the arrival of psychology and technology in action and adventure sports. "When I was starting out," says freestyle motocross great Travis Pastrana, "there were no coaches, no real training facilities. There was barely a sport." Tom Schaar, meanwhile, has coaches. He has trampoline rooms and foam pits and all sorts of high-tech equipment to train his body. And his mind. Schaar's been practicing visualization since the age of ten and had a working knowledge of flow at twelve.

And when it comes to applying this information in our lives, especially if we're interested in the kinds of accelerated performance showing up in action and adventure sports, there appears to be considerable benefit to starting young. "When you're talking about this next generation of athletes," says high-performance expert Dr. Leslie Sherlin (who we met back in Chapter Two), "their lack of age helps a great deal. They're too young to know what impossible means. Can you do something? Who knows? Let me go try. And they're too young to know what to be afraid of (Schaar, for example, has never had a serious injury). Plus, their brains aren't completely developed so there's less frontal lobe engagement. Long-term planning, critical thinking, a lot of these things aren't fully online."

As we learned earlier, one of the causes of flow is transient hypofrontality — the shutting down of large swatches of the prefrontal cortex. Children, as Sherlin pointed out, are *developmentally hypofrontal* — meaning portions of their neocortex are not fully formed (the brain keeps developing until age twenty-five) and this makes them even more flow prone. "More than that," he continues, "EEG studies of adolescents show their normal brain-wave pattern is much closer to the alpha wave/theta wave borderline that is baseline flow. No direct research has been done, but it looks like they're hovering on the edge of the state much of the time."

Putting flow-prone kids into high-flow environments means a lot of flow. Arming them with advanced flow-hacking techniques means even more. All this flow makes the activity deeply rewarding, both fulfilling a child's innate need for autonomy, mastery, and purpose and further increasing their sense of intrinsic motivation. When Tom

Schaar says, "I love being with my friends at the skate park — that's the greatest feeling," what he's saying is no one has to force him to practice, the autotelic nature of the activity — the fact that it drives him into flow — is the source code of his motivation.

But it's not just Tom Schaar. In fact, when it comes to examples of the accelerated progression that results from raising children in high-flow environments, we can look much closer to home: in the classrooms, gardens, and playgrounds of Montessori schools the world over. While exploring the threads of his seminal research on flow, Mihaly Csikszentmihalyi and his graduate students went on a quest to find the most "flow-prone" learning environments around. Montessori topped the list.

The educational philosophy pioneered by Maria Montessori in the early portion of the twentieth century is built around self-directed learning, long periods of intense concentration, and deep physicality (it's often called "embodied education") and has been repeatedly shown to produce far greater amounts of flow than more traditional methodologies. The results? While the data is still far from complete, a 2006 study published in the journal *Science* by University of Virginia psychologist Angeline Lillard found Montessori kids outperformed regular students on everything from academic tests to social skills to creative abilities to executive function. Other studies have extended these findings from the classroom to the boardroom. When professors Jeffrey Dyer of Brigham Young University and Hal Gregersen of the globe-spanning business school INSEAD surveyed over 3,000 executives and interviewed 500 people who had either started innovative companies or invented new products, they too found a Montessori connection. As Gregersen told the *Wall Street Journal:* "A number of the innovative entrepreneurs also went to Montessori schools, where they learned to follow their curiosity. To paraphrase the famous Apple ad campaign, innovators not only learned early on to think different, they act different (and even talk different)."

So if we take this next generation of action and adventure athletes as our test case, you've got to wonder: If Tom Schaar, raised in a high-flow environment, was able to best Tony Hawk by the age of twelve, what flow-hacking, Montessori-educated kid is now taking aim at Larry Page and Sergey Brin's achievements? And what are the very real possibilities for the rest of us? What happens when the source code of ultimate human performance becomes a cornerstone of education? When flow becomes central to culture? When achieving the impossible becomes par for the course? Hard to say for certain. But as Rainer Maria Rilke said, "Live the questions." And seriously, knowing what we already know about flow, who doesn't want to live these questions?

FLOW-HACKING TECHNOLOGIES

One idea central to this book is the ever familiar *knowledge is power*. If flow underpins optimal performance, then knowing the causes of flow — both where it comes from and why it comes — can help us achieve optimal performance more frequently. If we go one level deeper into this relationship, we'll get to the lineage of technology that supports this knowing. Thus, if we want to understand what's possible for the next generation of athletes — or, for that matter, for anyone interested in harnessing this state to improve performance — we also need to understand the revolution that technology is now bringing to flow research.

"Go back to Roger Bannister's time and the most sophisticated equipment we had was a stopwatch," says Michael Gervais. "Knowing how long it takes someone to do something is useful, but it's still a gross metric that explains little about the why. The stopwatch told us Bannister ran a sub four mile, yet we learned nothing about how he did it or how we could do it. But between then and now there have been six or seven measurement milestones. We moved from gross physical measures to more precise bio-data, from invasive bio-data procedures to noninvasive procedures. Until you get to where we are today — able to measure and quantify ATP (adenosine triphosphate — essentially cellular energy) levels in real time. This means that our ability to stalk elite performance has undergone a sea change."

As has our ability to stalk flow. In the 1990s, magnetic resonance imaging (MRI), which had been primarily used to study the body, gave way to functional magnetic resonance imaging (fMRI), which measures blood-flow activity in the brain. At Johns Hopkins, it was this technique that allowed Charles Limb to scan the brains of improv jazz musicians during flow — providing our first images of transient hypofrontality in action. At Emory, it was fMRI that helped Greg Berns map the dopamine system's relationship to flow triggers like risk and novelty. At Baylor, it was David Eagleman and time dilation. And this list goes on.

Neural feedback — the use of EEG to train performance — has undergone a similar transformation. Dr. Leslie Sherlin and his colleagues at Neurotopia, to offer one example, have developed an EEG-based system called "BrainSport" that, unlike earlier EEG systems, uses advanced hardware and sophisticated software to filter out extraneous noise. As of now, it can record the neuroelectrical activity of a golfer making a putt, a ballplayer swinging a bat, or a speaker giving a talk. Devices capable of working in action and adventure sports' environments are only a year or two away (Travis Pastrana is putting an early iteration through its paces). Even better, BrainSport is portable and simple to use. "The idea was to develop a robust neural-feedback system that works for everyone," says Sherlin. "People no longer have to come to the lab, get tons of sensors attached, and destroy their normal routines. A football player on the flight home after a game; a businessman about to enter a meeting; a housewife with a half-hour before the kids come home. They just put on the headset and start training."

Concurrently, a revolution in sensors, batteries, and connectivity has led to a flood of "quantified self" devices such as Nike Fuel band, Jawbone's UP, and the Basis Band. These wearable gadgets monitor an expansive array of biometrics, most of which can be used to hunt flow. And there are iPhone apps that do the same. We can now track cardiac coherence — when brain waves and heart waves synch up — which has been correlated with the state (but needs more research). Other apps let skiers and snowboarders calculate speed, helping them both dial in their challenge/skill ratio and pin down the exact miles per hour that trips their novelty and risk flow triggers.

At the Flow Genome Project we're taking advantage of both of these lines of development to build a series of dedicated flow research labs — a.k.a. Flow Dojos. Think Cirque du Soleil meets X Games meets the Science Exploratorium. The goal is to simulate all of the high-risk conditions that extreme performers rely upon to trigger flow — just without the risk. Our equipment is of the extreme playground variety, like a giant looping swing that lets almost anyone be *safely* upside down and twenty-five feet off the ground at the top of the loop, and pulling over three and half Gs at the bottom — which is enough risk and novelty to push most into flow.

Moreover, the swing is lined with LED lights that are connected to sensors like BrainSport. The closer a rider comes to the theta/alpha brain-wave border of baseline flow, the redder the lights turn. This allows the trainee to use real-time neurofeedback without having to break state to look at a data screen. Of course, with all these sensors, we're also data capturing along the way, and using this information to construct a more accurate "heat map of flow" — a map that will fine-tune our knowledge of the state and its triggers and thus provide everyone with easier access to the zone.

And ours is only one approach. There are many more, and from dozens of angles. But that's not even the half of it. Alongside these technological developments increasing our in-the-moment access to flow, there's also an entirely different line of development increasing the total amount of time we can stay in the flow-hacking game. Welcome to the world of bionics.

Hugh Herr, the head of the biomechatronics research group at MIT's Media Lab, is at the forefront of this world. He's already built the Rheo knee and the iWalk BiOM ankle, the world's first two artificially intelligent prosthetics. Both of these devices mimic natural movement patterns, are capable of learning (so they adjust to the user's gait and not the other way round), and were named Inventions of the Year by *Time* magazine (the Rheo in 2004, the BiOM in 2007). How durable and dynamic are these devices? The BiOM (the more sophisticated of the two) is already being worn by amputee soldiers returning to active duty.

But prosthetics for amputee soldiers are just the beginning. Herr has also designed the world's first true bionic exoskeleton, a revolutionary knee brace for able-bodied people that should be commercially available by 2015. "Right now," Herr says, "one of the worst parts of growing old is losing the ability to move around. So imagine taking the bionics in the BiOM and turning it into a strap-on device, something that can restore strength and function to the elderly or anyone with a bum knee."

Most of the athletes interviewed for this book didn't start exploring flow until their late twenties or early thirties, and none feel they have come close to utilizing the state's full potential. Unfortunately, as flow explorer skills improve over time, our physical abilities head in the opposite direction. But not for long. Herr's bionic knee brace can extend all of our athletic careers for years, possibly decades. And it's only the first in a torrent of biological enhancement possibilities now in the pipeline.

The standard metric for describing exponential growth rates in technology is Moore's law—the fact that the number of transistors on an integrated circuit doubles every twelve to twenty-four months while the price remains the same. Moore's law is the reason why today's smartphones are a thousand times faster and a million times cheaper than a supercomputer from the 1970s. Meanwhile, biotechnology—the category that underpins exoskeletons and other enhancement technologies—is currently accelerating at five times the speed of Moore's Law.

What is the adjacent possible for strap-on bionics? What promise do exoskeletons hold for the future of progression? What about flow hacking? Until recently, older and wiser meant creakier and slower. But with biotechnology expanding at an exponential rate, we can now refresh the physical line of development, while our cognitive and creative lines continue to grow. For the first time in history, anyone looking to push the upper edge of human performance will be able to combine the wisdom of the decades with the sprightliness of youth. So again, where do our limits lie?

"I'm certain we can't answer that question," says Michael Gervais. "At the world-class level, where talent differences are marginal, we estimate that 90 percent of success for elite performers is mental—yet this is the one measurement milestone we haven't hit. We don't know how to measure thought. What is it? Where does it begin? Where does it go? Can we track it? Can we track its effects? What's an accurate picture of its total impact on biology? Until we know these things, psychology remains a fuzzy science. But that's what's next. That's where this technological revolution is leading. That's why predicting limits is so difficult—because we're about to be able to take control of the one aspect of performance that trumps all others."

ALEX HONNOLD AND HALF DOME

If we do want to take a stab at predicting future limits, one place to turn is the sport of rock climbing. While most of action and adventure sports didn't become "extreme" until the early 1990s and skateboarding, our earlier example, not until 2002 (when Danny Way introduced the MegaRamp), rock climbers began free soloing (no ropes, you fall, you die) in the 1970s. This means that their knowledge base and baseline for reality got tipped toward the impossible a little ahead of the general action and adventure sports curve. In other words, meet Alex Honnold.

Alex Honnold started climbing at indoor gyms in 1996, when he was eleven years old. At nineteen, Honnold moved outdoors, where he soon developed a preference for big walls. Free soloing came next. In 2007, this twenty-two-year-old self-described "dork" and total climbing unknown free-soloed Yosemite's Astroman and the Rostrum in a day — a feat so difficult it's only been done twice before and both times by legendary hard men, Peter Croft and Dean Potter.

The following year, Honnold started thinking about free soloing the northwest face of Yosemite's Half Dome. It was a notion beyond the beyond. "When you talk about what the next generation of athletes considers possible," says Jimmy Chin, who has climbed with Honnold and directed a documentary on him for National Geographic, "Alex is the case study. His imaginative capabilities are just so far beyond everyone else in the sport. Back when he started thinking about Half Dome, no one else I knew — and I probably know most of the elite climbing community — was even considering a solo."

And for good reason.

Astroman and the Rostrum are medium-size climbs, both in the intermediate 5.11 range. Half Dome is a big wall — a 2,000-foot face that most teams take multiple days to complete — and the route Alex had in mind went expert-only, 5.12c. Worse, the route gets harder as it goes higher. Chin explains further: "The route Alex chose wasn't impossible for him. He could do the moves. But it's such an exhausting mental game. And with the hardest moves near the top, it's the equivalent of an NBA basketball player, under last game of the finals pressure, having to execute 1,000 free throws; step back to the three-point line and shoot 100 three-pointers; and then, after all that physical and mental exhaustion, step back and shoot one half-court shot. And this isn't about winning. All the shots have to go in, because any miss is fatal."

A week before Honnold decided to solo Half Dome, he climbed his desired route with a friend (and a rope) to dial in the moves. Normally, before attempting a hard solo, he would make repeat practice climbs, but a Half Dome lap took an entire day to complete. "Honestly," Honnold says, "I didn't want to have to explain to anyone why I was spending so much time on that route."

On September 6, 2008 — after a day spent sitting in his van and visualizing the climb — Honnold hiked to the base of Half Dome, set fingers to stone and pulled upward. He kept pulling. Up a zesty finger crack, then a few easier pitches, then one of the route's trickier sections — a nasty boulder problem above a small ledge. The ledge offers security, but the linkup requires six hard moves some 500 feet off the deck. "I don't remember much of the climb," says Honnold. "But I remember that corner. I almost flipped off the wall. That got my attention."

It also drove him deeper into the zone. Over the next few pitches, he used the state to establish an easy rhythm, trying to conserve his strength. He'd need it. Up ahead was a blank stretch of rock normally bypassed by an aid-climbing bolt ladder. Last time through, Honnold had done a 5.12c variation to avoid the bolts. But the holds were razor-thin and this time, without a rope, he didn't like those odds. Rumor told of a rarely used route circumnavigating the entire blank stretch. "I didn't know anything about it," says Honnold, "but I started wandering around, trying to not get lost. There was no sign that anybody had ever come this way. The holds were dirty, I was clawing through bushes. This was dead center Half Dome and I was probably off route."

Honnold wasn't off route, but it still took a 100-foot downclimb of a finger-wide crack to get him back to his line. Luckily, the next 500 feet were a comforting chimney system. Stem feet, palm wall, repeat. Finally, a small ledge. Two hours in, over a thousand feet up, Honnold took off his shoes to relax. Then he put them back on. It was time to head up the "Zig-Zags."

Last time through, this corner-crack system had caused some trouble; this time, not so much. "I climbed almost as if in a daze," Honnold later explained in an article for *Climbing*. "I knew what to do; I just tried not to think about it too much. I didn't think about the hard pitches above. I didn't think about the 5.11+ slab on top, a pitch above the Zig-Zags. I just moved steadily between small fingerlocks up the steep dihedral. The crux of the first Zig-Zag felt much easier than it had two days before, probably because now I had a sequence. Every hold felt crisp and perfect, and I pulled really hard."

He pulled up the rest of the Zig-Zags and onto the aptly named "Thank God Ledge." This fabled feature is thirty-five feet long, starting out plenty wide, but then the rock bulges and the path narrows, and, being 1,800 feet in the air, most people get on their knees and crawl. Honnold walked.

The ledge ends in a short chimney that guards the final slab. The slab is freaky hard. From his last trip, Honnold remembered two critical moves. But he was in the zone and sailed through the first move — then out of it completely, grinding to an absolute halt before the second. "I just came apart. I froze. *What the hell am I doing here* thoughts. A full-scale panic attack. It was really scary and really surreal. The move is barely 200 feet from the summit. There's always a crowd on top of Half Dome (you can hike up the other side). I could hear people talking and laughing. I was really glad they couldn't see me."

Worse, temptation was close at hand. For less ambitious climbers, a bolt ladder runs through this section as well. An enormous oval carabineer hung inches away. If Honnold snatched it, the solo would be tainted. If he didn't, he could die. "I stroked the biner a few times, fighting the urge to grab it, but also thinking how foolish it would be to die on a slab, sliding 2,000 feet to my death, when I could so easily save myself. My calves were slowly getting pumped. I knew I should do *something* soon, since treading water was only wearing me out. Downclimbing never occurred to me. I was going up — it was just a matter of how high — one way or another."

Sometimes the distance through impossible is nothing at all. Honnold smeared his toe on the rock, weighed the leg, then stood up — done deal. He took the final 5.7 section at a near run. There were some two dozen hikers on top, but few paid him much mind. Couples made out. Families ate lunch. Tourists snapped photos. Honnold had just become the first person in history to solo Half Dome, but it was only on the way down that he got any credit.

As he'd left his hiking boots at the base of the climb, Honnold had to hike down barefoot. "All these people kept coming up to me and asking where my shoes were," he says. "I had just spent three hours doing a huge solo and guys were: 'Dude, you're barefoot, that's hardcore.'"

Uh-huh, yup, hardcore. To put Honnold's accomplishment in different terms, when talking about Tom Schaar and his MegaRamp 1080, most feel his youth is more astounding than the leap forward in progression. The general reaction is "Sure, that's amazing, but just imagine what Schaar's going to be able to do when he's twenty."

Alex Honnold is the answer to that question. He's climbing's version of Tom Schaar, only all grown up. He was born into a world where both his baseline for reality and his spectrum for possibility were a quantum leap forward from the previous generation and he took full advantage. Isaac Newton wasn't wrong. We all see farther by standing on the shoulders of giants. In other words, asking what the future would hold if flow became central to culture is another way of asking how good the view is from Honnold's shoulders. Again, it's hard to say for certain, but it's worth pointing out that in 2012 Honnold repeated his Half Dome solo. This time twice as fast: finishing the route in one hour twenty-two minutes.

12

Flow to Abundance

STRATOS

The balloon was a marvel, ghostly silver, as thin as a dry-cleaning bag. Partially inflated, at the Roswell, New Mexico, launch site, it looked not unlike an amoeba dressed in haute couture. In the lower atmosphere, at full height, it rose a majestic fifty-five stories. In the stratosphere, pancaked by pressure, it stretched wider than a football field. And the stratosphere was where skydiver Felix Baumgartner was heading.

The date was October 14, 2012. The plan was for Baumgartner to ride that balloon some twenty-four miles above the Earth, higher than anyone has ever ridden a balloon before. To make this possible, he wore a one-of-a kind pressure suit designed to buffer temperatures as low as seventy degrees below zero and wind speeds of more than 700 miles per hour and to facilitate his ultimate goal: "space-diving" out of the balloon and falling back to Earth and along the way become the first human being to bareback the sound barrier — exceeding Mach 1 without aid of an engine or protection from a craft.

Initially conceived in 2005, the Red Bull Stratos Project, as this space dive was known, began as a joint venture between the energy drink company and Austrian skydiver and BASE jumper Baumgartner. The big idea was to "transcend human limits which have existed for fifty years," with those years being how long it's been since 1960, when Air Force pilot Joe Kittinger plunged nineteen miles out of a balloon as a test procedure for "extreme high-altitude" bailouts. The big question mark — of course — was could an energy drink company and an action sports hero accomplish what a half century of government-backed space programs could not?

Stratos was no small challenge. The technological issues were myriad, the list of catastrophic unknowns even longer. No one had any idea if the human body could go supersonic. Would the shock waves tear Baumgartner's body apart? Would the suit breach? Even bigger were the psychological hurdles. While an exceptionally talented skydiver, Baumgartner had zero experience with the do-as-you're-told rigors of a military-modeled space program. "Felix is an action sports athlete," explains Red Bull director of high performance Dr. Andy Walshe, who oversaw the project. "He's used to being able to control everything. He's not used to taking orders or trusting his life to a team of strangers."

Worse was the extreme claustrophobia produced by the space suit. In the capsule, on the way up, Baumgartner would have to endure long hours inside a vacuum-sealed straightjacket. Stratos was Baumgartner's lifetime dream, yet halfway through the testing phase, he freaked out, quit the project, and flew home to Austria — unable to shake the fear.

Eventually, Dr. Mike Gervais was brought in to help. In a testament to both how good our sports psychology techniques have become and how high a level of mental fortitude our top athletes now possess, it took three days for Baumgartner to get his phobia under control. "When Felix walked off the project," says Walshe, "it was the darkest moment in his life. But a phobia — that's deeply rooted fear. To face that, to come back, to trust strangers with his life, to put himself back into position to do something no one else had ever conceived of? I've seen plenty of astounding feats of human performance, but emotionally, Felix's journey is the farthest I've ever seen an athlete come."

And all this was before the actual jump took place.

The jump presented an entirely different suite of problems. Normally, skydiving is sensation rich — an exceptionally wide field of view and a full complement of air friction. But Baumgartner's face mask narrowed vision to a slit (as compensation, his gloves contained unbreakable chrome plates that function as side-view mirrors) and the suit, even deflated, puts four layers of thick protection between skin and sky. Instead of reacting to the air itself, flying the suit required reacting to the reaction — like playing a video game with a delay built in.

More alarming, in the nonexistent atmosphere of the stratosphere, falling objects have a tendency to spin — and keep spinning. If Baumgartner couldn't regain control, as he once told reporters: "At a certain RPM there's only one way for the blood to leave your body, and that's through your eyeballs."

To help Baumgartner avoid having to think about such things, and because redundancy was security, when the balloon reached its top altitude, Mission Control ran through a forty-item checklist: "Item twenty-six, move seat to rear of capsule; item twenty-seven, lift legs onto the door threshold." The whole process was designed to calm nerves with clear goals. Of course, 128,100 feet in the air, calm's a relative matter.

When the list was complete, Baumgartner stood outside the capsule, on a tiny exterior step, the Earth, quite literally, at his feet. He took a moment to take in the view, then said a few words into his microphone: "Sometimes you have to go up really high to understand how small you really are."

Next he saluted; next he leapt.

It took him thirty seconds to reach 600 miles per hour, less than a minute to shatter 700. He had just become the first human being to go supersonic. This was also when he started spinning. The Earth, some twenty miles below, whirled like a top. And kept whirling. Think shaken baby syndrome at Mach 1. But somehow — talk about flow or die — Baumgartner got everything back under control. He pulled out of the spin and locked into delta position: feet down, head up, and heading home.

In total, Baumgartner's free fall lasted four minutes nineteen seconds; his complete air time approximately ten minutes; his top speed 833.9 miles per hour — Mach 1.24. Baumgartner also took over the records for the highest manned balloon flight and the highest altitude jump and, with YouTube broadcasting a live feed of the event, the highest numbers of concurrent viewers — at 8 million.

Perhaps more interesting than these records is the deeper why. On the Stratos website there's a short list of potential applications for the knowledge gained from Baumgartner's jump: "Passenger/crew exit from space; developing protocols for exposure to high-altitude and high-acceleration environments; exploring the effects of supersonic acceleration and deceleration on the human body; and testing the latest innovations in parachute systems." To put this in plainer language, experts have said that if the passengers on the space shuttle Challenger had been equipped with Baumgartner's suit, they might have lived through their midair crack-up.

And along just these lines, some six months after Baumgartner's jump, Virgin Galactic's SpaceShipTwo powered up its engines for the first time. SpaceShipOne, you might remember, was the craft that won the Ansari X Prize in 2004. This original X Prize was a demonstration project, both proof that a private company could produce an affordable, reusable spaceship and the necessary first step in opening the space frontier. The idea behind SpaceShipTwo is the next step: tourism — taking paying customers on suborbital cruises.

And that goal is not far away. SpaceShipTwo's flight was a test burn, the first in a series that ends with actual space flights (some 550 people have purchased $200,000 tickets). According to Virgin Galactic founder Richard Branson, if everything goes according to plan, the plan is to have paying customers going rocket man before 2015.

This is why Baumgartner's jump is critical. We're going to space. That's what's next. Within a few years, human beings will be routinely visiting low-Earth orbit. In fact, Bigelow Aerospace, another private space company, is now developing an inflatable space hotel that's scheduled for 2017 deployment. With these developments around the corner, having basic space evacuation procedures in place — including a supersonic-capable space suit — just seems to make sense.

But if you want to really talk about the adjacent possible: the combination of Baumgartner's success and the birth of the space tourism industry means that space diving could be the next extreme sport frontier. It sounds silly, of course, but it wasn't too long ago that surfing a 100-foot wave or free-soloing Half Dome was equally ludicrous. Plus, consider the space-diving upside. Imagine having twenty-five miles of fall time to work with. Talk about possibilities for seeing lines. Talk about the potential for creative innovation. Baumgartner touched down in the desert, but sooner or later isn't someone going to try to land on a ski slope? How long then until we turn the space dive into the first stage of a double ski-BASE? How long until it gets stranger than that?

Somewhere, Shane McConkey is smiling.

LEARNING TO LEARN FASTER

Albert Heim fell off a mountain in the Swiss Alps in the late nineteenth century; Felix Baumgartner fell out of the stratosphere in the early twenty-first century, and in between an exceptional group of athletes and an extraordinary state of consciousness have teamed up to do the impossible — over and over again. It's been a real magical mystery tour. Danny Way jumped over the Great Wall of China on a shattered limb; Ian Walsh paddled into a wave the size of an apartment building; Dean Potter caught hold of a climbing rope while falling at terminal velocity into the Cellar of Swallows. "Any sufficiently advanced technology is indistinguishable from magic," Arthur C. Clarke famously told us. Hopefully one thing is now clear — flow is that advanced technology.

It is also very disruptive technology — which is exactly what we need right now.

In 2011, I cowrote a book with X Prize founder and Singularity University cofounder Peter Diamandis called *Abundance*. In it, we explore how exponentially growing technology combined with three other emerging forces gives humanity the power to significantly raise global standards of living over the next two to three decades. This is not the place for too much detail, but the most important thing to know is that abundance is not guaranteed. The four forces we describe create a wave of possibility — the possibility of solving society's grand challenges and exceeding the basic needs of every man, woman, and child on the planet. Yet if we want to ride this wave, we face the same issue as all surfers: first we have to paddle fast enough to catch it.

Without question, paddling fast enough to catch a possibility wave like abundance means we'll need the most capable versions of ourselves doing the paddling. We'll need to be better, faster, stronger, smarter. We'll need intrinsic motivation and incredible cooperation. Our imaginations will have to be deeply engaged; our creative selves operating at their full Picasso. In other words, if we're interested in forging a future of abundance, then we're going to need flow.

What's more, we know this strategy works. The athletes in this book already used flow to create an abundance of progression in the physical domain. By harnessing the state, the unlikeliest of suspects have turned themselves into Superman. In slightly more than two decades, action and adventure sports have ballooned from barely a blip on our collective radar to the most popular sports in the world save football, soccer, and autoracing.

This means an entire generation has grown up watching their heroes break barrier after barrier. Millions more saw it done with Project Stratos. Our children are now inculcated in a culture where the act of using flow to do that which has never been done before is actually done all the time. If you were creating a training program for people interested in tackling grand global challenges, you could do a lot worse.

If it seems too much of a stretch to connect individual athletes rewriting the rulebook on human potential to society as a whole solving the world's biggest problems, then consider the research of Arie de Geus. In the early 1980s, de Geus was the director of strategic planning for Royal Dutch Shell and deeply curious about corporate longevity. At the time, Shell was seventy-three years old—already an anomaly. The average corporate lifespan is twelve and a half years; the average multinational roughly forty. Yet, like Shell, a tiny fraction of corporations have *thrived* for centuries.

Why does this matter so much? Because, to thrive for centuries, these corporations have had to tackle wars, famines, plagues, droughts, floods, depressions, recessions, climate shifts, technological revolutions, political instability, and regime changes. Everything on this list is a variation of a woe the world now faces. These too are our grand challenges. So figuring out how these rare organizations succeeded in the past gives us a time-tested, battle-hardened strategy to do the same in the future.

To divine this secret, de Geus put twenty-seven corporations larger and longer lived than Shell under the microscope. He found a number of factors contribute to longevity, but one stood out far above the rest: *the ability to learn faster.* That was it — the secret to centuries of thriving. In an environment of turbulent change, as de Geus famously wrote: "The ability to learn faster than your competitors is the only sustainable competitive advantage."

As we already know, flow is the secret to learning faster. A lot faster. Data gathered everywhere from brick-and-mortar schools to virtual learning environments show that the state significantly increases positive learning attitudes and positive learning outcomes. The US military trained snipers in flow twice as fast as normal. McKinsey established that executives in flow are five times more effective than their steady-state peers. This is exactly what 150 years of flow research has revealed; this is what the recent revolution in action and adventure sports clearly demonstrates, flow brings out the very best in us — and for certain, it's that very best we'll need to create a world of abundance.

But these facts tells us something else equally important. This book has never really been about daredevil athletes doing impossible deeds. It's always been about us — all of us — doing impossible deeds. It is our future that is on the line. We can harness flow and ride the wave of possibility that is abundance or we can get dashed upon the rocks of halfhearted half measures. And like the trailblazers we met in this book, for us too, it's flow or die. "We are the ones," Pulitzer Prize–winning author Alice Walker reminds us, "that we have been waiting for."

Yet, if the waiting is over and the journey begun, remember that flow is strong medicine, and this path not one for the timid. Along the way, we would do well to remember the wisdom of our elders: the long lineage of academics and athletes and artists who have already broken this trail. Flow, they tell us, is the gateway to impossible, but this has never been take two pills and climb Everest in the morning. Committing to this path demands a radical restructuring of our days and our ways. It demands a considerable tolerance for risk and a considerable shift in culture. We must learn how to play with fire. We must learn to learn faster. We must learn to live thousands of lives in our lifetime — and not lives of quiet desperation, rather of raucous innovation (though naked spread-eagles are optional). But what those naked spread-eagles represent a relentless challenging of the status quo, an everlasting belief in our own possibility, a playful excellence in the face of mortal consequences, well, as mentioned, there's something to be said for the wisdom of our elders.

To put this in different terms, the most interesting thing about an acorn is that it contains a whole oak. But the most interesting thing about a human — well, we're not exactly sure. We do not know the full measure of what we might contain. We cannot yet leap tall buildings in a single bound, but the boldest among us are already throwing backflips off of them. And when he was hurtling through the vacuum of space, Felix Baumgartner was flying faster than a speeding bullet. So does catching the wave of abundance still sound impossible? Perhaps. But like all the athletes in this book — perhaps impossible is just the kind of challenge we've been waiting for. What the world needs most is Superman. What the world needs most is us.

Afterword

All revved up and nowhere to flow? Not at all. We've got you covered.

If you're interested in figuring out your own Flow Profile so you can create more of it in your life, check out www.flowgenomeproject.co/flowprofile.

Want to take a deeper dive and train your flow game, or bring the science of optimum performance into your company or organization? Check out Flow to Impact innovation and leadership workshops and keynotes: www.flowgenomeproject.co/flowtoimpact.

If you're interested in continuing this discussion, learning more about harnessing flow to raise your game, interacting with the author and many of the thinkers in this book, or even helping to drive citizen science flow research forward, join Flow Hacker Nation at www.flowgenomeproject.co.

And stay in touch with our latest thinking, commentary, and events on our Facebook page: www.facebook.com/Flowgenome.

Author's Note

I was lucky enough to become a journalist in the early 1990s, at roughly the same time that action and adventure sports became a story. Back then, if you could write and ski or surf or rock climb or whatever, there was work. I couldn't do many of those things very well, but a collection of wonderful editors were kind enough not to notice. As a result, I got to spend a sizable chunk of that decade chasing professional athletes around mountains. It was an amazing amount of fun. It was also flat-out amazing.

It was during that period that I first got to know many of the people in this book; this also means I owe many of them a significant debt of gratitude. Not only do their impossible deeds fill these pages, many of their ideas do as well. Without the generous help of Laird Hamilton, Dean Potter, JT Holmes, Jeremy Jones, Travis Rice, Ian Walsh, Chris Miller, Danny Way, Doug Ammons, Tao Berman, Mike Horn Alex Honnold, Dave Kalama, Miles Daisher, Jon Devore, Andy Farmington, Mike Swanson, Travis Pastrana, Tom Schaar, Kirk Krack, and Mandy-Rae Cruickshank, this book would not have been possible.

An incredible special thanks to Jamie Wheal, my great friend and partner in the Flow Genome Project. Jamie's ideas are literally everywhere in this book. At least four chapters (five, six, seven, and twelve), were essentially cowritten. He also helped plot out the original outline, repaired a frightening amount of the final product, and provided considerable inspiration throughout. Talking flow with Jamie has been one of the true joys of my life. I also need to thank his wife, Julie, and great kids, Emma and Lucas, for being exceptionally patient with this whole process.

I also owe a debt to longtime action sports writer/editor Micah Abrams — without his friendship and ideas about the accelerated progression in action sports, this book would have never gotten off the ground. Albert Baime, my editor at *Playboy*, assigned the original story about action sports progression that ended up becoming this work. Joe Donnelly, Jimmy Chin, Chris Malloy, Dirk Collins, and Jon Klaczkiewicz were all steady sources of wisdom. Jacob Rosenberg graciously let me see outtakes of his great Danny Way biopic, *Waiting for Lightning*, and talked skateboarding theory and history for hours on end. Matt Warshaw suffered through way too many Millennium Wave conversations. Dave Stanton designed a great cover, was a constant sounding board for ideas, and, when we were out on the hill, generally ensured that I never backed away from the gnar (he also drove me to the hospital when things didn't work out so well). Scott Gaffney, Robb Gaffney, Sherry McConkey, and Steve Winter were all incredibly generous with their memories of Shane and their insights into action sports. Of course, a giant tip of the hat to Shane McConkey, thank you for lighting the way.

On the research side, I started looking into flow in 2000 (long story; if curious, see my earlier book *West of Jesus*) and have been seriously aided in this effort by a collection of gifted, generous scientists. Pretty much any time I've had a flow question, James Olds, David Eagleman, Andy Newberg, Andy Walshe, Mike Gervais, Leslie Sherlin, Jeff Krichmar, Rick Granger, Arne Dietrich, and Reese Jones have made themselves available. Susan Jackson and Greg Berns, both of whom have done great flow research and were incredibly helpful with this book, sadly ended up on the cutting-room floor. Andrew Hessel first talked me into starting a flow research organization and has been a fantastic idea factory along the way.

I'd also like to mention that I've been writing about flow science and action and adventure sports for a long time. This means that bits of this work have appeared elsewhere (*Forbes, Discover, Playboy, Outside, Popular Science, Psychology Today,* and in my books *West of Jesus, A Small, Furry Prayer,* and *Abundance*). In the majority of cases, I've tried to rewrite the words and freshen things up. In a few cases, the way I initially wrote about these ideas still represents the best possible way I know how to communicate them, and thus have left those sentences in their original form.

More generally, debts of gratitude are owed to Rick Theis for reading countless drafts and keeping me sane. Laura Edwards, Jason Silva, Joe Donnelly, Burk Sharpless, and Rafe Furst let me bounce ideas off them endlessly. At DC, Maria Boschetti helped track down athletes and set up interviews. The same goes for Ryan Snyder, Maddie Zeringue, and Jordan Miller at Red Bull. Rolando Garibotti was a great source of information about climbing in Patagonia. And Scott Serfas for the amazing shot of Travis Rice that graces this cover.

There are also quite a few people who were kind enough to speak to me at great length but whose names didn't make it into the book. A heartfelt thanks to: Kai Lenny, Kristin Ulmer, Scott Bradfield, Patrick Brady, Greg Stump, Nic Sims, Michael Marckx, Michael Ham, Paula Tallal, Nick Perata, Michael Posner, Gavin McClurg, Ben Stookesberry, Darren Berrencloth, Brett Leemaster, Daryl Franklin, Michael Reardon, Thayer Walker, Jeff Spencer, Charles Murray, Shane Dorian, Kevin Maney, Ken Block, Brett Tippie, Ritchie Schley, Dangerous "Dan" Cowan, Art Thompson, Marvin Zuckerman, Jaimal Yogis, and Katie Ives.

My agent Paul Bresnick has been with me since my second book and wonderful at every step. Everyone at Amazon has been fantastic as well. My exceptionally talented editors, Julia Cheiffetz and Carly Hoffmann, tightened prose, pushed hard on ideas, and generally ensured this book made sense to those who don't routinely hurl themselves down mountains. Larry Kirshbaum, Justin Renard, Amy Michaels, and Courtney Dodson were lovely as well. Thank you all.

Finally, as always, my wife, Joy, has been my inspiration, best friend, frontline editor, and ceaseless supporter. Moreover, as we co-run a special-needs/elder-care dog sanctuary together (www.ranchodechihuahua.com), while I was writing this book, Joy not only had my back, she also had the backs of an enormous pack of dogs. As mentioned, I've been very lucky.

Notes

"AI" in citation indicates an author interview.

Page   **PREFACE**

vii   "Twenty-First-Century Skills": Founded in 2002, the Partnership for 21st Century Skills is a coalition of the business community, education leaders, and policymakers to position twenty-first-century readiness at the center of US K-12 education. The complete list of twenty-first-century skills includes: creativity and innovation, critical thinking and problem solving, communication and collaboration information literacy, media literacy, information and communication technology literacy, and life and career skills. For more info, check out its website, http://www.p21.org.

viii   "Flow naturally catapults you to a level you're not naturally in": Ned Hallowell, AI, December 2012.

       Flow is an optimal state of consciousness: Mihaly Csikszentmihalyi, *Flow* (HarperPerennial, 1990), pp. 4–5; or see his TED talk, http://www.ted.com/talks/mihaly_csikszentmihalyi_on_flow.html.

       Researchers now believe flow: The full list of what people believe flow can accomplish could go on for days. For a good short summary, see: "The Art of Work," *Fast Company*, August 2005, or http://www.fastcompany.com/53713/art-work.

ix   a recent Gallup survey: "Majority of American Workers Not Engaged in Their Jobs," Gallup.com, October 28, 2011, or http://www.gallup.com/poll/150383/majority-american-workers-not-engaged-jobs.aspx.

       "A decade of research in the business world": "Is Happiness the Secret to Success?" CNN.com, March 19, 2012, or http://www.cnn.com/2012/03/19/opinion/happiness-success-achor.

x   The great civil rights leader: Gil Bailie's *Violence Unveiled* (Crossroad Publishing Company, 1996), p. xv.

INTRODUCTION

xi Steve Winter: Steve Winter, AI, May 26, 2011. A version of this story and a great article about McConkey's importance to action and adventure sports appears in "Skiing Will Never Be the Same: The Life and Death of Shane McConkey," *Skiing*, August 2009, or http://www.skinet.com/skiing/fondue-party/athletes/2009/08/skiing-will-never-be-the-same-the-life-and-death-of-shane-mcconkey.

xii "Shane did one and a half rotations": Winter, ibid.
    According to Dictionary.com: http://dictionary.reference.com/browse/genius?s=t.

xiii Salomon introduced the 1080: For a great history of the 1080, check out http://www.youtube.com/watch?v=AKkyygSGaoU.
    world's first Triple Cork 1440: See: http://espn.go.com/video/clip?id=6383920 or 2011 Poor Boyz release (www.poorboyz.com).
    Tao Berman: For starters, check out his website: www.taoberman.com. Also: "The Tao of Tao Berman," *Men's Journal*, April 2004.
    Shannon Carroll popped off Oregon's Sahalie Falls: "Superheroes," *Outside*, December 2000.

xiv according to *Canoe & Kayak* magazine: "Again," *Canoe & Kayak*, March 2009, or see: http://www.canoekayak.com/canoe/new-waterfall-record.
    Pedro Olivia's 127-foot launch: "Pictured: The Moment Record-Breaking Kayaker Plunged 127 FEET Off Waterfall . . . and Survived," *Mail Online*, March 2009, http://www.dailymail.co.uk/news/article-1164101/Pictured-The-moment-record-breaking-kayaker-plunged-127-FEET-waterfall — survived.html.
    Tyler Bradt plunged 189 feet: http://www.youtube.com/watch?v=MmeFkkqnWdg.
    new illegal-hits rules: "League's Official Player Safety Rules," NFL.com, November 30, 2010, http://www.nfl.com/news/story/09000d5d81c8823a/article/leagues-official-player-safety-rules.
    The 2011 technical-foul changes: "NBA Expands Rules on Technical," ESPN.com, September 23, 2010, or http://sports.espn.go.com/espn/print?id=5609817&type=story.
    NBA enforcer Ron Artest: "Ron Artest Now Metta World Peace," ESPN.com, September 16, 2011.
    "In this day and age": Micah Abrams, AI, 2011.

xv Mike Gervais: Mike Gervais, AI, 2011.
    The sport of platform diving: *The Complete Book of the Summer Olympics* (Sports Classics Books, 2004).
    a difficult and dangerous dive: "History of Diving," USA Diving, see: http://www.usadiving.org/about/diving-101/history-of-diving.

xvi Canada's JF Cusson: There's some old video footage available at http://www.newschoolers.com/watch/307492.0/JF-Cusson — First-X-Games-Big-Air; also see "Olympic Big Air," *PowderMag*, February 16, 2010.

Double Cork 1620: Google "TJ Schiller Dub 1620" or try: http://www.youtube.com/watch?v=2UOoRKIbCP8.

The Baker Road gap: "Recognize: The Mt. Baker Road Gap," TransworldSnowboarding.com, April 20, 2004.

Mads "Big Nads" Jonsson, launched 187 feet: "Kickers that Changed Snowboarding," *White Lines*, December 2010.

xvii backflip has been: For a great little history of the backflip in motocross, see http://www.fmxschool.com/fmx_trick_history.htm.

"There's just no easy way to describe . . .": Andy Walshe, AI, 2011.

xviii The epicenter of this shift was Maverick's: Matt Warshaw, *The Encyclopedia of Surfing* (Harcourt Books, 2003), pp. 370–71.

Surfer magazine once . . . : Ben Marcus said this in *Surfer* back in 1992, but it's requoted in Mark Kreidler, *The Voodoo Wave: Inside a Season of Triumph and Tumult at Maverick's* (Norton, 2011).

Maverickssurf.com: One of the most difficult things about using the Internet to source anything is how quickly stuff goes up and comes down. The original quote is now gone, but the Maverick's Invitational 2012–13 announcement it came from is viewable here: http://www.eventbrite.com/org/2877839845 and reprinted here: http://www.wavescape.co.za/news/contests/solid 20-foot-in-thick-fog-at-mavs.html.

"Since the beginning of modern surfing": Chris Malloy, AI, 2010.

"Jeff Clark was crazy enough": See jeffclarkemavericks.com for Clarke's description of these events.

Jon Krakauer penned in *Outside*: "Mark Foo's Last Ride," *Outside*, May 1995.

xx "Waves are not measured in feet and inches": "How to Measure Wave Height in Surfing," Surfer.com, January 2013

Jason Borte at Surfline: http://www.surfline.com/surfing-a-to z/mark-foo-biography-and-photos_809/

xxi *Inside Maverick's*: Bruce Jenkins, Grant Washburn, and Doug Acton, *Inside Maverick's: Portrait of a Monster Wave* (Chronicle Books, 2006), p. 62.

psychologist Ernest Becker: Ernest Becker, *The Denial of Death* (Free Press, 1973).

xxii "Death is told so clearly to fuck off": Thomas Pynchon, *Gravity's Rainbow* (Penguin Books, 1973), p. 10.

1. THE WAY OF FLOW

3   women's team gymnastic competition: Nancy H. Kleinbaum, *The Magnificent Seven: The Authorized Story of American Gold* (Bantam Books, 1996).

"Strug . . . does not possess . . .": "100 Most Memorable Moments of the Past 25 Years," ESPN.com.

5   "It was like three times the size of anything I had ever seen in skateboarding": "A Skateboarding Ramp Reaches for the Sky," *New York Times*, November 1, 2006.

"It's the widest spot in the wall": Danny Way, AI, June 2012. He also says this in Jacob Rosenberg's great 2013 biopic *Waiting for Lightning.*

"Nothing's too gnarly": *Waiting for Lightning,* ibid.

7   He broke two world records along the way: Height and length.

freestyle motocross legend Travis Pastrana: Travis Pastrana, AI, June 2012.

8   Albert Heim found the zone as well: There are various translations of Heim's original work available. The entire Santis story appears in Douwe Draaisma, *Why Life Speeds Up As You Get Older: How Memory Shapes Our Past* (Cambridge University Press, 2004), pp. 244–51, or "The Experience of Dying from Falls," *Omega — Journal of Death and Dying,* Volume 3, Number 1, 1972, pp. 45–52.

11   those experiments involved psychedelics: "The Nitrous Oxide Philosopher," *Atlantic,* May 1996, pp. 93–101.

"Most people live . . .": William James and Henry James, *The Letters of William James* (Atlantic Monthly Press, 1920), p. 253.

"Our normal waking consciousness": Ibid., p. 254.

12   Walter Bradford Cannon: Walter Bradford Cannon, *Bodily Changes in Pain, Hunger, Fear, and Rage: An Account of Recent Researches into the Function of Emotional Excitement* (Appleton, 1915).

13   Way won his first contest at age eleven: For a breakdown of his entire career, see www.dannyway.com.

"Danny Way single-handedly invented sports medicine . . .": Jacob Rosenberg, AI, June 2012.

Chris Malloy tells a story . . . : Chris Malloy, AI, June 2012.

14   "I've gotten really good at pulling the veil down": Danny Way, AI, June 2012.

Jake Brown: "Stepping Aside as His Creation Soars," *New York Times,* July 29, 2009. Also, for a look at this entire X Games battle, check out *X Games 3D: The Movie,* August 2009.

15   "second Wind": William James, "The Energies of Men," *Science,* No. 635, pp. 321–32.

Invented by Christian Hosoi in 1986 . . . : For a little video of Hosoi talking about inventing the trick, try http://www.youtube.com/watch?v=osgP5L_-v7U.

16   "That's part of the problem with trying to discuss . . .": Travis Pastrana, AI, June 2012.

"I've been shooting action sports for twenty years": Mike Blabac, AI, June 2012.

17   Mihaly Csikszentmihalyi: Csikszentmihalyi's history can be found in a number of places. See his TED talk at http://www.ted.com/talks/mihaly_csikszentmihalyi_on_flow.html, or "Interview: Mihaly Csikszentmihalyi," *Omni,* 17(4), p. 73. Also see "The man who found the flow," *Shambhala Sun,* September 1998.

19   "During a peak experience": Abraham Maslow, *Motivation and Personality* (Harper & Row, 1970), p. 164.

The birth of his happiness study . . . : Mihaly Csikszentmihalyi, *Flow: The Psychology of Optimal Experience* (HarperPerennial, 1991).

20 "It was clear from talking to them . . .": Mihaly Csikszentmihalyi, *Creativity: Flow and the Psychology of Discovery and Invention* (HarperPerennial, 1996), p. 110.

being so involved . . . : "Go with the Flow," *Wired*, September 1996.

21 A ten-year study: "Increasing the 'Meaning Quotient' of Work," *McKinsey Quarterly*, January 2013.

James Slavet: "Five New Management Metrics You Need to Know," Forbes.com, December 2011. See: http://www.forbes.com/sites/bruceupbin/2011/12/13/five-new-management-metrics-you-need-to-know.

"There are moments that stand out . . .": Mihaly Csikszentmihalyi and Susan Jackson, *Flow in Sports: The Keys to Optimal Experiences and Performances* (Human Kinetics, 1999), p. 3.

Flow was a groundbreaking . . . : "The Art of Flow," ibid. Also, for a look at flow's impact on business, see: Keith Sawyer, *Group Genius: The Creative Power of Collaboration* (Basic Books, 2007).

22 Michael Sachs: Michael Sachs, AI, 2006. This originally appeared in Steven Kotler, *West of Jesus: Surfing, Science, and the Origin of Belief* (Bloomsbury, 2006).

"It's either find the zone or suffer . . .": Danny Way, AI, June 2012.

2. THE WAVE OF FLOW

23 Surfers describe Teahupoo . . . : Warshaw, *Encyclopedia of Surfing*, pp. 632–33; also Jason Borte, "Surfing A to Z," Surfline.com, see: http://www.surfline.com/surfing-a-to-z/teahupoo-history_925

"Jaws is all about the hold down": Susan Casey, *The Wave: In Pursuit of the Rogues, Freaks, and Giants of the Ocean* (Random House, 2010), p. 52.

24 "Anything bigger is simply moving too fast": Ibid., p. 14.

wrote surf historian Matt Warshaw in *Surfriders* . . . : Matt Warshaw, *Surfriders: In Search of the Perfect Wave* (Collins Publishing, 1997), p. 79.

25 "The day started out with us being told . . .": All the Laird Hamilton quotes, unless otherwise noted, come from a series of interviews between the author and Hamilton conducted during June and July 2012.

26 "On any normal wave": Matt Warshaw, AI, June 2012. It's also worth pointing out that Warshaw is one of the foremost experts on surf history and that all of the surfing anecdotes recounted in this book were informed by Warshaw's considerable wisdom.

"Laird had to drag his backhand": Sam George speaking in *Riding Giants*, directed by Stacy Peralta, Sony Pictures Classic and Studio Canal, 2004.

28 Scientists describe it either as a "state of consciousness": For questions on flow and consciousness, much of the basics (and much of my thinking on the matter) can be found in six different books: Charles Tart, *Altered States of Consciousness* (HarperCollins, 1969); Arne Dietrich, *Introduction to Consciousness* (Palgrave, 2007); Rita Carter, *Exploring Consciousness* (University of California Press, 2002); Jeff Warren, *The Head Trip: Adventures on the Wheel of Consciousness* (Random

House, 2007); Tor Norretranders, *The User Illusion: Cutting Consciousness Down to Size* (Penguin, 1999); and Mihaly Csikszentmihalyi's *Flow: The Psychology of Optimal Experience* (New York: HarperPerennial, 1991). Much of my thinking here was also shaped by discussions with scientists: Baylor's David Eagleman, Krasnow Institute's James Olds, Los Alamos Labs' Steve Smith and Marko Rodriguez, and applied complexity researcher Stephen Guerin.

Charles Tart's classic description: Tart, *Altered States of Consciousness*, pp. 1–20.

29 "When you're in that moment": This quote from Laird Hamilton comes from the outtakes to Jacob Rosenberg's *Waiting for Lightning.*

"I remember letting go of the rope . . .": As mentioned, this Hamilton quote, like all the others in this section, comes from AI conducted June and July 2012. But for a great description of these events, also see: Paul Jones, "August 17, 2000: Laird Hamilton's 'Millennium Wave' at Teahupoo," Surfline.com, http://www.surfline .com/surf-news/this-day-in-surfing — -august-17th-2000 — -laird-hamiltons -millennium-wave-at-teahupoo_46530/.

30 Here's his list: Csikszentmihalyi, *Flow*, pp. 48–70.

31 Moreover, flow exists on a continuum: Mihaly Csikszentmihalyi, *Beyond Boredom and Anxiety: Experiencing Flow at Work and Play* (Jossey-Bass, 1975). These ideas were also further informed by lengthy discussions with *Flow in Sports* coauthor and sports psychologist Susan Jackson.

32 Leslie Sherlin: I first met Leslie Sherlin at Red Bull's 2012 Glimpses Conference (a high-performance conference held every summer), and we have been talking flow and brain waves ever since. The ideas in this chapter are based on over two decades of research by Sherlin and two years of discussion between the author and Sherlin. For an introduction to Sherlin's work, see: http://www.neurotopia.com.

33 There are five major brain-wave types: And there are plenty of places to learn about each. For a more general discussion, see Warren, *The Head Trip*.

Csikszentmihalyi used EEG: "In the Zone: A Biobehavioral Theory of the Flow Experience," *Athletic Insight: The Online Journal of Sports Psychology*, 2001. See: http://www.athleticinsight.com/Vol3Iss1/Commentary.htm#Introduction; also: "Scientists Zap Brains to See if It Will Help Trigger 'Flow,'" *Washington Post*, February 13, 2012.

34 Human beings have evolved two distinct systems: For a great but brief description, see: Arne Dietrich, "Neurocognitive Mechanisms Underlying the Experience of Flow," *Consciousness and Cognition*, Vol. 13, 2004, pp. 746–61. For a much lengthier (and more general) discussion, see: David Eagleman, *Incognito: The Secret Lives of the Brain* (Pantheon, 2011).

"When the brain finds a task it needs to solve": Eagleman, *Incognito*, pp. 71–72.

35 Red Bull's director of athletic high performance, Andy Walshe: If you want to see what this looks like, Google "Andy Walshe and Neurotopia." There's a YouTube clip of football player Devin Hester going through basic brain-wave training.

use EEG to figure out what the brains: Leslie Sherlin, Michael Gervais, and Andy Walshe, "Where Fear, Risk, Thrill, and Performance Mastery Meet: Action Sport

Athlete Brain States." Poster presentation at the annual meeting of the American Psychological Association, Washington, D.C., August 2011. Also: N. C. Larson, L. Sherlin, A. Baker, and J. Troesch, "Randomized, Controlled Cross-Over Research of Performance Brain Training Effects in Elite College Golfers," oral paper presentation at the 20th Annual Conference of the International Society for Neurofeedback and Research, Orlando, FL, September 2012; L. Sherlin, N. C. Larson, and R. M. Sherlin, "Developing a Performance Brain Training Approach for Baseball: A Process Analysis with Descriptive Data," *Journal of Applied Psychophysiology and Biofeedback*, 2012 (DOI) 10.1007/s10484-012-9205-2.

a six-stage cycle: This idea is based on Sherlin's research.

37   got nauseous just looking at the place . . . : Casey, *The Wave*, p. 24.

38   "When you let go of the rope . . .": "Surfing into Jaws," *National Geographic Adventure*, July 2002.

"[L.]ike all sets of Jaws": Casey, *The Wave*, p. 24.

"We were definitely in the zone": Dave Kalama, AI, May 2012.

40   Creativity has a brain-wave signature as well: This is based on a lot of longstanding research (that is now starting to be questioned). One of the earliest major studies was: "Creativity and Cortical Activation During Creative, Intellectual, and EEG Feedback Tasks," *Biological Psychology*, Vol. 3, Issue 2, September 1975, pp. 91–100. Also, see James Kaufman and Robert Sternberg, *The Cambridge Handbook on Creativity* (Cambridge University Press, 2011). That said, there's been some interesting work pointing out that theta is also key for creativity. Check out: "Free Your Mind: A Scientific Approach to Unleashing Creativity," *The Independent*, October 2006.

EEG shows a burst of gamma waves: Mark Beeman, Edward Bowden, Jason Haberman, Jennifer Frymiare, Stella Arambel-Lui, Richard Greenblatt, Paul Reber, and John Kounios, "Neural Activity When People Solve Verbal Problems with Insight," *PLOS Biology*, 2004, 2(4). Also, for a great overview, see Beeman's Northwestern website: http://groups.psych.northwestern.edu/mbeeman/research.htm. Harvard Business School professor Teresa Amabile: Teresa Amabile, Sigal Barsade, Jennifer Mueller, Barry Straw, "Affect and Creativity at Work," *Administrative Science Quarterly*, 2005. Vol. 50, pp. 367–403.

41   "Everybody who has ever spent any time in flow": Chris Miller, AI, June 2012.

an interview with *Bon Hawaii*: "An Interview with Laird Hamilton, Dave Kalama, and Don King," *Bon Hawaii*, April 27, 2008. Check it out: http://www.bonhawaii.com/interview-laird-hamilton-dave-kalama-don-king.

3. THE WHERE OF FLOW

42   On the list of the world's most dangerous climbs: See: http://matadornetwork.com/trips/11-most-dangerous-mountains-in-the-world-for-climbers, or http://opishposh.com/10-hardest-mountains-to-climb, or http://smashinghub.com/20-most-dangerous-mountains-peaks-in-the-world.htm.

"Patagonia's weather is terrible": Dean Potter, AI, a series of interviews conducted between July 2012 and May 2013.

"Up on the High Lonesome": John Long, *The High Lonesome: Epic Solo Climbing Stories* (Falcon Guides, 1999), p. 1.

43   "There's someone in my head, but it's not me": David Eagleman, AI. Eagleman used this phrase in his book *Incognito*, but he also used it in conversation with me when I was reporting "How Time Flies," *Popular Science*, April 2010. See: http://www.stevenkotler.com/articles/how-time-flies.

44   Jiddu Krishnamurti refers to this someone as "the Tyrant": Jiddu Krishnamurti, "The Kingdom of Happiness," Talks of Jiddu Krishnamurti in Eerde Castle, Holland, 1926. Viewable on his website: http://www.jiddu-krishnamurti.net/en/1926-the-kingdom-of-happiness/jiddu-krishnamurti-the-kingdom-of-happiness-01.

Carl Jung defined intuition as "perception via the unconscious": Carl Jung, *Psychological Types* (Princeton University Press, 1971), p. 133. Viewable here: http://psychclassics.yorku.ca/Jung/types.htm.

a career that's had few parallels: There's a ton of great Potter info out there, but I would suggest "The Aerialist," *Outside Magazine*, July 2011.

Potter took his one-man band down to Patagonia: A lot of the information about Potter's trip through Patagonia was based on interviews with Potter himself. But Patagonia climbing historian Rolando Garibotti helped me work out details about the routes and the magnitude of the accomplishment. Also, a series of articles that ran in the *Alpinist*, including "The Call," Fall 2002; "Falling," Winter 2004–05; "The Space Between," Fall 2007.

48   "After a wholly uneventful time in college": See Dietrich's online biography here: http://www.harford.de/arne/pages/biography.html (Inactive).

49   The PFC is the heart of our higher cognitive abilities: C. D. Frith and R. Dolan, "The Role of the Prefrontal Cortex in Higher Cognitive Functions," *Cognitive Brain Research* 5 (1996), pp. 175–81; C. D. Frith and U. Frith, "Cognitive Psychology—Interacting Minds—a Biological Basis," *Science*, November 26, 1999, pp. 1692–95; J. M. Fuster, "Temporal Processing—Structure and Function of the Human Prefrontal Cortex," *Annals of the New York Academy of Sciences* 769 (1995), pp. 173–81; J. M. Fuster, "Executive Frontal Functions," *Experimental Brain Research* 133 (2000), pp. 66–70.

"The prefrontal cortex is where thinking happens": Arne Dietrich, AI, a series of interviews starting in May 2012 and running through July 2013.

transient hypofrontality: Arne Dietrich, "Functional Neuroanatomy of Altered States of Consciousness: The Transient Hypofrontality Hypothesis," *Consciousness and Cognition* 12 (2003), pp. 231–56.

"If there is a sudden danger": "Watching the Brain 'Switch Off' Self-Awareness," *New Scientist*, April 2006. Or Ilan Goldberg, Michal Harel, and Rafael Malach, "When the Brain Loses Its Self: Prefrontal Inactivation During Sensorimotor Processing," *Neuron* Vol. 50, Issue 2, April 2006. Also, see: http://wis-wander.weizmann.ac.il/making-the-self-disappear#.Ue6BTY42XTQ.

50 Charles Limb began using fMRI: Monica Lopez-Gonzales and Charles Limb, "Musical Creativity and the Brain," *Cerebrum,* February 2012. Also "Charles Limb and Allen Braun, "Neural Substrates of Spontaneous Musical Performance: An fMRI Study of Jazz Improvisation," *PLOS One* 2008, 3(2).

the medial prefrontal cortex: Limb and Braun, "Neural Substrates of Spontaneous Musical Performance."

Penn State kinesiologist Vladimir Zatsiorsky: Vladimir Zatsiorsky and William Kraemer, *The Science and Practice of Strength Training,* Second Edition (Human Kinetics, 2006). Also see Jeff Wise, *Extreme Fear* (Palgrave, 2009).

51 Potter didn't even know how to skydive: Again, all the Potter quotes and information from this section comes from a long series of interviews conducted in 2012 and 2013.

54 The same events that erase our sense of self also distort our sense of time: David Eagleman, AI 2011. Also, Kotler, "How Times Flies." Lastly, see Maria Coffee's excellent *Explorers of the Infinite: The Secret Spiritual Lives of Extreme Athletes — And What They Reveal About Near-Death Experiences, Psychic Communication and Touching the Beyond* (Penguin, 2008). Also, for a very cool discussion about the enhanced perception that comes with time dilation, see Nobuhiro Hagura, Ryota Kanai, Guido Orgs, and Patrick Haggard, "Ready Steady Slow: Action Preparation Slows the Subjective Passage of Time," *Proceedings of the Royal Society: Biology,* September 5, 2012.

elegant fMRI experiments: David Eagleman, "Human Time Perception and Its Illusions," *Current Opinions in Neurobiology* April 2008, 18(2), pp. 131–36. Also Chess Stetson, Matthew Fiesta, and David Eagleman, "Does Time Really Slow Down During a Frightening Event?" *Plos One* 2(12), December 2007.

55 variations of it are not that uncommon in action and adventure sports: Steven Kotler, *West of Jesus: Surfing, Science, and the Origins of Belief* (Bloomsbury, 2006). Also: *Explorers of the Infinite.*

professional kayaker Sam Drevo: Coffee, *Explorers of the Infinite,* p. 57.

neuroscientist Andrew Newberg and University of Pennsylvania neuropsychologist Eugene D'Aquili: I have been talking flow with Andrew Newberg longer than just about anyone else. That said, all of the information in this book can be found in Andrew Newberg, Eugene D'Aquili, and Vince Rause, *Why God Won't Go Away: Brain Science and the Biology of Belief* (Ballantine, 2002). Also see: Kotler, "The Neurology of Spiritual Experience," *H+,* September 16, 2009, http://hplusmagazine.com/2009/09/16/neurology-spiritual-experience.

4. THE WHAT OF FLOW

59 *60 Minutes:* "I am flying," *60 Minutes,* October 11, 2009. See: http://www.cbsnews.com/video/watch/?id=5377292n.

The earliest attempts at "human-powered flight": Michael Abrams, *Birdmen, Batmen, and Skyflyers: Wingsuits and the Pioneers Who Flew in Them, Fell in Them, and Perfected Them* (Three Rivers Press, 2006), pp. 13–27.

60 Frenchman Patrick de Gayardon: Abrams, *Birdmen,* pp. 211–25.
Birdman International: See: www.bird-man.com.
Super Terminal: The flick is all over YouTube, just search for "Super Terminal." For impact, see: http://www.flylikebrick.com/wingsuit-history.php.
JT Holmes: This chapter is based on extensive interviews with JT Holmes, Andy Farmington, Mike Swanson, and Jon Devore conducted between May 2012 and July 2013. A very special thanks to JT Holmes who allowed me to call him whenever I had a question (and this included waking him up in the middle of the night on several occasions).
Red Bull Air Force: See: redbullairforce.com.

62 decided to play a little *Frogger:* For a very cool video of this experiment, check out "Fit Hearts Have Street Smarts," at Sciencenow.com. See: http://news.sciencemag .org/sciencenow/2012/02/video-fit-hearts-have-street-sma.html.

63 For the experiment: Laura Chaddock, Mark Neider, Michelle Voss, John Gaspar, and Arthur Kramer, "Do Athletes Excel at Everyday Tasks?" *Medicine and Science in Sports and Exercise,* Vol. 43, No. 10, pp. 1920–26, 2011.
New York Times: Gretchen Reynolds, "How Sports May Focus the Brain," *New York Times,* March 23, 2011.
Jeff Hawkins and Sandra Blakeslee in *On Intelligence:* Jeff Hawkins and Sandra Blakeslee, *On Intelligence* (Times Books, 2004), p. 89.

64 the brain's pattern-recognition system: A lot of neuroscientists are starting to believe that the basic function of the brain is pattern recognition. For a great book on the subject, see: Ray Kurzweil, *How to Create a Mind: The Secret of Human Thought Revealed* (Viking, 2012).
the feel-good neurochemical dopamine: Lots to choose from here. See: C. R. Clarke Clarke, G. M. Geffen, and L. B. Geffen, "Catecholamines and Attention I: Animal and Clinical Studies," *Neuroscience and Biobehavioral Reviews* 11(4), 341–52 (1987). P. Krummenacher, C. Mohr, H. Haker, and P. Brugger, "Dopamine, Paranormal Belief, and the Detection of Meaningful Stimuli," *Journal of Cognitive Neuroscience,* 22(8), pp. 1670–81 (2010). Georg Winterer and Daniel Weinberger, "Genes, Dopamine and Cortical Signal-to-Noise Ratio in Schizophrenia," *Trends in Neuroscience,* Vol. 27, No. 11, November 2004. And: Sven Kroener, L. Judson Chandler, Paul Phillips, and Jeremy Seamans, "Dopamine Modulates Persistent Synaptic Activity and Enhances the Signal-to-Noise Ratio in the Prefrontal Cortex," *PLoS One,* August 2009, 4(8):e6507. Also, Michael Sherman gave an excellent TED talk on how too much dopamine/pattern recognition leads to strange beliefs, see: http://www.ted .com/talks/michael_shermer_on_believing_strange_things.html.
it's why learning happens: P. R. Montague, P. Dayan, and T. J. Sejnowski, "A Framework for Mesencephalic Dopamine Systems Based on Predictive Hebbian Learning," *Journal of Neuroscience* 16(5): 1936–47; P. R. Montague, S. E. Hyman, and J. D. Cohen, "Computational Roles for Dopamine in Behavioral Control," *Nature* 431:760–67 (2004).
the dopamine dumped in our system . . . : There's a ton of stuff out there on

dopamine and learning reinforcement, but Martha Burns wrote a nice blog on the subject for *The Science of Learning Blog* entitled "Dopamine and Learning: What the Brain's Reward Center Can Teach Educators," September 18, 2012. See: http://www.scilearn.com/blog/dopamine-learning-brains-reward-center-teach -educators.php.

65   very complicated predictions about the future: For a great discussion on pattern recognition, chunking, and future prediction, see Vivek Ranadive and Kevin Maney, *The Two-Second Advantage: How We Succeed by Anticipating the Future — Just Enough* (Crown Business, 2011).

66   Flow is an extremely potent response: Of all the research presented in this book, the neurochemistry of flow presents the greatest challenges. For starters, the researchers are balkanized, so forget about a consensus opinion. Secondly, there are huge question marks everywhere. What is the exact order of the neurochemical cascade? Do neuroelectrical changes trigger neurochemical changes, or visa versa? (Appears to depend on initial conditions.) Is the neurochemistry of flow the same in every person? (Doubtful.) Does neuropeptide Y play a role? Does the neurochemistry differ for sensation seekers — do blunted dopamine receptors play a huge role? And on and on. That said, what I've tried to do in this chapter is present the ideas that most researchers agree on at least most of the time. The good news is we are getting better and better at measuring neurochemical response, and these issues should start to resolve themselves over the next decade.

The process includes *dopamine:* For a great discussion on dopamine and flow, see Gregory Berns, *Satisfaction: The Science of Finding True Fulfillment* (Henry Holt and Company, 2005), pp. 146–74

67   *Norepinephrine* provides another boost: For a norepinephrine overview, see Eddie Harmon-Jones and Piotr Winkielman, *Social Neuroscience: Integrating Biological and Psychological Explanations of Social Behavior* (Guilford Press, 2007), p. 306. Also, for a great look at all of the neuroscience surrounding attention, see Michael Posner, *Cognitive Neuroscience of Attention* (Guilford Press, 2004). Finally, for a look at the relationship between norepinephrine and flow, Harvard cardiologist Herbert Benson. For the lay version of this work, see Herbert Benson and William Proctor, *The Breakout Principle: How to Activate the Natural Trigger That Maximizes Creativity, Athletic Performance, Productivity, and Personal Well-Being* (Scribner, 2003), pp. 46–68.

Endorphins, our third flow conspirator: The research pointing in this direction dates back to the 1980s, but it wasn't actually proved until much more recently. See Henning Boecker, Till Sprenger, Mary E. Spilker, Gjermund Henriksen, Marcus Koppenhoefer, Klaus J. Wagner, Michael Valet, Achim Berthele, and Thomas R. Tolle, "The Runner's High: Opioidergic Mechanisms in the Human Brain," *Cerebral Cortex*, 2008, 18 (11), pp. 2523–31. Also see Henning Boecker, "Brain Imaging Explores the Myth of Runner's High," *Medical News Today*, March 4, 2008.

The next neurotransmitter is *anandamide:* Arne Dietrich and W. McDaniel, "Endocannabinoids and exercise," *British Journal of Sports Medicine* October 2004, 38(5), pp. 536–41, and D. A. Raichlen, A. D. Foster, G. L. Gerdeman, A. Seillier, and A. Giuffrida, "Wired to Run: Exercise-Induced Endocannabinoid Signaling in Humans and Cursorial Mammals with Implications for the 'Runner's High,'" *Journal of Experimental Biology,* 215, 2012, pp. 1331–36.

the brain releases *serotonin:* This one is certainly up for debate. Most researchers seem to agree that serotonin is somehow involved in flow, but direct work has not been done. We do know for sure that serotonin shows up with exercise, so the chemical is certainly in the mix when it comes to action and adventure sports athletes in flow. For a general look at serotonin and exercise, see Simon Young, "How to Increase Serotonin in the Human Brain Without Drugs," *Journal of Psychiatry and Neuroscience,* 2007. Also, John Ratey and Eric Hagerman, *Spark: The Revolutionary New Science of Exercise and the Brain* (Little Brown, 2008).

Philip Cowen told the *New York Times:* Natalie Angier, "Job Description Grows for Our Utility Hormone," *New York Times,* May 2, 2011.

68   "Every so often a Celtic game would heat up": Bill Russell and Taylor Branch, *Second Wind: The Memoirs of an Opinionated Man* (Ballantine Books, 1980).

69   it accelerates social bonding: If you want the layperson version of this idea, see Helen Fisher, *Why We Love: The Nature and Chemistry of Romantic Love* (Holt, 2004). For the very technical version, see Jaak Panksepp, *Affective Neuroscience: The Foundations of Human and Animal Emotions* (Oxford University Press, 1994).

It was time for their trip round Suicide Corner: There's really great footage of these jumps; see "Birdmen Fly Through Chicago for 'Transformers,'" *CBS News,* June 28, 2011.

70   Tao Berman's sentiment: Tao Berman, AI, 2011.

The fight-or-flight response: Obviously, there's tons of stuff out there, but Jaimal Yogis does an excellent job with the science in his recent book *The Fear Project: What Our Most Primal Emotion Taught Me About Survival, Success, Surfing . . . and Love* (Rodale, 2013).

71   that's flow's real trigger: Benson and Proctor, *The Breakout Principle.*

72   psychologists call "situational awareness": Mica Endsley, "Towards a Theory of Situational Awareness in Dynamic Systems," *Human Factors,* 1995, 37(1), pp. 32–64.

74   purportedly for ADHD: Alan Schwartz, "Risky Rise of the Good Grade Pill," *New York Times,* June 9, 2012.

number one cause of accidental death: "Drug Deaths Exceed Traffic Deaths," *ABC News,* September 20, 2011.

a trillion-dollar public-health problem: "DrugFacts: Nationwide Trends," National Institute on Drug Abuse, December 2012. See http://www.drugabuse.gov /publications/drugfacts/nationwide-trends.

5. THE FLOW SHORTCUT

75 naked spread eagles: Much of the research for this section is based on conversations with Scott Gaffney and JT Holmes. Also see: Rob Story, "Skiing Will Never Be the Same: the Life and Death of Shane McConkey," *Skiing*, August 2009.

76 the website Tahoetopia: "Tahoe Resorts A-to-Z: Squaw Valley USA," Tahoepia .com, http://www.tahoetopia.com/news/tahoe-resorts-z-squaw-valley-usa.
cult-classic ski flick *Daydreams:* http://www.tahoetopia.com/news/squaw-val ley-palisades-daydreams-film. Also see: http://craigbeckproductions.com/Day dreams_History.html.
Rob Story in *Skiing* magazine: Story, "Skiing Will Never Be the Same."

77 Vail, in their wisdom, banned him for life: Bill Gifford, "Dying to Fly," *Men's Journal,* June 10, 2009.
"Every morning he'd be the first up . . .": "Fellow Pros on What Shane Meant to Them," Powdermag.com, August 18, 2009.
"Pretty much it's always a bad idea to try to do something Shane can do": Ingrid Backstrom, *Push* (Matchstick Productions, 2005).
"McConkey turn": See ibid. Skier Eric Hjorleifson gives a pretty great description. Leslie Anthony once fittingly described . . . : Leslie Anthony, *White Planet: A Mad Dash Through Modern Global Ski Culture* (Greystone Books, 2010), p. 204.

78 Doug Coombs: This comes from interviews with Dirk Collins, but there's a great old *Ski* magazine interview with Coombs available here: http://tailgatealaska .com/node/52.
straight-lined Python. You can see the run in Matchstick production's 1998 film *Sick Sense.* The sixty-miles-per-hour tidbit comes from Steve Winter, who was shooting that day.

79 University of Chicago educational psychologist Benjamin Bloom launched the Talent Project: K. Anders Ericsson, Neil Charness, Paul Feltovich, and Robert Hoffman, *The Cambridge Handbook of Expertise and Expert Performance* (Cambridge University Press, 2006), pp. 287–301.
As Bloom later told reporters: Ibid.

80 "A lot of us were from broken homes": John Roos, "Skateboarding, Punk Inspire a Hunn's Salvation," *LA Times,* December 5, 2000.
Anders Ericsson performed: Ericsson et al., *Cambridge Handbook of Expertise and Expert Performance,* and Malcolm Gladwell, *Outliers: The Story of Success* (Little, Brown, 2008), pp. 35–68.
"They work much, *much* harder": Gladwell, *Outliers,* p. 39.

81 Walter Mischel performed: Philip Zimbardo and John Boyd, *The Time Paradox: The New Psychology of Time That Will Change Your Life* (Free Press, 2008), pp. 216–20.

82 *Outside* magazine profile of Shane McConkey: Tim Sohn, "The Life and Death of Shane McConkey," *Outside,* June 2009.
"From this experience": This entire section is based on Zimbardo and Boyd's *The Time Paradox.*

84   UCLA psychologist Steven Berglas: Steven Berglas, *Reclaiming the Fire: How Successful People Overcome Burnout* (Random House, 2001).

85   Psychologists describe flow as "autotelic": Csikszentmihalyi, *Creativity,* p. 113.
"Because flow involves meeting challenges and developing skills": Mihaly Csikszentmihalyi, *Good Business: Leadership, Flow, and the Making of Meaning* (Penguin, 2003), p. 50.
"The person I became . . .": Rob Schultheis, *Bone Games: Extreme Sports, Shamanism, Zen, and the Search for Transcendence* (Breakaway Books, 1996), pp. 10–11.

87   high-performance sports psychologist Michael Gervais: Mike Gervais, AI, August 2012.
South Korean researchers looking at e-learning: Li-An Ho and Tsung-Hsien Kuo, "How Can One Amplify the Effect of E-Learning?: An Examination of High-Tech Employees' Computer Attitude and Flow Experience," *Computers in Human Behavior* January 2010, 26(1), pp. 23–31.
military snipers trained in flow: Sally Adee, "Zap Your Brain into the Zone: Fast Track to Pure Focus," *New Scientist,* February 6, 2012.
it literally shortens the path: A lot more has been written about flow and learning. For a decent wiki on the subject, check out: Udo Konradt, "Flow Experience and Positive Affect During Hypermedia Learning," *British Journal of Educational Technology,* 2010, 34(3) http://edutechwiki.unige.ch/en/Flow_theory.
Dr. Rob Gaffney explains in *Squallywood*: Robb Gaffney, *Squallywood: A Guide to Squaw Valley's Most Exposed Lines* (Westbridge Publishing, 2003), p. 120.

88   Official Canadian Ski Museum biography: See: http://www.skimuseum.ca /biodata.php?lang=en&id=33.

89   "During his big-mountain competition days": Micah Abrams, "It's Totally Doable," *Freeze,* February 2003, Issue 8.2.
"In one particular scene Shane . . .": "Fellow Pros on What Shane Meant to Them."

90   "Shane brought everyone hope": See: http://www.sessions.com/blog/2012/12/30 /happy-birthday-shane-mcconkey.

6. OUTER FLOW

93   "They would have told me I was committing suicide": All Doug Ammons quotes are based on a long series of interviews/e-mail exchanges between Ammons and the author. These took place between July 2012 and June 2013.
Outside made a list of the ten greatest adventurers since 1900: "Game Changers: The Ten Greatest Adventurers Since 1900," *Outside,* March 10, 2010.

94   "Perhaps the most beautiful experience in kayaking": Doug Ammons, *Whitewater Philosophy* (Water Nymph Press, 2009).
"A Brief History": See: http://www.dougammons.com/other-stories-stikine _short.html.

97 an altruism-triggered flow state: Allan Luks and Peggy Payne, *The Healing Power of Doing Good* (iUniverse, 2001), pp. 17–18. Also: http://allanluks.com/helpers_high.

98 the lure of the joystick: Ben Cowley, Darryl Charles, Michaela Black, and Ray Hickey, "Towards an Understanding of Flow in Video Games," *Computers in Entertainment*, 6(2), July, 2008; Penelope Sweetser and Peta Wyeth, "GameFlow: A Model for Evaluating Player Enjoyment in Games," *Computers in Entertainment* 3(3), July 2005.

"Placing players in flow": Erik Gregory, "Understanding Video Gaming's Engagement: Flow and Its Application to Interactive Media," *Media Psychology Review*, 1(1), 2008.

Oracle's *Developer Insight Series:* Janice Heiss, "The Developer Insight Series, Part 3: The Process of Writing Code," *Oracle*, May 2009. See: http://www.oracle.com/technetwork/articles/javase/devinsight-3-139847.html.

flow-based accounting: Tom DeMarco and Timothy Lister, *Peopleware: Productive Projects and Teams*, 2nd ed. (Dorsett, 1999), pp. 62–68; also see: http://javatroopers.com/Peopleware.html.

99 "All of the basic activities that led to today's high-tech revolution": Reese Jones, AI, January 2013.

"The peak experience in sport": Ken Ravizza, "Qualities of the Peak Experience in Sport," *Psychological Foundations of Sport* (Human Kinetics, 1984), pp. 452–62.

2000 study run on kayakers: Christopher Jones, Steven Hollenhorst, Frank Perna, and Steve Selin, "Validation of the Flow Theory in an On-Site Whitewater Kayaking Setting," *Journal of Leisure Research* 2000, 32(2), pp. 247–61.

100 Greylock Partners venture capitalist James Slavet: James Slavet, "5 New Management Metrics You Need to Know," Forbes.com, December 13, 2011. See: http://www.forbes.com/sites/bruceupbin/2011/12/13/five-new-management-metrics-you-need-to-know.

101 the amygdala: Joseph LeDoux, *The Emotional Brain: The Mysterious Underpinnings of Emotional Life* (Simon & Schuster, 1996), pp. 138–78.

"There was a rush": Ammons, *Whitewater Philosophy*, p. 6.

102 neuropsychologist Barbara Sahakian: Barbara Sahakian, AI, May 2012. Also see: Steven Kotler, "Training the Brain of an Entrepreneur," Forbes.com, May 14, 2012, http://www.forbes.com/sites/stevenkotler/2012/05/14/training-the-brain-of-an-entrepreneur.

an even bigger neurochemical response is facilitated: There's a ton of literature about the relationship between risk and dopamine. Greg Bern's aforementioned book *Satisfaction* is a great place to start. Also see Peter Gwin, "The Mystery of Risk," *National Geographic*, June 2013. Moreover, it appears that certain people are more hardwired than others for sensation seeking. For example, see: Alice Park, "Why We Take Risks — It's the Dopamine," *Time*, December 30, 2008; Susanne Piet, "What Motivates Stunt Men," *Motivation and Emotion* 11(2), 1987.

Harvard psychiatrist Ned Hallowell: Ned Hallowell, AI, March 2013.

consequences of betting on a bad idea: For a great look at the neuroscience of mental risk taking, see: Greg Berns, *Iconoclast: A Neuroscientist Reveals How to Think Differently* (Harvard Business Press, 2008).

104   hold our attention much like risk: Brian Knutson and Jeffrey Cooper, "The Lure of the Unknown," *Neuron*, 2006, 51 (3), pp. 280–81; Nico Bunzeck and Emrah Duzel, "Absolute Coding of Stimulus Novelty in the Human Substantia Nigra/VTA," *Neuron*, 2006, 51 (3), pp. 369–79; also Jonathon Benjamin, Lin Li, Chavis Patterson, Benjamin Greenberg, Dennis Murphy, and Dean Hamer, "Population and Familial Association Between the D4 Dopamine Receptor Gene and Measures of Novelty Seeking," *Nature Genetics*, 1996, 12. pp. 81–4.

awe is a state of total absorption: Dacher Keltner and Jonathan Haidt, "Approaching Awe, a Moral, Spiritual, and Aesthetic Emotion," *Cognition and Emotion* 2003, (17)2, pp. 297–314. Also: Melanie Rudd and Kathleen Vohs, "Awe Expands People's Perception of Time, Alters Decision Making, and Enhances Well-Being," working paper, available here: http://faculty-gsb.stanford.edu/aaker/pages/documents/TimeandAwe2012_workingpaper.pdf.

105   James Olds: James Olds, AI, April 2013.

Deep embodiment: Jamie Wheal, "Free Your Ass and Your Mind Will Follow: Embodied Leadership," *Change This* 42(6), January 2007. To get at the heart of this idea also requires a decent understanding on new thinking about embodied cognition. For a great overview: Louise Barrett, *Beyond the Brain: How Body and Environment Shape Animal and Human Minds* (Princeton University Press, 2011). "[T]asks that require real-time": Arne Dietrich and Michel Audiffren, "The reticular-activating hypofrontality (RAH) model of acute exercise," *Neuroscience and Biobehavioral Reviews* 2011, 35, pp. 1305–25.

107   "million-dollar hole": Gerry Moffett, AI, July 2012.

"paradox of control": Csikszentmihalyi, *Flow*, pp. 59–62.

"It is this absence of . . . emotion": Martin Seligman, *Authentic Happiness: Using the New Positive Psychology to Realize Your Potential for Lasting Fulfillment* (Free Press, 2002), p. 116.

108   "When you're arrogant and egotistical": James Olds, AI, March 2013.

7. INNER FLOW

109   Mandy-Rae Cruickshank never intended to become a superhero: All Mandy-Rae quotes and details come from an interview conducted June 2002.

110   Alec Wilkinson explained in the pages of *The New Yorker:* "The Deepest Dive," *The New Yorker*, August 24, 2009.

"I had zero free diving technique at the time": Kirk Krack, AI, June 2012. Also see: http://www.performancefreediving.com.

113   "[W]e tend to exist in a distracted present", Douglas Rushkoff, *Present Shock: When Everything Happens Now* (Penguin, 2013), p. 4.

114 the three most critical: Csikszentmihalyi, *Flow*, pp. 48–93.

most of the students didn't see the gorilla: Christopher Chabris and Daniel Simons, *The Invisible Gorilla* (Harmony, 2011).

doctors tested failed to spot the animal: Alix Spiegel, "Why Even Radiologists Can Miss a Gorilla Hiding in Plain Sight," NPR.org, February 11, 2013.

116 "In the mountains, feedback is instant": John Gans, executive director of NOLS. Lecture delivered at High Mountain Institute, CO, 1999.

professions with less direct feedback loops: Stephen Dubner and Steven Levitt, "A Star Is Made," *New York Times*, May 7, 2006.

about 4 percent: Chip Conley, AI, September 2013. The real ratio, according to calculations performed by Csikszentmihalyi, is 1:96.

Yerkes-Dobson law: Robert Yerkes and John Dodson, "The Relation of Strength of Stimulus to Rapidity of Habit Formation," *Journal of Comparative Neurology and Psychology*, 1908, 18, pp. 459–82.

117 "Ever since you were a little kid": Miles Daisher, AI, January 2013.

118 "Mindset" refers to: Carol Dweck, *Mindset: How We Can Learn to Fulfill Our Potential* (Ballantine Books, 2007).

119 they were the winning drivers: Lisa Trei, "Fixed versus Growth Intelligence Mindsets: It's All in Your Head, Dweck Says," Stanford News Service, February 7, 2007.

"When you think about it": Dweck, *Mindset*, p. 11.

120 Four part flow cycle: Benson and Proctor, *The Breakout Principle*. You will also note that the flow cycle looks an awful lot like Alex Osborn and Sidney Parnes's "Creative Problem-Solving Model." It also bears a lot of similarity to most "learning cycles." This is not accidental. Certainly more research needs to be done, but it seems like we're looking at versions of the same process.

"For a businessperson": Benson and Proctor, *The Breakout Principle*, p. 18.

121 Norwegian skier and BASE jumper Karina Hollekim: Karina Hollekim, AI, February 2013.

Jamie Wheal: Jamie Wheal, AI, July 2012.

123 "I grew up watching the greatest show on earth": All of the Ian Walsh quotes and details were garnered in an interview conducted February 2013.

124 The article: Michael Shapiro, "On One Breath," *Hana Hou! The Magazine of Hawaiian Airlines*, August/September 2008.

125 the ride was his: See: http://xxl11.billabong.com/archive/roty.

126 "Careers are a jungle gym, not a ladder": Sheryl Sandberg, *Lean In: Women, Work, and the Will to Lead* (Knopf, 2013), p. 53.

8. THE WE OF FLOW

128 Mark Powell who first solved these issues: Steven Roper, *Camp 4: Recollections of a Yosemite Rock Climber* (The Mountaineers, 1994), pp. 83–87.

"He knew that a person who didn't mind a little hardship": Ibid.

129   "Powell distinguished himself": Joseph Taylor III, *Pilgrims of the Vertical: Yosemite Rock Climbers and Nature at Risk* (Harvard University Press, 2010), p. 134.

130   "When you play in ensembles": Unless otherwise noted, all Keith Sawyer information in this chapter comes from a series of interviews conducted between August 2012 and July 2013.

131   "Surgeons say that during a difficult operation": Csikszentmihalyi, *Flow*, p. 65.
        "My years of playing piano": Keith Sawyer, *Group Genius: The Creative Power of Collaboration* (Basic Books, 2007), p. x.

132   if those conversations happen at work: Csikszentmihalyi, *Flow*, pp. 157–59.
        St. Bonaventure University psychologist Charles Walker: Charles Walker, "Experiencing Flow: Is Doing It Together Better Than Doing It Alone?" *Journal of Positive Psychology*, 2010 5(1), pp. 3–11.
        "group flow were the highest performers": Sawyer, *Group Genius*, p. 43.

133   ways to alter social conditions to produce more group flow: Ibid., pp. 39–58.

134   the very first time in the 120-year history: Ibid., p. 53.

135   deep solidarity and togetherness: Richard Celsi, "Transcendent Benefits of High-Risk Sport," *Advances in Consumer Research*, 1982, 19, pp. 636–41.

136   "Two of Camp 4's boulders": Roper, *Camp 4*, pp. 151–52.

137   the moment the technology truly exploded: Aaron Nmungwun, *Video Recording Technology: Its Impact on Media and Home Entertainment* (Routledge, 1989), pp. 168–70.
        article for *Slate*: Matthew Malady, *The Search for Animal Chin*, Slate.com, July 27, 2011.

139   "You can't really describe the impact": Joe Donnelly, AI, June 2012.
        "Mayor of the Dirtbags": Rob Buchanan, "Climbing at the Speed of Soul," *Outside*, December 2002.
        JT Holmes explains: JT Holmes, AI, October 2012.

9. THE FLOW OF IMAGINATION

140   Primal Crew got to work: This story is based on a series of Miles Daisher interviews conducted in January 2013.
        "They called it the Primal House": David Miller, "The Primal Crew: A Group of Friends Who Redefined Gravity Sports," MatadorNetwork.com, October 24, 2008.

141   Frank "The Gambler" Gambalie: Janet Reltman, "Last Base," *ESPN The Magazine*, February 21, 2000.

143   "That was a big deal": JT Holmes, AI, March 2012.
        Jimmy Chin explains: Jimmy Chin, AI, January 2013.

144   global survey conducted by IBM: "IBM 2010 Global CEO Study: Creativity Selected as Most Crucial Factor for Future Success," IBM.com, May 2010.
        Partnership for 21st Century Skills: See: http://www.p21.org.

"the process of developing original ideas that have value": Ken Robinson, *Out of Our Minds: Learning to Be Creative* (Capstone, 2011), pp. 1–7.

There's significant risk involved in every step of this process: Greg Berns, *Iconoclast: A Neuroscientist Reveals How to Think Differently* (Harvard Business Review Press, 2010).

"Creativity is just connecting things": Gary Wolf, "Steve Jobs: The Next Insanely Great Thing," *Wired,* April 2002.

145   the creative act: For links between creativity and dopamine, see: S. A. Chermahini and B. Hommel, "The (B)link Between Creativity and Dopamine: Spontaneous Eye Blink Rates Predict and Dissociate Divergent and Convergent Thinking," *Cognition* June 2010, 115(3), pp. 458–65; Also: "Parkinson's Treatment Can Trigger Creativity," ScienceDaily.com, January 14, 2013.

"When you're concentrating on something that matters": Ned Hallowell, AI, May 2013.

flow state itself acts like a force multiplier for creativity: See: Csikszentmihalyi, *Creativity.* Also, Alison Gopnik, "For Innovation, Dodge the Prefrontal Police," *Wall Street Journal,* April 5, 2013.

low alpha/high theta state also boosts creativity: There's obviously a ton to choose from, but for a solid review of the field Narayanan Srinivasan, "Cognitive Neuroscience of Creativity: EEG Based Approaches," *Methods,* 2007, 42, pp. 109–16; Also: Andreas Fink et al., "The Creative Brain: Investigation of Brain Activity During Creative Problem Solving by Means of EEG and fMRI," *Human Brain Mapping,* 2009, 30(3) pp. 734–48.

"When you're out skiing or skating with your friends": Micah Abrams, AI, June 2013.

146   "Shane desperately wanted": Scott Gaffney, AI, February 2012.

147    $500,000 to build: Daryl Franklin, AI, June 2012.

148   shot at the double ski-BASE on March 25, 2009": The details in this section are based on interviews with both JT Holmes and Steve Winter (both of whom were there at his death) conducted May and June of 2011.

149   Leslie Anthony wrote in *White Planet:* Ibid.

10. THE DARK SIDE OF FLOW

153   ten times voted *Snowboard* Big Mountain Rider of the Year": Max Klinger, "A Soft-Spoken Snowboarder Blazes Icy Trails," *New York Times,* February 23, 2013.

"Without the sponsors and support": See: http://www.oneill.com/#/men/asiapacific/teamriders/g.global_team½jeremy_jones.

154   "Alaska was a different planet": All Jeremy Jones quotes come from a series of author interviews conducted between March 2013 and July 2013.

155   the "Deeper" experiment: http://www.tetongravity.com/films/deeper.

159   "I felt I could not be hurt": Pelé and Robert L. Fish, *My Life and the Beautiful Game: The Autobiography of Pelé* (Doubleday, 1977).

ESPN called 2011 the "grimmest year in [action] sports": Devon O'Neil, "No One Is Immune to Risk," ESPN.com, December 28, 2011. Also see: Andrew Keh, "Sarah Burke, Freestyle Skier, Dies from Injuries in Training," *New York Times,* January 19, 2012; "Arne Backstrom: 1980–2010," *PowderMag,* June 4, 2010. And for why 2013 looks grimmer than 2011, see: http://snowboardsecrets.com/deaths.

160 "Not less than everything": T. S. Eliot, *Four Quartets* (Mariner Books, 1968).

ramifications are soul-sucking: What we're really looking at here is the incredibly addictive power of neurochemistry. See: Ting-Jui Chou and Chih-Chen Ting, "The Role of Flow Experience in Cyber-Game Addiction," *CyberPsychology and Behavior* December 2003, 6(6), pp. 663–75; Vaughan Bell, "The Unsexy Truth About Dopamine," *The Observer,* February 2, 2013; "Getting Your Endorphin Fix," *New York Times,* June 24, 2013; Dan Peterson, "Runner's High Can Turn into a Real Addiction," *NBC News,* August 29, 2009; Susan Perry, "Did You Know These 7 Surprises About Slots?" PsychologyToday.com, November 4, 2012.

"No question about it": All the Jamie Wheal quotes in this chapter come from a series of interviews/discussions between April 2011 and July 2013.

"When I feel that really draining": Dean Potter, AI, March 2013.

161 "I hope you talk a little about how utterly fucked": Chris Malloy, AI, February 18, 2012.

162 we have decided that play: Johan Huizinga, *Homo Ludens: A Study of the Play-Element in Culture* (Beacon Press, 1971); Kenneth Ginsburg, "The Importance of Play in Promoting Healthy Child Development and Maintaining Strong Parents-Child Bonds," *Pediatrics,* January 1, 2007, 119(1), pp. 182–91; Margarita Tartakovsky, "The Importance of Play for Adults," PsychCentral.com.

163 Red Bull, for example, has teamed up with the Navy SEALs: Mark Anders, "The River of Pain," *The Red Bulletin,* January 5, 2013.

"All my friends who have been lost": "The Death Zone," *NBC News,* February 23, 2012. See: http://unofficialnetworks.com/msnbcs-rock-center-brian-williams-speaks-dr-robb-gaffney-sherry-mcconkey-risk-fatalities-sport-skiing-78051.

164 a $750 billion lifestyle industry: "The Outdoor Recreation Economy," Outdoor Industry Association, 2012. See: http://www.outdoorindustry.org/pdf/OIA_OutdoorRecEconomyReport2012.pdf.

166 snowboarding legend Craig Kelly died: Frank Litsky, "Craig Kelly, 36; Helped Redefine Snowboarding as Sport and Art," *New York Times,* January 25, 2003.

"Kelly was the pioneer": All the Travis Rice quotes in this section come from an author interview conducted May 2013.

168 "You've got to be kidding me": *The Art of Flight,* Brain Farm Digital Cinema and Red Bull Media House, 2011.

11. THE FLOW OF NEXT

170 *fast followers:* Steven Blank, "You're Better Off Being a Fast Follower Than an Originator," *Business Insider,* October 5, 2010.

The X Games were in San Francisco: Statista.com. See: http://www.statista.com
/statistics/205228/total-x-games-attendance; Elizabeth White, "Wonder Where
the Fans Went? Think X Games," *Media Life Magazine*, January 2001.

skateboarding's Best Trick competition: Tony Hawk and Sean Mortimer, *Hawk:
Occupation: Skateboarder* (Regan Books, 2001), pp. 1–5.

171 It was a show, all right: http://www.youtube.com/watch?v=1vInHTvNX6Q.

"Everything blanked out except the 9": Hawk and Mortimer, *Hawk*, pp. 2–3.

He started skating by the time he was five years old: All the Tom Schaar details
come from an author interview conducted April 2013, but also see: http://blog
.dcshoes.com/us/en/skate/the-team/tom-schaar.

172 "I remember thinking": *Bones Brigade: An Autobiography*, directed by Stacy Peralta, 2012.

landed the world's first 1080: Keith Hamm, "12-year-old Tom Schaar Lands 1080,"
ESPN.com, March 30, 2012.

"I can't believe I can do something Tony Hawk can't": "Skateboarder Tom
Schaar/'My First X': The Evolution of the 1080," *Network A*, June 25, 2012.

173 "I try not to think about anything": "X Games Los Angeles 2012: Mitchie Brusco
Silver Medal Interview," X Games, July 3, 2012.

174 it was bound to happen: Neal Bascomb, *The Perfect Mile: Three Athletes, One Goal,
and Less Than Four Minutes to Achieve It* (Mariner Books, 2005).

"Most people considered running": Ibid., p. 1.

175 "If you want to understand the Bannister effect": Mike Gervais, AI, April 2013.

Edmund Jacobson who first discovered this link: F. J. McGuigan and Paul Lehrer,
"Progressive Relaxation: Origins, Principles and Clinical Applications," in *Prin-
ciples and Practices of Stress Management*, Third Edition, edited by Paul Lehrer,
Robert Woolfolk, and Wesley Sime (Guilford Press, 2008), pp. 57–71.

lifting weights was enough to increase strength: Guang Yue and K. J. Cole,
"Strength Increases from the Motor Program: Comparison of Training with Maximal Voluntary and Imagined Muscle Contractions," *Journal of Neurophysiology*
67, no. 5 (May 1992), pp. 1114–23.

176 further amplifying flow: Angie LeVan, "Seeing Is Believing: The Power of Visualization," PsychologyToday.com, December 3, 2009.

177 "When I was starting out": Travis Pastrana, AI, March 2012.

"When you're talking about this next generation of athletes": Leslie Sherlin, AI,
February 2013.

178 far greater amounts of flow than more traditional methodologies: Kevin Rat-
hunde, "Montessori Education and Optimal Experience: A Framework for New
Research," *The NAMTA Journal* Winter 2001, 26(1), pp. 11–43.

University of Virginia psychologist Angeline Lillard: Angeline Lillard and Nicole
Else-Quest, "The Early Years: Evaluating Montessori Education," *Science*, September 29, 2006, 313(5795), pp. 1893–94.

When professor Jeffrey Dyer . . . and Hal Gregersen: The innovators Dyer and
Gregersen are referring to include everyone from high-tech pioneers like Ama-

zon founder Jeff Bezos, SimCity creator Will Wright, Wikipedia founder Jimmy Wales, and Google cofounders Sergey Brin and Larry Page to culture-shaping creatives like rapper/entrepreneur Sean Combs, chef/entrepreneur Julia Child, and Nobel laureate author Gabriel García Márquez. In 2004, when Barbara Walters interviewed Page and Brin, she asked if the fact that their parents were both college professors was the major reason for their success. Page felt otherwise: "We both went to Montessori schools, and I think it was part of that training of not following rules and orders, and being self-motivated, questioning what's going on in the world, doing things a little bit differently."

they too found a Montessori connection: Jeffrey Dyer, Hal Gregersen, and Clayton Christensen, "The Innovator's DNA," *Harvard Business Review,* December 2009.

179 "Go back to Roger Bannister's time": Mike Gervais, AI, April 2013.

180 "The idea was to develop": Leslie Sherlin, AI, February 2013.

"quantified Self" devices: Lila Battis, "Fitness Trackers Compared!" *Men's Health.* See: http://www.menshealth.com/techlust/new-fitness-trackers.

181 Hugh Herr, the head of the biomechatronics: Steven Kotler, "Bionic Man," *Playboy,* June 2012.

"anyone with a bum knee": Ibid.

182 five times the speed of Moore's Law: Peter Diamandis and Steven Kotler, *Abundance: The Future Is Better Than You Think* (Free Press, 2011).

183 meet Alex Honnold: Honnold quotes and details came from a series of interviews conducted by the author between March 2013 and July 2013.

Peter Croft and Dean Potter: Douglas MacDonald, "Astroman and Rostrum Free-Solo," Climbing.com. See: http://www.climbing.com/news/astroman-and-rostrum-free-solo.

"When you talk about what the next": Jimmy Chin, AI, March 2013.

186 first person in history to solo Half Dome: "NG LIVE!: Free Soloing with Alex Honnold," *National Geographic Live.* See: http://video.nationalgeographic.com/video/specials/nat-geo-live-specials/chin-bonus-nglive.

finishing the route in one hour twenty-two minutes: Joshua Weatherl, "Honnold Solos, El Cao, Half Dome and Mt. Watkins in Eighteen Hours," Alpinist.com, June 7, 2012.

12. FLOW TO ABUNDANCE

187 skydiver Felix Baumgartner was heading: See: www.redbullstratos.com.

188 "Felix is an action sports athlete": Andy Walshe, AI, April 2013.

189 "At a certain RPM": John Tierney, "24 Miles, 4 Minutes and 834 M.P.H., All in One Jump," *New York Times,* October 14, 2012.

190 lived through their midair crack-up: See *Summary Report: Findings of the Red Bull Stratos Scientific Summit,* California Science Center, January 23, 2013.

Ansari X Prize in 2004: See: www.xprize.org.

SpaceShipTwo's flight was a test burn: "Virgin Galactic's SpaceShipTwo Makes Test Flight," USAToday.com, April 29, 2013.

Paying customers going rocket man before 2015: Elizabeth Howell, "Virgin Galactic: Richard Branson's Space Tourism Company," Space.com, December 20, 2012.

192   Arie de Geus: Arie de Geus, *The Living Company: Habits for Survival in a Turbulent Business Environment* (Harvard Business Review Press, 2002).

193   "We are the ones": Alice Walker, *We Are the Ones We Have Been Waiting For: Inner Light in a Time of Darkness* (New Press, 2006).

About the Author

Steven Kotler is a *New York Times* best-selling author and an award-winning journalist. His books include the nonfiction works *Abundance; A Small, Furry Prayer; West of Jesus;* and the novel *The Angle Quickest for Flight.* His articles have appeared in more than seventy publications, including the *New York Times Magazine,* the *Atlantic, Wired, Forbes, GQ, Popular Science,* and *Discover.* He is also the cofounder and director of research for the Flow Genome Project, a transdisciplinary, international organization dedicated to decoding flow and open sourcing it to everyone (www.flowgenomeproject.co). You can find him online at www.stevenkotler.com or writing *Far Frontiers,* his blog for Forbes.com: www.forbes.com/sites/stevenkotler.